©orporate
cultures and
global
b®ands

orporate
cultures and
global
bands

edited by

Albrecht Rothacher

Asia-Europe Foundation

 **World Scientific**

NEW JERSEY · LONDON · SINGAPORE · BEIJING · SHANGHAI · HONG KONG · TAIPEI · CHENNAI

Published by

World Scientific Publishing Co. Pte. Ltd.

5 Toh Tuck Link, Singapore 596224

USA office: 27 Warren Street, Suite 401-402, Hackensack, NJ 07601

UK office: 57 Shelton Street, Covent Garden, London WC2H 9HE

British Library Cataloguing-in-Publication Data
A catalogue record for this book is available from the British Library.

First published 2004
Reprinted 2005

CORPORATE CULTURES AND GLOBAL BRANDS

ISBN 981-238-856-7 (pbk)

Printed in Singapore by World Scientific Printers (S) Pte Ltd

Contents

Acknowledgements

The rise and fall of corporate empires, national companies going global, changing their governance in the process and creating products which purposefully elicit emotional consumer reactions as brands, all this is fascinating stuff not only for successful practitioners, but also for readers and researchers alike. All participants of the seminar on "Comparative Business Cultures" held at the Economics Department of the National University of Singapore during 2003 shared this spirit of intellectual excitement and discovery of the most diverse corporate and marketing worlds which are captured in the contributions of this volume. Hence I am most obliged to my young researcher colleagues for their interesting and lively chapters. My thanks go to Asmizar bin Abu (McDonald's), Chia Peng Theng (Nokia), Melissa Chin (Disney), Chua Sin Lay (Mars), Annalisa Dass (Nike), Pauline Javani (Zubrowka Bison Vodka), Cheryl Lim (Benetton), Lim Jia Woon (Toyota), Lim Teck Nam (Virgin), Ong Wei Ling (Ikea) and Michelle Phua Yifei (Coca-Cola).

As the author of the remaining chapters I am also deeply grateful to Jenny Tan and Zareen Tia of the Asia Europe Foundation (ASEF) for their meticulous secretarial skills when putting my scribbles into a decent typewritten draft. Last but not least my thanks go to my long suffering family for enduring yet another book project.

Corporate Identities and Successful Branding

Until recently global brands have been seen as licence to print money. With the right label and generous PR budget, sugary lemonades, greasy meat buns, tee-shirts or sports shoes could be sold for a multiple of the original manufacturing costs to an ever growing number of credulous, happy and somewhat simple-minded consumers.

Yet quite a few of the world's most celebrated brands face unforeseen difficulties, which seem unrelated to direct management mistakes or largely ineffective boycott calls: McDonald's, Coke, Disney and the U.S. car makers are all struggling with reduced sales and slimmed margins.

The most prominent American brands stood for both the fear and the promise of a homogenised global way of life along U.S. patterns, leveling national tastes and cultural preferences towards the smallest common denominator of mankind.

For backward industrial, many developing and former Communist countries, these brands surely offered progress in terms of reliable qualities, services and the notion to participate in the American way of life: Even the concept to eat, drink, make and to enjoy any product at any moment was seen as liberating.

Once however, the memory of scarcities was overcome, discretionary incomes increased and a basic familiarity with the U.S. way of life and consumption was established, the novelty value and compulsive attractivity of U.S. mass brands began to decline.

Rather than striving for uniformity, consumers recently begin to opt for greater freedom of choice and ever-greater diversity and product segmentation to express their personal likes and individuality, including a revival of national and regional brands, including in the U.S. (very visible, e.g., in Lone Star Texas).

U.S. mass brands, that bogeyman of anti-globalisers, may have had their golden days of the 1990s, the decade after the fall of the Iron Curtain, behind them. But a much larger crowd of more differentiated, well-focused and properly managed national and multinational brands are still very much alive and kicking with a great future ahead of them. Newly branded consumer sectors, like in telecoms, financial services, or IT operators, or even in capital goods producers are being added to the classical staples.

What then are brands, that elusive buzzword of corporate visionaries, marketers, ad men, retailers, addicted teenagers and globalisation critics?

Simply put, a brand is the soul of a product. It facilitates consumer choice as it represents reliable qualities, images and pricing. If properly communicated and maintained, it can also evoke powerful emotional qualities for a consumer, which enhances his possibly even lifelong loyalty to the product.

A brand owner thus needs to keep its focus, value its brand, avoid the pitfalls of reckless stretching, discount selling, excessive national product differentiation and of abrupt modernisations.

Clearly, companies with successful brands grow quicker and are more profitable than commodity producers or companies with their inconsistent and ineffective brand policies.

It remains, however, imperative that during often rapid growth, the corporate identity remains in harmony with the brands and their professed core values. The pitfalls of corporate history are many-fold. From the original over-life sized founding fathers (typically the inventors of the brand) generational succession is rarely smooth. Bureaucratisation by professional managers in public companies which often succeed the 3rd to 5th generation of founder–owner families represents the risk of brand illoyalty, as hired CEOs and greedy shareholders may be more loyal to themselves than to their brands. Corporate mergers and takeovers (typically motivated by too large a war-chest by a bored top management) usually spell more trouble than gain, as corporate cultures and frequently brand identities are being damaged irreparably by wild diversifications, which look intelligent on paper only or by mergers whose "synergies" usually destroy the brands which have been taken over as unloved stepchildren.

The concept of corporate culture is possibly even more elusive. According to John Middleton it is related to the atmosphere at work: "the way we do things around here" reflecting "patterns of shared values and beliefs created over time". They set norms for acceptable behaviour in organisations, change and conservatism, creativity and conformity, group orientation and individuality, customer service and in-house orientation....

Society at large and national business culture plays a significant role with respect to social knowledge, rituals, ideologies and values as they apply to hierarchy, information sharing, employee participation, negotiation and communication behaviour, the roles of men and women, to career patterns, remuneration and labour relations. There are also significant regional variations. Even within a homogenous national culture like the U.S., the Californian way of doing business varies from how it is done in Dallas, Texas, in Atlanta, Georgia, let alone in New York City or in Detroit. These differences are even more pronounced in countries with more historical regional differences. Sectoral styles also play their roles: a bank has a different corporate culture from a steel plant or a trucking company or a design studio.

Charles Handy differentiated four types of organisational cultures:

1. *Power Cultures*: with one central source of power, typically exercised by a charismatic founder or his successors in a fairly authoritarian fashion. The company is led in a strong, decisive and forceful way, can react quickly, and leaves little initiative to middle management. All this is good for quick growth if the decisions are vindicated by market acceptance. But it could equally be a recipe for disaster if they turn out wrong. Typical are start-up firms in their early decades.

2. *Role Cultures*: practiced in large bureaucratic companies with prescribed roles, procedures, and delegated authority. Job descriptions and procedures count rather than personalities. The organisation becomes predictable, routinized, but also inflexible and slow. Established banks, insurance companies, big conglomerates (like the Japanese keiretsu), public companies and firms with high capital intensity are classical examples.

3. *Task Cultures*: small work groups who get their jobs done by networking and human interactions. Individuals have high control over their work. Hierarchies are flat; the work style is informal. This is typical for PR agencies, real estate agents, marketing firms.

4. *Person Cultures*: individual operations dominate, personal values and professionalism counts. Institutional loyalties are weak: This applies to consultancies, law firms, academia, research and journalism.

More than any meaningless mission statement a robust corporate culture is an asset. It guarantees long-term performance of an organisation, as it has carefully been built-up and evolved in line with the business environment and in harmony with the national culture of its home country. Oral corporate history, including gossip, heroic myths and corporate philosophy plays a role as does personnel policy: "Who gets in, who gets fired, and who gets promoted?", as does preferred management behaviour which could oscillate between authoritarian, *laissez faire* and participative styles, and between formality and informality in procedures. For long-term employees this leads to a sense of belonging and motivation beyond the job description and allows the formation of important communication networks for action and quick information.

Corporate cultures are put at risk by reckless downsizing and outsourcing and by mergers and takeovers. Ultimately in view of Terrence Deal and Allan Kennedy, it is the bottom line orientation of fund managers, who overemphasize short-term shareholder value and thus destroy the social fabric essential to a company's long term organisational health and prosperity.

As employment becomes insecure and "me first" being the only rational strategy for survival, corporate loyalty is the first casualty. Downsizing and outsourcing betrays the trust of employees. In-house skills and corporate memory are lost. Outsourced contract workers feel alienated doing the same job for lower wages. Those who survived feel guilty, operate with lower morale, higher absenteeism, low profile and greater outward conformity. Product and service quality and customer relations suffer. The same applies to corporate takeovers, in which the losing side's corporate culture is being forced out as fund managers expect rapidly reduced payrolls as evidence of promised "synergies" (which in reality hardly ever materialize).

For brand management corporate identity is of key importance: in order to be successful as a credible brand both must remain in harmony. Disney's family values must be practiced in corporate behaviour, Virgin's studied youthfulness be reflected in corporate informality, the approachable PR of Ikea and Lego be practiced in actual customer relations, or a bank be seen as a respectable and more formal organisation. Thus when Dresdner Bank, a solid institution of reserved German bankers was taken over by the brash insurance salesmen of Allianz, not only did their corporate culture go down the drain, but so did their customers' confidence, their volume of deposits and their bottomline.

National business cultures play an important role for corporate identities and for brand images. German and Japanese products stand for engineering prowess, reliable qualities and their business organisations for participative bureaucracies ("role cultures"). French and Italian products are reputed for their design, flair and creativity, their business organisations are typically power cultures with great authoritarian distance and an alienated work force. While the designs are brilliant, problems in manufacturing quality, delivery and after sales service can be expected.

There is nothing wrong with neither national style — but what happens if you blend them? The chemical and pharmaceutical producers Hoechst and Rhone Poulenc merged to form a hybrid synthetic called Aventis. Two established well-branded companies disappeared to form a face — and flavourless neuter: a company without an identity. Its product sales, regardless of their individual qualities, had to suffer, and so they promptly did. Having become an object for takeovers, in 2004 Aventis was swallowed by the much smaller Sanofi with French government support.

We have assembled 18 case studies in seven core consumer sectors (foodstuffs, drinks, distribution, apparel, electronics, transportation and entertainment) to demonstrate the close interconnection between corporate growth, corporate identity and brand development. Stories of qualified success are matched with those of failure, of dented prospects and of still unfulfilled expectations.

Some features are unique to the brand or to the corporate history in question. But there are also common trends, which with all due caution, could be distilled into more universal observations.

Mars, the company and its products (confectionery and pet food) were created by Forrest Mars, the founder's son. It still remains a well-focused family-owned company. The same applies to Sprüngli-Lindt as the only surviving independent Swiss quality chocolate dynasty. It overcame its 5th generation crisis and manages a smooth and focused global quality positioning for its Lindt brands.

Kikkoman is a few centuries older. During the past decades the Mori clan succeeded to make soy sauce a world condiment. With only moderate and a fairly focused diversification, the traditional family-owned company remained on track. It survived a wine scandal in time to re-establish sound management prior to Japan's wild binge of capital misallocation and destruction of the 1980s, thus escaping unhurt from the bubble burst of 1992 and after.

Coca-Cola certainly is the world's best-known contemporary brand. After the original inventors were bought out, it was systematically built up by Robert Woodruff, but still remained quintessentially a very U.S. Southern product. As Coke seems to have reached its limits to growth, the company has diversified into a multitude of juices and drinks, including very local brands like, for instance, Almdudler, an archtypical Austrian herbal lemonade, which nobody would ever associate with the Atlanta giant.

In East Europe only very few brands survived Communist mismanagement. One of the best with global potential is Poland's Vodka Zubrowka. Unfortunately political hiccups during Poland's privatisation and a certain reticence by the new brand owner Pernod Ricard, which has many promising drinks on its shelves, so far prevented the effective utilisation of this potential.

McDonald's is surely a most unlikely success of U.S. management style worldwide. Its emphasis on automation, standardized qualities, cleanliness and quick service represented progress in most of the world's fast food industry. After having bought out the McDonald's brothers, Ray Kroc assured McDonald's success by strength of image creation and toughness of guidance and control over franchises and employees. It is only recently that people in the more effluent markets lost their appetite for fatty hamburger buns. McDonald's reacted with a more varied menu, but mainly with reduced prices, a down-market move with little future.

In distribution, Ikea is the product of Ingvar Kamprad's marketing genius: the relentless global expansion of a low cost furniture retailer with knock down sets and a very spartan service. The company cultivates the Swedishness of its origins in both marketing and management style. Informality, frugality and approachability rule — and are successful worldwide.

The Seibu-Season chain of Seiji Tsutsumi did it the other way round: it started out as an increasingly avant gardist trendy upmarket department store and supermarket chain. Highly successful during Japan's asset inflation period, Seiji led it on a mad credit financed diversification drive into overpriced real estate development and went global with the Intercontinental chain. In the end, Seibu collapsed spectacularly. His brother

Tsutomu Tsutsumi, who in his heydays bought the Nagano Winter Olympics, was saved only narrowly by marginally sounder finance due to the bigger capital base of his inherited hotel and railway businesses.

One of Italy's postwar textile successes was set up by Luciano Benetton and his siblings. He subcontracted production, delegated sales to exclusive franchises and focused on design and image creation by stirring public controversies. Benetton's messages of multiculturalism and cosmopolitan lifestyles, are however, not matched by his autocratic traditional family-oriented corporate culture and his Italian dominated personnel and marketing policies. Yet he manages to succeed with these inconsistencies, perhaps not by accident *à l'Italiana*.

Nike is an even younger company founded by running academics in Oregon in the 1960s. It has similarly outsourced all production and concentrates on R&D and brand management only. It maintains a forever youthful and informal corporate style, and with a huge marketing budget pushes for an unapologetic U.S. masculine 'can do' spirit in its corporate image.

Nokia, the Finnish forestry processor turned electronics makers since its re-focusing effort in the mid 1970s has cultivated an entrepreneurial management style with a strong customer, design and R&D focus and continuous product innovation. Although claiming to be cosmopolitan with its high tech commitment, with its hardworking and egalitarian management style and business ethics it remains distinctly Finnish.

Sony, which also claims to be cosmopolitan, is similarly unmistakably Japanese. Built up by Akio Morita as one of Japan's post-war miracle companies, it diversified from a successful electronics manufacturer through ill-fated U.S. acquisitions into electronic entertainment. Although still marginally profitable, since Morita's death Sony has lost its way and is in search of focus.

Sir Richard Branson's Virgin group is purposefully anti-establishment and anti-textbook. In line with its rebellious non-conformist image it happily overstretches its low budget brand with three airlines, soft drinks ('Virgin Cola'), cosmetics and record 'Megastores", often with very mixed results. It operates on free press publicity generated by its flamboyant founder and finds acceptance notably by British and Australian underclass feelings of solidarity and their strange sense of fun. Virgin companies are bought on credit and later sold to get out of financial predicaments to no apparent purpose. Yet against all odds Virgin survives under Sir Richard somewhat autocratic, spontaneous and fun-loving leadership.

Toyota was built up by Kiichiro Toyoda, who had inherited Toyoda Automated Loom Works, into the world's largest car manufacturer. Different fron Nissan, its less successful competitor, it entered overseas production only reluctantly and very much remained a traditional conformist Japanese family-owned company.

Fiat, Italy's foremost car maker, after a hundred years of turbulent corporate history is still controlled by the Agnelli family. Under their autocratic management it had more than its fair share of labour troubles and as a one-model company went through pronounced cycles of boom and bust. Unfortunately funds generated during the good years were spent on unfocused diversifications to create an unwieldy conglomerate. Attempts to establish lasting footholds outside the Italian market equally came to naught, thus threatening Fiat Auto's long-term survival.

The merger mania hit two German premium car markers, BMW and Daimler-Benz, in the mid 1990s. The two entered into unhappy marriages of convenience with Rover and Chrysler, respectively. Daimler had just divested itself from an earlier wild loss-making diversification, which had attempted to create a high tech conglomerate. On paper synergies of both mergers looked wonderful: permitting access to new markets with an attractive portfolio of mass market cars. Yet cultural management and brand incompatibilities let both deals go sour very quickly. BMW opted for a quick divorce and remains a happy single ever after with an expanded albeit focused premium car strategy, while Daimler Chrysler remains locked in its unhappy loss inducing marriage, losing brand focus and national corporate identity in consequence. Neither German engineering prowess nor U.S. patriotic corporate citizenship remain very credible for either.

Lego remained a family-owned quality toy maker, faithful to its philosophy of creative play, very Danish in its informal and participative leadership style and its adherence to its corporate values, although a new generation of children and middle-class parents seems to have abandoned them. In response Lego now seems to chase trends, instead of leading them as it did in the past.

Disney did it the other way round. It also had its "family values" but aimed at the lowest common denominator of a melting pot society. Built up by the Disney brothers, it expanded into a comprehensive entertainment, media and merchandising empire under the autocratic rule of long-term CEO, Michael Eisner. In the fickle and rough entertainment business it seems, however, very difficult to keep on smiling in line with its childish cartoon characters of origin. Intellectual brand consistency thus remains a persistent problem, notably when violent movies and tough corporate lawyers promise instant profits.

In order to generate a global brand, a middle-of-the-road consensual approach of common wisdom never worked. At the beginning there is always (or nearly always) a founding father, a marketing and production genius, who pushed things through and persisted against all odds. In our sample these were men like Forrest Mars, Ingvar Kamprad (Ikea), the Tsutsumi brothers (Seibu), Luciano Benetton, Phil Knight (Nike), Akio Morita

(Sony), Sir Richard Branson (Virgin), Giovanni Agnelli (Fiat), Koiichiro Toyoda, the Christiansen family (Lego) and the Disney brothers.

There were also those playing a similar role, who bought out the original innovator and perfected a struggling infant brand and build up and harnessed its potential. These were people like Ray Kroc (McDonalds) and Robert Woodruff (Coca-Cola). Clearly, the owner-brand founders' management style is regularly characterised as autocratic, often as idiosyncratic as well. It usually took the form of classical authoritarianism, regardless of whether it is in the U.S. (Mars, Disney/Eisner, McDonald's/Kroc, Coke/Woodruff), in Europe (Agnelli, Sprüngli, Benetton) or in Japan (Morita, Toyoda, Seibu/Tsutsumi). Even when informality and flat hierarchies were instructed, there was still a charismatic boss like Kamprad (Ikea), Branson (Virgin), Knight (Nike), and Christiansen (Lego) who discouraged middle management bureaucrats and insisted on his perception of a consistent corporate and brand culture.

While they were irreplaceable in the take off stage, the second big-price question always refers to corporate succession. Owner-founders typically prefer dynastic succession. Their sons (daughters usually don't enter the picture) suffer from a double handicap: Their larger-than-life successful fathers in their patriarchal-authoritarian ways typically overshadowed the sons (or grandsons). Often enough they were polygamous and treated family members, including their sons, badly, or laid the ground for paralysing succession struggles between their sons, who on occasion appear as spoilt, overcharged, overeducated or simply disinterested in management. Fiat and Sony are examples. On occasion, the inevitable strikes at a later generation.

Yet almost all of our successful brands remain in family control: Mars, Benetton, Lego, Sony, Ikea, Sprüngli, Kikkoman, Fiat, Toyota and Virgin: Brand management by committee-like

Pernod Ricard for Zubrovka Vodka or by managerial consensus of the Japanese sort (Toyota, Kikkoman) appears as much less effective.

Obviously one-man decisions are high-risk decisions: They carry the prospect of a stroke of genius but with at least equal probability the likeliness of utter failure. The diversification strategies of Seibu, Sony and Fiat are examples of the latter, as were the takeover decisions of Daimler and BMW. Sir Richard's Virgin group represents the institutionalised permanent risk. Yet without the vision and the drive of founding fathers and their successes, Sony would still be a radio repair shop in Osaka, Lego do carpentry work in Billund, Seibu sell obento travel provisions at Ikebukuro station, Benetton knit home-made sweaters, and Nike organise cross-country runs in Oregon forests. In fact, without them most companies, including Coke, Disney and McDonald's would surely have gone out of business long ago.

As brands succeed, corporations grow and the founder hero inevitably fades from the scene. Then bureaucratization sets in. Some, like Nokia, Sprüngli and Nike, managed to set up the rare feat of an entrepreneurial corporate culture. Mostly, however, hired hands take over as CEOs whose fate through share options is increasingly decided by short-term oriented fund managers, who care about quarterly bottom lines and about little else. All the founding fathers knew that short termism and profitable fire sales spell the death of any brand. It hence should come as little surprise that many global brands, especially those of U.S. origin, are in trouble today. They also knew that corporate bureaucratization and committee decisions for brand definitions usually imply dilution: In the spirit of compromise typically they are intended to mean too many things to too many people.

A case in point are the pronounced national identities of most successful brands. The American dream and the U.S. way of life are part and parcel of Disney, Coca-Cola, Nike, Mars and

McDonald's. Kikkoman, Toyota, Seibu and Sony are clearly Japanese. Ikea is Swedish, Lego Danish, Nokia Finnish, Benetton and Fiat Italian, Virgin British, Zubrowka Polish, and BMW and Daimler German. National brand origins reflect distinct corporate national identities and brand images, firmly held by consumers. Dilution by mergers and misguided globalist corporate mission statements and PR efforts (practiced by Sony, Benetton, Nokia and DaimlerChrysler) only risks to hurt the brand's integrity.

Claims of newly created artificial corporate identities may flatter the vanity of senior management. They do not, however, reflect the expectations and daily experiences of their customers and their employees. Managerial delusions of global grandeur produced by hired PR hands may be corrected at relatively little cost. More dangerous are well filled war chests which allow takeovers and diversifications as a seductively easy shortcut to empire building for bored senior managers. Brand management is patient work of incremental subtle innovation and modernisaton, not the stuff to generate managerial glory in business magazines and corporate case studies, let alone to excite fund managers insistent on quick bottomline results. Fiat, Daimler, BMW, Sony and Seibu all fell victim to this most frequent case of managerial hubris, which never generated the profits promised but only served to threaten their core brands and their companies' survival.

As global markets for uniform products did not really emerge, global operators returned to the time-proven model of international operations: Local management was again encouraged to modify products, marketing and management accordingly to local preferences.

There remains an intrinsic need for consistency between corporate cultures and their brand images. A caring family value company like Disney cannot produce violent films or go aggressively after copyright violators. Fiat should not permit its Iveco subsidiary to produce trucks for mobile executions in China

(*The Straits Times*, 13.3.2003). Charges of child labour in Third World countries follow all sportswear makers, who like Nike, have outsourced their manufacturing. McDonald's which wants to be a family restaurant is haunted by lawsuits of fattened teenagers, which have generated the worst possible publicity for a restaurant chain.

Globalisation critics since decades have leveled an earful of complaints against global brands, charging Nestle infant formula to kill babies, oil multinationals to destroy nature and to exploit their oilfields for little local benefit with the help of corrupt dictatorships, Chiquita bananas (United Fruits) to instigate wars in Central America, pharmaceutical companies to use slum dwellers as guinea pigs, and apparel makers to exploit child labour. Naomi Klein's 'No Logo' (2000) has become the slogan of anti-globalists.

Yet politically inspired boycotts so far have failed to make a dent. Companies like Coca-Cola, McDonald's and Nike generate 50% of their turnover in Europe, Asia, and in the Middle East. Yet even at the height of the highly unpopular U.S. war against Iraq, there was no visible impact on sales outside the Middle East. Similarly fears of German and French brand producers of effective boycott calls in the U.S. did not materialise in 2003. Possibly giant Stars & Stripes at German car dealership and plants helped to placate hurt nationalist feelings.

Twenty years ago, Theodore Levitt in the *Harvard Business Review* famously predicted the globalisation of markets: mass transportation and communication would make distinct national tastes and cultural preferences disappear. There would be global markets for standardised consumer products.

Today, we know that with increased income levels and varied personal experiences in mature markets the opposite happens: Consumers reject standard fare and opt for wider choice and their national, regional and personal preferences instead.

This does not automatically mean 'big brand, big trouble'. Rather there remains a bright future for well managed, well focused brands as we have seen.

In fact, in the field of consumer products and services, the existence of well-established national brands of international repute is a considerable asset in terms of international competitiveness. Other things being equal, a country with strong brands across the board will do better in international trade than one which produces faceless commodities.

Apart from Japan, which still has strong if no longer overly exciting brands, most of Asia has a problem, as Asian brand owners typically care very little for intangibles like product or corporate image, especially when it costs money first. Lee Kuan Yew put this perceptively: East Asia needs "maverick generals" to generate sustainable brands (*The Straits Times* 6.6.2003). In his view it is handicapped by its Confucian heritage which with its conformist discipline was good to organise big regiments for reliable mass productions, but not to encourage the stubborn creativity of individuals. The subsequent case studies offer plenty of evidence of how to do this, but also about pitfalls to avoid.

Bibliography

Batey, Ian, *Asian Branding*, Singapore: Prentice Hall, 2002.

Blasberg, John and Vishnamath, Vijay, "Making Cool Brands Hot", *Harvard Business Review*, June 2003, 20–2.

Deal, Terrence and Kennedy, Alan, *The New Corporate Cultures*, London: Texere Publishing, 2000.

Fuyuno, Ichiyo, "Japan's McTrouble", *Far Eastern Economic Review*, 12.9.2002.

Handy, Charles, *Understanding Organizations*, Harmondsworth: Penguin, 1999.

Hofstede, Geert, *Culture and Organizations*, London: McGraw-Hill, 1997.

Keller, Kevin Lane, et al., "Three Questions You Need to Ask about Your Brand", *Harvard Business Review*, September 2002, pp. 81–6.

Lewis, Richard D., *When Cultures Collide, Managing Successfully across Cultures*, London: Nicholas Brealy, 1999.

Middleton, John, *Culture*, Oxford: Capstone Publishing, 2002.

Shah, Reshma, "Summer School: Branding", *Financial Times*, 21.8.2002.

Temporal, Paul, *Branding in Asia*, Singapore: John Wiley, 2000.

Tomkins, Richard, "As Hostility towards America Grows, Will the World Lose Its Appetite for Coca-Cola, McDonald's and Nike?", *Financial Times*, 27.3.2003.

Tomkins, Richard, "When a Big Mac Is No Longer Good Enough", *Financial Times*, 21.12.2002

Werner, Klaus and Weiss, Hans, *Schwarzbuch Markenfirmen*, Vienna: Deuticke, 2001.

"Fast Food in America", *The Economist*, 7.12.2002.

"Marken — Image, Produkte, Unternehmen", Verlagsbeilage, *Frankfurter Allgemeine*, 25.6.2003.

Mars Inc.: More Than Candies and Cat Food

Mars Inc. started out as a candy factory but is today a company with offices and factories worldwide. They make and market a variety of products, ranging from candies to pet food to processed rice. Their products are marketed globally, and consumed in more than 100 countries. Mars Inc., despite being a multi-national company, continues to be family owned and is managed by third-generation descendants, John, Forrest Jr. and Jacqueline Mars. The company was listed as the third largest private company in America in 2002 by Forbes and the family was listed as 21st on the list of the richest in the world, with a net worth of $10 billion.[1]

The company's business interests include snack foods (M&Ms, Snickers, Mars, MilkyWay, Dove Chocolate, Skittles, Combos, etc.), main meals (Uncle Ben's rice, pasta and sauces), pet care (Whiskas, Pedigree, Cesar), drinks (vending machines: Flava and Klix), electronics (automated payment systems) and information technology.

[1] http://www.forbes.com/2003/02/26/billionaireland.html

The company is a highly private company. It does not grant many interviews to the media and is also reluctant to release its financial reports even to its banks. It should also be noted that Mars Inc. is one of the world's biggest private companies, and a big spender in the realm of global advertising to market its products.

History

According to the Mars website, Mars history has two main themes, one of which is innovation and the other to transfer successful innovations around the world. These two themes defined the nature of the company's operations till today.

The company was founded by Frank Mars in 1923, his first success after a series of failures. The company was then known as the Mar-O-Bar Co. In the beginning, he manufactured an item of the same name at the factory, which was a combination of caramel, nuts and chocolate and a butter cream concoction known as Victorian Butter Cream. In 1924, Frank Mars ran into his son Forrest, whom he has not seen since his divorce from his first wife Ethel. Forrest Mars claims to have suggested the idea of a portable version of the chocolate malt drink, which turned into the Milky Way Bar. This new chocolate creation was a stunning new debut in the candy market at that time. The chocolate coating kept the candy bar fresh, in an era where candies did not keep well for long periods of time; and also because the bar did not cost much to produce but tasted as good as chocolate. The bar provided the company with the start it needed.

By 1927, the company was renamed Mars Inc. and the factory relocated to Chicago's west side, where the freight charge was half of that in Minneapolis. The factory was built on a former golf course and Frank Mars turned the factory into a showplace, blending well with the rich suburban neighborhood. It did not give any hint that it was a factory. The factory was automated with what was considered state-of-the-art at that time. In 1930, Frank Mars invented the Snickers bar, and in 1932, he introduced the 3 Musketeers bar, which gave Mars Inc. the reputation of being the second largest candy maker in America, after Hershey (Brenner, 2000).

Frank Mars was contented with the success of his company, perhaps due to his string of failures, but Forrest was bent on expansion and constantly pushed his father to expand the business. However, Forrest's meddling attitude in the company and constant push for expansion into Canada caused Frank to throw him out of the business. Frank Mars died fifteen months later and the company went into the hands of his second wife (another Ethel) and daughter.

With $50,000 and the foreign rights to Milky Way given by his father, Forrest went to Europe to try his luck. His interest in the chocolate business prompted him to study with many masters in Europe, such as the factories of Jean Tobler and Henri Nestlé by working in their factories. Later in 1933, he went to England to launch the Milky Way Bar. However, the market was dominated by Cadbury Brothers Ltd. and Rowntree & Co. This prompted him to scale down his plans for a big factory and start a small one instead. He devoted all his money and attention into the company, so much that his father-in-law had to bring his wife and son back to America to feed them. He adjusted the taste of the Milky Way Bar to suit British taste and even marketed it egoistically as the Mars bar. Sales of the Mars bar took off and even though Forrest Mars' attempt to introduce new candy bars failed, the company in England was nevertheless a success (Brenner, 2000).

With the success of the Mars Bar, Forrest Mars turned his attention to other things. In 1934, he bought Chappel Bros., a British company that canned meat by-products for dogs. At that time, there was no specialized food for pet dogs and cats; they simply ate scraps from the dinner table. Forrest Mars saw an opportunity and he marketed Chappie's canned food as being more nutritious. Without any competitors, he dominated the market easily.

By 1939, Mars Ltd. was the third largest candy manufacturer in Britain, and Forrest had also set up a factory in Brussels to sell Mars bars across Europe. However, with the onset of the Second World War, he had to leave his successes because the British government started taxing foreigners. By then he had an idea that was to become later M&Ms and when he returned to America, he looked to Hershey's for a joint venture.

Forrest Mars convinced the then right-hand man of Milton Hershey, William Murrie of the possibilities of making a chocolate that does not melt. He had seen these candies in Spain during the civil war and was very impressed by them. Mars put up 80 percent of the investment, while Murrie provided the other 20 percent and the chocolate for the venture. Murrie's son Bruce was sent to work with Mars on this venture. The product that was launched in 1941 was M&Ms, which stood for Mars and Murrie. However, the venture soon turned sour, as Bruce Murrie found Forrest Mars a difficult person to work with and soon sold out his shares to Forrest. The information on Mars and M&Ms websites today make no mention of Hershey's help in making M&Ms.[2]

The candies first appealed to American soldiers, because of their ability to withstand temperatures without melting. While it was a good idea, M&Ms did not sell very well initially. It made money, but it did not match up to Snickers. Therefore, in 1950, Forrest Mars hired the advertising firm Ted Bates & Co. to do a detailed study of the sales of M&Ms. Forrest was an innovator in using research as a marketing tool. He was the first in the candy business to do so, and it paid off. The study found that M&Ms were appealing to children, but children did not have the money. Thus,

---

[2] http://global.mms.com/us/about/history/index.jsp

the company changed its pitch to appeal to parents. The agency came up with the famous tagline of M&Ms, "Melts in your mouth, not in your hands". This appealed to parents, as they saw M&M candies as clean and non-messy. With advertising slots on TV during popular shows like the Mickey Mouse Club, this candy became the most popular candy in 1956.

With M&Ms gaining success, Forrest Mars took off to start another business, as he saw potential in a new process of processing rice. The owner of a rice mill discovered parboiling, a process that resulted in a more nutritious grain. Forrest saw potential in branding and selling the rice for a premium, which was a radical idea at that time. Nevertheless, he went forward with his plans and went off to learn about rice-making. He finally named the product Uncle Ben's Rice, after the owner of the mill. The rice contributes to Mars' revenue by around $400 million as of 1999 (Brenner, 2000).

While Forrest Mars had been successful thus far with his company, he viewed his father's company as the ultimate challenge. He saw the company as rightfully his, since he inspired the Milky Way bar and had encouraged his father to build the Chicago factory. Under the control of Frank Mars' second wife Ethel and daughter Patricia, Mars Inc. was slow to innovate (Brenner, 2000). After the death of Ethel Mars, half of her share in the company passed over to Forrest and with this inheritance, he waged a war for control against William "Slip" Kruppenbacher, Ethel Mars' half brother. Forrest Mars fought to modernize the technology of the factory, introducing a mechanized candy production process in 1953. By 1959, Mars Inc. was the largest producer of candy coated bars in the world, thanks to the new technology brought in by Forrest Mars. However, Forrest still wanted complete control over the company.

With the retirement of Kruppenbacher in 1959, James Fleming, Patricia Mars' husband was appointed president and chief executive officer. Quality suffered under his management as he skimmed on expensive ingredients, such as peanuts and chocolate and profits got thinner (Brenner, 2000). Forrest Mars finally convinced Patricia to sell her shares to him, thus obtaining 80% of the company shares in exchange for placing his own companies under the Mars Inc. umbrella. Subsequently, he convinced the rest of the shareholders to sell their shares and obtained complete control over Mars Inc. In December 1964, Forrest Mars became the chairman, president and chief executive officer of Mars Inc.

Upon taking control, Forrest Mars made radical changes to the company structure according to his management style. He took away all the frivolous aspects of the company: the executive dining hall, the French chef, the oak paneling, the art collection, rugs, stained glass and corporate helicopter. He increased salaries by 30%, replaced annual compensation with incentive pay and gave each employee a time card. There were sweeping changes made to the company that miffed some employees. Quality control was improved, undoing the cost-cutting measures put up by James Fleming. Forrest Mars next sought to achieve self-sufficiency by producing its own chocolate. He believed in controlling all aspects of the production of his products and even today, Mars Inc. do not contract out any aspect of its production.

Forrest Mars made many radical changes to the company after acquiring it, but he only held power for a relatively short period of nine years. In 1973, at the age of 69, he retired and turned over the reins of the company to his sons, Forrest Jr. and John Mars and his daughter, Jacqueline. It was through the efforts of these two men that the company was made a truly global company. In spite of handing power over to his children, Forrest Mars continually criticized the performance of his sons and kept tight tabs on the company. As a result, the brothers appear to have held a tighter grip over the company than Forrest Mars ever did.

Forrest Mars the Man

Much of Mars Inc. success is directly attributed to Forrest Mars, his insight and his management style. He built the company into the second largest candy producing company in America and had visions of a global corporation. He had a peculiar style of managing people, which perhaps stemmed from his drive for success. As a young man, he showed signs of entrepreneurship, when he sold meat that he bought at discounts to the school cafeteria in the University of Berkeley for a profit. He made so much profit that he canceled his business classes. He later transferred to Yale University to study economics, and once again, on the sidelines, he had a small business. This time, he sold neckties that were meant to be discarded to students, even setting up a booth in the students' union.

Forrest Mars was also an early fan of management guides, as he read books on famous entrepreneurs, like Ford and was fascinated by their principles of doing business, paying particular attention to tiny and obscure details (Brenner, 2000). In his business attempts, from the Mars bar in Europe to dog food, Forrest Mars was always more interested in starting up than managing the business. As he was often quoted saying, "I'm not a candy maker, I'm empire-minded." He has had thoughts of global expansion already in the 1920s, when he failed to convince his father to expand the business into Canada.

In his company, Forrest Mars was known for his high demands on workers, and his obsession with quality. Many associates of the company who were interviewed by Brenner for her book provided anecdotes of how demanding Mars could be. His demand for perfection went to the extent that he called up an associate in the middle of the night to request a batch of M&Ms be taken off the shelves when he bought a packet of M&Ms whereby the legs of the M were missing (Brenner, 2000).

He was also ahead of his time in empowering his employees, long before such practices were generally adopted by corporations worldwide. He paid high salaries to his employees, and made each associate feel important. In a sense, each associate was a mini engineer in his own right, as they were given complete power over their workspace, even the ones on the factory lines. Each associate knew how to maintain their machines and if there was a question of quality, it was the responsibility of the employee to halt the production line.

Forrest Mars has always been an entrepreneur, and even after handing the company over to his children in 1973, he continued to dabble in businesses. In 1980, he set up another candy business, specializing in liqueur-filled chocolates. He named the company after his mother Ethel M. This venture was successful, like most of Forrest Mars' ventures, and he managed it the way he did Mars Inc. The Company today falls under the umbrella of Mars Inc.

However, despite having management ideas that were ahead of his time and having built a multi-national corporation, Forrest Mars remained relatively unknown. He and his family were strictly private, few knew about Forrest Mars the man until his death in 1999 and that was the way he wanted it.

The Five Principles

Forrest Mars' management style forms the cornerstone of the company. Today, his ideas have been written into the management philosophy of the company and are known as the five principles of Mars. They take the form of a brochure which is available in all Mars offices. It has also been translated into many different languages for their overseas offices and factories. These five principles are that of Quality, Responsibility, Mutuality, Efficiency and Freedom.

The first principle is probably the most important out of the five. It states "the consumer is our boss, quality is our work and value for money is our goal." Quality control has always been important to the company. Forrest Mars had regular checks at his factories and offices, as he believed that a neat and clean environment is important for efficiency. Also, employees are expected to maintain a high level of cleanliness. For example, at the M&Ms factory in Hackettstown, New Jersey, its floors are scrubbed every 45 minutes. Another example is that of having exactly 15 peanuts on top of each Snickers bar, and maintaining a smooth surface on the chocolate coating. Mars Inc. was also the first manufacturer of confectionary who dated their products and seized them from distributors if unsold by the expiry date, thus maintaining the freshness of the product. Also, every grain of Uncle Ben's rice is inspected by laser beams. All this is done as they believe that "quality means guaranteeing consumers that our brands will live up to their expectations — time after time, without deviation".[3]

The entire operation of Mars is centered on the concept of quality, as they view that quality results from "unremitting attention to detail at every stage [of production]".[4] Mars takes the quality of its raw material seriously. It even has a division (the Information Services) that monitors the potential harvest of each crop, be it cocoa, peanuts, and advises the company on its long range supply strategy. In fact, Mars engineers found means of predicting the harvest of an entire crop, and today, the division even rents satellite time to monitor weather patterns and hires the best statisticians to calculate its effects on crops. All this is done to maintain the quality of Mars' products and also to benefit the company and its consumers, a principle known as mutuality.

[3,4] http://www.mars.com/quality.asp

The second principle states that "As individuals, we demand total responsibility from ourselves; as associates, we support the responsibility of others".[5] This principle manifests itself in the nature of the corporate structure, as all employees are seen as individuals, and each employee is an associate. There are no fancy titles for senior management and the owners of the company today continue to punch their timecards when they arrive at work. In this company, employees are all of equal status, address each other on a first-name basis, meetings held only "as needed", and view fancy presentations as a waste of time. Also, there are no secretaries or big offices for the management; each person takes his own phone calls, makes his own photocopies and uses a coach when needed. To further compound the idea of responsibility, each associate has a personal responsibility in the company as the salaries are tied to the performance of the products. If profits go up, salaries go up, but if the profits decline, so does the salary.

The third principle refers to mutuality, which is defined as "a mutual benefit is a shared benefit; a shared benefit will endure". This is described on the Mars website as "the standard to which everyone... aspires in all our business relationships".[6] Mars believes in benefiting everyone that they deal with, be it associates, consumers or the community at large. For example, they provided refrigerated candy bar display case for merchants in Kuwait, which allows the merchants to display Mars products prominently without fear of melting, while candy bars from competing companies had to remain in the freezer. This would benefit both the merchant and Mars, as both are able to earn money from this. Mutuality also speaks for itself in the quality control exercised by the company. Consumers are assured of the quality of Mars' products and Mars

[5] http://www.mars.com/responsibility.asp

[6] http://www.mars.com/mutuality.asp

continues to have loyal customers. In addition, Mars has built several information portals that provide information for pet owners, such as My Pet Stop, which provides general information pet care. The community also benefits as Mars also sponsors fund-raising initiatives on its fund-raising site.

The fourth principle advocates efficiency, "We use resources to the full, waste nothing and do only what we can do best."[7] In Mars, much of their efficiency comes from the fact that they are very much self-sufficient in terms of production and its control over all its resources. Moreover, machines at the factories are kept running 24 hours a day, and the products that do not pass the quality checks are put back into the mix, such that nothing is wasted. A very clear example of how Forrest Mars promoted efficiency was how he managed to put efficiency in every aspect of the production of Uncle Ben's Rice. The hulls of the unprocessed rice were burned to generate part of the electricity for the plant, and he even managed to sell the ash to power plants and steel industries. According to information on Uncle Ben's Rice, the factory even recycles 53% of the water in processing rice. Associates' desks also had to be kept clean, as he believed that this was the only way to work efficiently.

The final principle is that of freedom. Mars believes that "we need freedom to shape our future; we need profit to remain free".[8] This is reflected in how it regards its employees. Employees of Mars Inc. are given much liberty, and separate divisions of the company are usually given free rein over their decisions. There is only intervention by top management when something is very wrong with the division. In fact, Forrest Mars often left his employees to do their work, *laissez-faire* style, as he was more

[7] http://www.mars.com/efficiency.asp

[8] http://www.mars.com/freedom.asp

concerned with empire-building then with actual management. In the larger sense, the private nature of the company also allows the company to have freedom, as it is not answerable to any shareholders. This also allows for investments that have long-term yield rather than having profits dictate the growth of the company. Perhaps as a result, Mars Inc. has never been in debt.

These five principles are the underlying philosophy that guides the actions of the company and its employees. They continue to be in use, assuring consumers of quality and teaching associates how to behave.

Corporate Structure of the Company

The corporate structure of Mars Inc. is that of an open-style management, which Forrest Mars implemented when he took over control of his father's company in 1964. He defined the structure of the company by his string of actions that eliminated all aspects of status between white-collar and blue-collar workers, such as office partitions and the executive dining area. Today, the company views every employee as an associate, regardless of their status within the company. There is no differentiation of status and each associate, including the members of the Mars family, has to use timecards. Each associate is given a ten percent bonus for punctuality. Also, formality is discouraged and everyone is on a first-name basis.

There is virtually no bureaucracy existent in the company. Meetings and memos are discouraged, and the arrangement of the furniture in offices emphasizes a non-bureaucratic environment. Mars managers are seated in a wagon-wheel fashion and surrounded by subordinates, to encourage communication. Employees simply had to approach their managers when they needed something, reducing the need for bureaucracy. Forrest Mars believed in openness, and he believed that with such an arrangement, everyone knew what everyone else was doing, thus increasing efficiency.

Another aspect of the corporate structure was that the organization of the company is flat. There are only six rungs to the corporate ladder, with the top three rungs occupied by the family, the executives and senior managers. There appears to be only a relatively small number of people in these top three rungs, which is surprising for a global organization. The rungs correspond to the pay scale and are made public, such that the associates know exactly where they stand. It is also intended as a motivation for advancement.

The use of the six rungs of corporate ladder also allows for easy transfer of managers from one division to another, for example from M&Ms to Pedigree. Managers are also transferred to and from overseas divisions. This practice allows for crossbreeding of ideas and also familiarizes the manager with all aspects of Mars' operations. This practice of transferring people around is made possible with the salaries being pegged to the six rungs of the corporate ladder.

The company is also divided along seven distinct and universal functions, which are manufacturing, marketing, sales, research and development, goods and services, finance (accounting) and personnel. These departments are now known as commercial, engineering, finance, information technology (IT), logistics, manufacturing, marketing, personnel, research and development and sales. These departments are also situated next to each other, so that each is informed of what the other is doing. This flat and simple organizational structure thus helps to produce more efficient communication lines.

With such a vast organization, coupled with the freedom given to it, it would appear to be difficult to keep tabs on the organization. However, Forrest Mars had a central committee to oversee the operations of the company and its diverse divisions.

The remuneration of the employees of Mars Inc. is competitive, also to inspire loyalty. The salary is also tied to the profits of the company in order to instill a sense of personal responsibility in the associates. This came from Forrest Mars' belief that "to get the best, you had to pay the best" (Brenner, 2000). As a result, a job interview with Mars is highly coveted and many Mars managers are said to have retired as millionaires. The system of high pay also meant that many managers stayed with Mars Inc. till their retirement.

While the corporate structure of the company appears to be good for the employees, there were nevertheless problems. Despite the high pay and the freedom given to the managers, many of them found it difficult to move to higher ranks. The family management tends to trust only a select few, and with Forrest Mars' children at the helm of the company now, they have been unwilling to delegate and tend to cling to corporate power. As a result, many ambitious and outstanding executives have become frustrated and moved to other companies, despite having to take a pay cut (Brenner, 2000).

Expansion Globally

Mars Inc. is today a multi-national corporation, with offices in 47 countries, and worldwide product marketing. The idea of global expansion started as early as in the 1920s, when Forrest Mars failed to convince his father to expand operations to Canada. Today, Mars Inc. produces a myriad of products worldwide, with products to suit the palate and demands of the different countries.

When bringing their products into other countries, Mars Inc. likes to be the first to arrive before the other competitors. When the Soviet Union opened up, Mars was there first, to generate publicity for its products such that they had a consumer base before they even set up a factory there. In fact, when Mars is establishing an overseas division, they will send a senior manager over to 'scout' the area for advertising potential and recruit people. In many cases, this person is with the new establishment for only a short period of time, essentially to pass on American corporate culture and leave. Effectively, there is no on-site American overseer. In theory, the foreign establishment is supposed to follow the American corporate culture of Mars but in practice, there are nuances in the foreign corporate cultures.

It appears that the corporate culture of the company has not changed much from the times of Forrest Mars, but it is the foreign establishments that have been allowed to deviate somewhat from the framework of the American corporate culture. The fact that these overseas divisions are left largely under the charge of a foreign counterpart allows the foreign manager to promote his own culture in this company, while the basic management principles are similar. The overseas division does not promote the fact that it is an American company and they hire mainly locals. In fact, the French division of the company tends to act as if Mars Inc. was a French company. Moreover, there is typically no US overseer, except the family, which tours around the world to inspect the different divisions overseas. Besides these visits, the overseas divisions are largely left to their own to innovate and to run their business. Such attitudes held by the Mars brothers has allowed the growth of foreign corporate cultures. It shows the extent to which the corporate cultures in Mars' foreign divisions have deviated from the American style and adapted various styles of their own.

The five principles are also used in other countries, where they are being translated and adhered to by associates overseas. Overseas divisions also maintain a flat hierarchical structure that mirrors the management style of Mars. The management philosophy does not change much, as it takes on a task culture in all its divisions. In fact, the foreign offices even have a similar office layout.

Thus, in their attempt to achieve global reach of their products, Mars has set up foreign establishments, all of which follow the Mars management culture, but with slight cultural variations. Therefore, it is evident that the corporate culture has only changed culturally, in line with foreign norms but the bulk of it remains close to the American model. Today, Mars Inc. has overseas divisions in Europe, the former Soviet Union, China, Poland and Australia.

The extent of Mars Inc.'s global reach is evident in the popularity of its products worldwide. Being the first American confectionary maker to arrive in Russia has its benefits, as Snickers is now a recognized word in the Russian dictionary, while its American competitor Hershey's is nowhere to be seen (Brenner, 2000). Mars Inc. also has successful international marketing in pushing its products worldwide. Their advertising strategy is generally similar worldwide, making use of identical themes for its products. One particular example is the use of the M&Ms "spokescandy" to advertise its products worldwide. The M&Ms television advertisements are similar worldwide, with the "spokescandies" speaking in the different languages of that country. To cater to a global consumer, there are also websites created for the various continents and these are written in their native languages.

The company also uses advertising in global events to make the brand known. The Snickers bar has been the official candy for the World Cups 1994 and 1998. Mars Inc. also supposedly paid $5 million for the Snickers Bar and M&Ms to be the official snack food of the 1984 Olympics games. They also sponsored the Olympics for 1988 and 1992. Such advertising makes the brand known globally and helps entering new markets. Besides, Mars also integrates its advertising with partner websites, such as Warner Home Video and Flipside network. Even though it does not sell anything online, it has nevertheless raised awareness of its products. Moreover, Mars Inc. ran a highly successful internet campaign for the introduction of a new color in its M&Ms mix, which resulted in a 145% increase in traffic on the M&Ms website. For this campaign, surfers were alerted by the Mars Inc. Masterfoods website about the poll and there were also large amounts of budget put into advertising. This increased awareness of the brand by raising impressions by 170%. The questions were asked in 15 different languages.

The company also achieved its global reach by adopting the same standards for their brands worldwide. Previously, Mars products are marketed differently and went by different names in different countries. For example, the Snickers Bar were known as Marathon in Britain. This made global advertising campaigns difficult. The process of standardizing the diverse brands came about after the sponsorship of the 1984 Olympics. Subsequently, names and packaging have been standardized, as were advertisements. Mars even took on a project to "teach" consumers the correct pronunciation of its candies. All these were part of a global strategy that made Mars products recognizable worldwide.

Another means of its global expansion strategy was to introduce products which were successful in one country to other markets, though this did not always work out. For example, Suzie Wan, a series of Asian foods that was popular in Australia and New Zealand, was subsequently launched in America, but it did not enjoy the same success. Managers in Mars are asked why a product should not be launched in another country, rather than why it should. This is due to the company's belief in "the transfer of best practice", which is the simple belief that what works well in one country will also work well in another (Brenner, 2000). Today, the company has several best-selling brands, most of which are sold worldwide.

With an arsenal of bestselling worldwide brands, Mars Inc. is surely successful, especially since the brands are genuine global brands put forth by a "truly international company managed by international people".[9]

Future Prospects

Mars Inc. today continues to be a private company. It is listed by Forbes as the largest American food related company on its list, ahead of other companies such as Wrigley's and Nabisco.[10] It is also ranked third on the list, with estimated annual revenues of 1.75 billion. Yet it remains a family business. The Mars family continues to take the top management positions. However, it appears that there is no one in the third generation who is really interested in the business. There could be a problem of leadership handover as Forrest Mars' children are aging and there seems to be no designated successor (Brenner, 2000). In April 1999, Forrest Mars, Jr. quietly retired. His brother John Mars is now the chairman, president and CEO of the company.

It appears also that the old man, Forrest Mars had little hope in the company. It was speculated that he was so concerned about the sharing of ownership and control over his ten children that he approached the chairman of Nestlé to discuss a buyout in 1992 at the age of 88.[11]

---

[9] Quote given by Phil Forster, the overseer of the company's confectionary brands worldwide, in Brenner, 2000, p. 289.

[10] http://www.forbes.com

[11] Brenner, Joel Glenn, "A Candy King Bar None; Forrest Mars Sr.", *The Washington Post*, July 6, 1999.

The company has been steadily losing ground, as they have been unwilling to acquire smaller companies for fear of clashes between corporate cultures. As the senior executives of the company continually affirm, the company "[does] not buy and sell, [it] builds."[12] The reluctance to buy smaller firms has resulted in the growth of Hershey's in the United States. Hershey's has bought over many smaller family-owned confectionary firms, such as Leaf North America, Henry Heide Inc. and the Friendly Ice Cream Corp. The Hershey's Food Corp has also acquired stakes in foreign candy companies for joint venture overseas, in Mexico and Sweden. As a result, Hershey's has surpassed Mars Inc. as the top candy producer in America. The only recent acquisition made by Mars was the DoveBar International Inc., and 56.4 percent of the French animal food company, Royal Canin SA. The acquisition of Royal Canin SA proved to be beneficial to the company, as it now adds $360 million to the company's annual sales. But these acquisitions appear to be few and rarely happen. The most recent was probably that of the formation of a partnership between Effem Mexico SA de CV, a Mars company and Mexico's Grupo Matre, focused on producing candy for Hispanic markets. While its competitors have expanded aggressively, Mars has been left in the dust.

Moreover, the Mars' family's personal preferences dictate to a certain extent the introduction of new products. For example, the family, having grown up in England, does not like peanut butter. Therefore, there are few peanut butter products in the Mars line of products, the only prominent one being the Peanut Butter M&Ms, but insiders claim that the Mars brothers are extremely critical of its sales. In contrast, the family enjoys hazelnuts and has tried to introduce many hazelnut products, but these do not appeal to the American palate. This is detrimental in a climate of product

[12] Quote from Phil Forster in Brenner, 2000, p. 292.

innovations pushed by Mars' competitors. By holding certain products back, the family has, to an extent, undermined the competitiveness of the company.

In addition, the conservative and reactive nature of the brothers has caused some marketing *faux pas*. For example, in 1976, the brothers withdrew the red colored M&Ms from the mix because of a controversy over the discovery of carcinogens in certain red food coloring. The colorings in question were not used by the company, but the brothers nevertheless withdrew the red M&Ms, a move which many saw as wrong and which also failed to reassure consumers. It took ten years for the red candies to return to the mix (Brenner, 2000).

The use of global advertising and astute marketing techniques has made Mars Inc. a multi-national company today, one of the biggest players in the confectionary industry. Coming from humble beginnings, this family-owned company has managed to survive for two generations and its results speak for themselves. It remains to be seen what the future holds for the company, when the current familial management retire and the future directions that will be taken by this corporation, as the next generation takes over, if they take over.

Bibliography

Barnes, Bart, "Master Candymaker Forrest Mars Sr. Dies; Imperious Leader Built Secretive Family's McLean-Based Company", *The Washington Post*, July 3, 1999.

Blank, Christine, "Advertisers Back New Push for Brand Awareness", Dynamic Logic in *iMarketing News*, <http://www.dynamiclogic.com/press_coverage_imark041202.php>.

Blank, Christine, "M&M Web Site Skyrockets 145 Percent as Surfers Vote for New Candy Color, according to Nielsen/Netratings", <newsroom.ribbitt.com/pdf/mm.pdf>.

Blank, Christine, "Listing of Private Companies", *The Washington Post*, April 29, 2002.

Bredemeier, Kenneth, "Mars Buys French Pet-Food Maker", *The Washington Post*, July 11, 2001.

Brenner, Joel Glenn, "Appreciation; A Candy King Bar None; Forrest Mars Sr", *The Washington Post*, July 6, 1999.

Brenner, Joel Glenn, *The Chocolate Wars: Inside the Secret Worlds of Mars and Hershey*, New York: HarperBusiness, 2000.

Online Sources

—, "Company CV — Mars" *Marketing, September 12, 2002.*

http://www.forbes.com/2002/11/07/privateland.html

http://www.forbes.com/2003/02/26/billionaireland.html

http://www.mars.com/index/products.asp

http://www.mars.com/about/index.asp

http://global.mms.com/us/about/history/index.jsp

http://www.mars.com/

http://www.mars.com/quality.asp

http://www.mars.com/responsibility.asp

http://www.mars.com/mutuality.asp

http://www.mypetstop.com

http://www.marsfundraising.com

http://www.mars.com/efficiency.asp

http://www.unclebens.com/about/environment.asp

http://www.mars.com/freedom.asp

http://www.mars.com/careers/index_teams.asp

http://www.snickers.com/

http://www.forbes.com

The Bitter Sweet Chocolates of Sprüngli-Lindt

Sprüngli-Lindt as a sixth-generation Swiss chocolate maker has weathered extraordinary turbulences in its corporate past and still miraculously managed to survive as the only family-controlled Swiss chocolate makers from amongst a unique crowd of 19th century quality chocolate innovators like Cailler, Peter, Suchard and Tobler. Profitable for more than 100 years, it now enjoys global sales of SFrs 1.7 billion with 6,000 employees in Europe, Asia and the Americas.

Its brand names include Caffarel, Fioretto, Ghirardelli, Lindor, Lindt, Nouvelle Confiserie and Swiss Tradition. Products cover full range chocolates like pralines, liquor bonbons, chocolate bars and wafers, Easter eggs and bunnies....

The company started in Zürich as an artisanal sugar bakery in 1845 serving the sweet tooth of local citizenry. In 1892, it transformed itself into an innovative industrial chocolate maker, with marketing forays into France, Germany and Italy in the 1920s. In the 1960s these European ventures were revived and consolidated. Since 1992, when its three main markets Switzerland, Germany and France still accounted for 80% of its turnover, it has since expanded into a truly global operator, with markets outside its core marketing region now achieving more than 55% of sales. The U.S. and Canadian market alone accounts for 24% with exclusive sales outlets ("Lindt Boutique") achieving double digit growth rates.

Lindt's premium branding strategy, which uses only first grade materials, focuses on purity, freshness and flavours, has worked miracles in the globally stagnating chocolate market. In general the market is hurt by excessive cocoa prices following the turmoil and civil war in the Ivory Coast, the major commodity producer country. Further, producers have begun to destroy their brands in the endemic resort to discount sales.

With almost "refreshing boredom", as Switzerland's leading daily *Neue Zürcher Zeitung* put it, Lindt manages increased profits and dividends in an ever tougher environment since a decade ago.

This positive development was by no means assured. Since its humble beginnings Lindt & Sprüngli was frequently rocked by turmoil. Yet in the Darwinian struggle of modern capitalism it ultimately survived, expanded and prospered.

The Lindt & Sprüngli story started when in 1819 when David Sprüngli, then a poor journeyman baker joined a locally well-established Zürich sugar bakery. When his principal died in 1836, Sprüngli at the mature age of 60 bought out the widow and himself became a locally respected 'confiseur' and an honourable member of Zurich's then small town bourgeoisie. The story might have ended here, if it had not been for his son, Rudolf, who in 1845 began experiments with improved chocolate production. At the time, this was a trading secret of North Italian 'Cioccolattieri', who however produced too limited amounts of inconsistent quality to satisfy the then fashionable craze among women to sip hot chocolate. Then this was the only acceptable activity for a lady of good standing to do when in a coffeehouse alone or without related male company. The challenge was to mechanise production: How to crush and mill the roasted cocoa beans, mix the bitter paste with sugar and aromatic condiments (vanilla notably) and to create brown chocolate paste in a mechanised process with the help of water power.

Rudolf Sprüngli was one of a handful of Swiss inventors and tinkerers active in innovating chocolate production. Among them were Francois-Louis Cailler in Vevey, Philippe Suchard in Neuchatel (who in 1879 set up his first foreign production in Lörrach, Southwest Germany, had his trademark registered and started modern marketing by inserting collectable pictures in his chocolate packs), and Henri Nestlé, who in 1867 invented milk powder ("farine lactee") which made milk durable. Daniel Peter then managed to combine milk with chocolate inspite of their incompatible fats. He solved the dilemma by withdrawing fats from cocoa, added milk powder and sugar while heating up, then put the cocoa butter back in: Thus in 1825 'Chocolate au lait' was born. Most of these inventors lived in Suisse Romande, French speaking Switzerland. There were workaholic pioneers imbued in the Calvinist ethic, who in a curious apparent contradiction devoted themselves to an indulgent luxury product, one of the few sins upon which puritan Calvinism did not frown upon.

With increased production and reduced retail prices Swiss chocolate makers in the 1880s justified their mass production of the newly found "people's food" as contributing to popular health by offering a nutritious wholesome food supplement to an undernourished population.

Given their disagreements over production styles, marketing outlook and capital needs, in 1892 Rudolf Sprüngli's sons split into a "Confiserie line" (which still operates a high class, top quality coffee house at Zürich's Paradeplatz) and a "factory line". The latter, in order to finance the new industrial facility with its expensive, new machinery and refrigeration in rural Kilchberg near Zürich, in 1898 was turned into a shareholding company, with most shares of the new "Chocolat Sprüngli AG" being held by family members, senior managers and friends. (Henceforth, in good Swiss tradition, the supervisory board continues to be packed with family and corporate friends, and shareholders assemblies are made happy with regular dividends and sweet gift packs).

In 1899, Sprüngli undertook a fateful merger with the chocolate maker, Rodolphe Lindt of Berne. In return for a sizable amount of cash and Sprüngli shares, Lindt promised to share his elusive top quality production secret, his customer base and production facilities. A creative but irascible and unpredictable character, Lindt had invented a special blend of his liquid chocolate paste, which not only was exquisitely tasteful but also as "chocolate fondant" melted when consumed (and did not have to be bitten off and chewed like traditional chocolate). As a somewhat erratic "gentleman producer" uninterested in sales and in the systematic commercial exploitation of his invention, Lindt soon clashed with the Sprüngli people. He began to ignore his merger obligations and resumed to produce his own chocolates on his own account. It took a decade long legal battle, which in 1927 confirmed Sprüngli's terms of this ultimately unfriendly takeover. Since 1930, the company in consequence is named "Chocolatefabriken Lindt & Sprüngli AG". In the meantime however, Lindt & Sprüngli and the Swiss chocolate industry had to survive World War I, the loss of the Russian market due to revolution, and of the German market due to hyper-inflation and the world economic crisis of 1929. All Swiss chocolate makers had used the inter-war years to expand rapidly abroad. Yet in the aftermath of Black Friday, Peter and Cailler were swallowed by Nestlé. Suchard and Tobler ended in today's Philip Morris (recently aka Altria) portfolio.

Lindt & Sprüngli which had only cautiously entered into a joint venture with Rowntree in Berlin (1928) and later (1932) in the UK, was the only Swiss chocolate maker to survive independently.

The Second World War again led to the loss of most export markets and to the disruption of supplies for landlocked Switzerland. War rationing limited sales to one bar per person per month. Yet "Lindt & Sprüngli" managed to remain profitable as a medium sized regional producer. The company would have remained in that position had not Rudolph Sprüngli won in a 5th generation power struggle in 1962. He had written his Ph.D. thesis on the financial and strategic recklessness of their failed Tobler competitors and embarked on a cautious course of European market expansion. Having married the heiress of a cash rich construction company, he was able to buy out dissenting family members and minority shareholders, which suited his autocratic and increasingly egocentric management style. He strengthened his control with the quick entry and exit of hired managers.

Twenty years later, "Lindt & Sprüngli" had acquired Chocolate Gison AG in Chur, Chocoladefabrik Gubor in Langenthal, Nago Nährmittel AG in Olten (all in Switzerland). It had maintained its joint venture with Rowntree ("Lindt England Ltd") in the UK, started production in France with its "Consortium Français de Confiserie". In Italy it held an 11% share in Bulgheroni SpA in Varese. Following a political bribery scandal in Italy, Sprüngli bought out the remaining 89% of the discredited Bulgheroni management. In 1993, the plant was renamed "Sprüngli & Lindt SpA". Their German license producer, Leonard Monhard in Aachen, owned by a famous contemporary art collector, Peter Ludwig, who probably cared more about his paintings than about the profitability of his chocolates, faced bankruptcy in 1986. Hence Lindt & Sprüngli bought him out for DM120 million in 1987. They subsequently had to invest DM220 million for new production sites to replace the old obsolete postwar facilities.

In 1989 in Stratham, New Hampshire, production and distribution facilities for the U.S. East Coast were set-up, as was a distribution company in Hong Kong to service the Far East.

By the late 1980s, troubles set in for 'Lindt & Sprüngli' at both corporate and private levels. Branding was inconsistent in the then four core markets: with Lindt premium branding in Germany and Italy, frequent rebates in France, and "anything goes" in Switzerland.

The 'group council' of Swiss and foreign managers found foreign operations to be profitable, but the traditional Kilchberg manufacturing centre to be an inefficient loss-maker. This was anathema to the traditionalist Rudolph Sprüngli. The aging autocrat had come under the influence of an attractive faith-healing lady, with a past of ill repute, a certain Heidi Gantenbein (she still offers her spiritual services on the internet for a fee). He divorced his long-term wife, married Miss Gantenbein and subsequently fired scores of managers upon spiritual guidance of his new wife. The new management was forced to attend spiritual sessions with Ms Gantenbein. Witnessing the culinary bastion of corporate Switzerland in the hands of a faith-healing former striptease dancer sent shock waves around Lake Zurich. By 1993, Dr Rudolph Sprüngli was retired as an honourary chairman. A no nonsense new CEO, Ernst Tanner was appointed and Rudolph's son, Rudolf Konrad Spruengli who also fallen into disfavour with Ms Gantenbein and his father, was rehabilitated as a board director. Proper Euro-branding was now undertaken, reticent joint venture partners turned into subsidiaries, and cost-effective reforms undertaken at the Kilchberg site.

With a decade of sustained solid improvements, consistent production, marketing investments and innovations, the efforts of

Ernst Tanner showed a steady stream of results, thus effectively defending 'Lindt & Sprüngli's' independence, which had already been traded as a takeover candidate during the scandal years of the early 1990s.

Bibliography

Lüchinger, René, *Kampf um Sprüngli*, Frankfurt/Main: Verlag Ullstein, 1995.

"Lindt & Sprüngli — ein mastiges Praliné", *Neue Zürcher Zeitung*, 2.4.2003.

Lindt of Switzerland, http://company.monster.com.Lindt/.

"Lindt & Sprüngli liefet erneut Resultat von der Schokoladenseite", *eBand aktuell*, 1.4.2003.

"Lindt & Sprüngli steigert Umsatz 2002", *Basler Zeitung*, 29.4.2003.

"Lindt & Sprüngli — "Group Structure", http://www.lindt.com/international/aboutus/group.asp.

Kikkoman: Far Travelled Sauces

Kikkoman today is a $2-billion company, the world's largest soy sauce producer with 4,000 employees worldwide and sales in nearly 100 countries. It is the only Japanese company which has managed to expand in the drinks and seasonings sector internationally. In fact Kikkoman succeeded to make its soy sauce variants world condiments beyond the traditional confines of Japanese and Chinese cuisine.

The founding myth has it that Kikkoman soy branding started in Noda along the Edo River near Tokyo after Shige Maki, the clan's tough and resourceful ancestral mother made a narrow escape from besieged Osaka Castle in the 17th century civil wars. In any event, it is well documented that in 1661 the Mogi-Takanashi clan began brewing shoyu (natural soy sauce) in Noda, a small town in Chiba Prefecture. It was one of the typical rural industries developing in Tokugawa Japan, when urbanisation created increasing demand for rurally produced textiles, pottery and processed foods. (One should recall that in the 18th century, Tokyo had become the world's largest city.) Yet production patterns were distinctively premodern. Until the Meiji era (beginning 1868) the Mogi as owners hardly exercised any managerial functions. Toji (foremen) were in charge of the (decentralised) production, oyakata (labour recruiters) hired and paid the fluctuating day labourers, and a separate front office staff did clerical and sales work. This semi-autonomous and loosely coordinated production structure lasted well into the 20th century.

A first step towards a more consolidated owner-management system was taken in 1887 when a local cartel, the Noda Shoyu Brewers' Association, was formed in response to the oversupply and excessive competition in the Kanto shoyu market, where the Noda producers jointly held a share of 5% to 10%. The cartel was to last thirty years and set common purchasing, price, wage and shipping arrangements to Tokyo, their major market outlet. In 1911 the cartel built a railroad link to Noda, thus expanding the brewers' regional marketing to a national scale.

Yet, the requirements of modern fermentation technology, enabling more economic high-volume, low-cost production required ever-closer cooperation for the needed capital intensive investments. At this point in 1917 the nine Mogi-Takanashi clan families decided to bolt the cartel and to form their own "Noda Shoyu Corporation" putting up as flagship brand "Kikkoman", the most successful among the various family brands. The merger created by far the largest Japanese soy sauce producer at the time. Its stocks and directorships were divided and exclusively held among the principal families of the clan, all related by century-old descent and intermarriage.

By 1925 the toji directed work groups were abolished and replaced by formal production structures supervised by recently recruited managers who introduced rigid work supervision and discipline. This period of organisational transformation coincided with the emergence of union activities, which found the all-male labour force in the food industry (Japan's second largest industrial sector then after the textile industry, which employed largely dormitory-locked country girls) more congenial. Resenting the aggressive modernisation, Noda workers in 1923 under Sodomei, a reformist union's leadership went on a month long strike over work conditions. The strike was settled by Chiba's prefectural governor with a face-saving compromise for both sides. Four years later, the Great Noda Strike was to make social history in Japan. The Sodomei union branch, having recruited 1500 out of 2000 employees and accumulated a considerable war chest, felt challenged by more radical unionists and by wage cuts ordered by the Mogi management. The strike lasted 218 days and ended in total failure. The union ran out of money, while Noda Shoyu through non-unionised plants and by hiring new labour managed to keep its output unaffected throughout. The pay claims had to be abandoned, the union disintegrated, and most fired workers were not reinstated.

Only after this strike — coinciding with the nationalist appeals of the new right-wing government of General Tanaka — did the Mogi clan adopt a conscious "corporate family" ideology, introducing in the 1930s the usual paternalist symbolic and material fringe benefits to regular employees and a seniority-based payments system. By that time Noda Shoyu Corporation had well developed into a rural zaibatsu, directed by a clan-owned holding company, comprising a local bank, a transport company, a railroad, production facilities in Korea and Manchuria, exporting to Hawaii and the U.S. West Coast, and dominating Noda, its corporate town of 20,000 inhabitants.

During the war years, the company continued to produce and was even able to pay dividends to is clan owners.

After the war the U.S. occupation's anti-zaibatsu drive forced the holding company's assets to be sold, stripped the clan family heads off their formal power to enforce the family codes, and brought a new union to the Noda Shoyu Co. Yet, the corporation found its way around some of the new rules. Found guilty of price fixing and as a "price leader" by the recently founded anti-trust "Fair Trade Commission", the company responded by acquiring its own fully owned distribution network. Top management positions — unaffected by the 1964 renaming to "Kikkoman Shoyu" (1980: "The Kikkoman Corporation") — continued to be (and still are) exclusively held by members of the Mogi clan. The Mogi/Takanashi families still hold 25% of Kikkoman's shares, "friendly enterprises" like Nihon Seimei Insurance and Mitsubishi Bank control another 20%. Only the relation to the company union seems to have reversed. Contrary to what we know about Japan's labour history, the Noda Shoyu union started as a management-run union in 1946, but turned Socialist in 1949 and remained so. In the early 1960s, the union and the allied Socialist Party took over the Noda mayoralty and the majority of the municipal assembly, and thereafter started to dissociate the corporate town from the ruling clan and its enterprise.

With the Westernisation of Japan's diet, the need for shoyu flavoring declined, and so did its per capita consumption in Japan. Up to 1962 the clan management responded by buying up the market shares of traditional competitors in this contracting market. Then adopted sons took over the presidency and pursued more innovative strategies for corporate survival: Promoting overseas sales of soy sauce to non-Japanese consumers as an "all-purpose, international seasoning" and securing their U.S. market share by opening a plant in Wisconsin in 1972. The new Kikkoman management further diversified in both traditional products, like sake, shochu (a vodka-like liquor), plum wines, and in other seasonings, as well as in imported brand ketchups, juices, soups, wines and brandies. With 60% of sales in the early 1980s still accruing from soy sauce (and holding a 40% share of its Japanese market), Kikkoman at a sales volume of then $600 million was one of the few internationally competitive Japanese food processors. They are usually handicapped by the country's high level of agricultural protection pushing up input prices.

In 1969, JFC International Inc. was acquired. It produces some 8,500 oriental foodstuffs mostly under the Dynasty brand name, but also Nishiki Premium Grade Rice and Ozeki Sake. In 1990, Kikkoman strengthened its partnership with Del Monte (for whom it acted as an importing agent to Japan since 1963). It acquired permanent marketing rights for the Asia-Pacific region (except for the Philippines) for all Del Monte products, which are notably fruit juices, canned pineapple and peaches, tomato ketchup and dried raisins.

Different from many Japanese companies, Kikkoman's diversification remained focussed on the food sector proper. Its international drive also proceeded cautiously over the decades thus avoiding the pitfalls of many other Japanese companies in the boom years of pre-1992.

When the Japanese bubble finally burst, Kikkoman survived as it had an early warning signal to which it reacted well. In the mid-1980s, Kikkoman's attempt at internationalising almost proved its undoing. It sold its Mann's wine as a premium high-quality wine in Japan trusting that its customers' connaisseurship did not go very far. Unfortunately at the time glucol anti-freeze was found in diluted Austrian wines. Promptly traces were also found in Mann's wine, proving that the claimed high-quality vintage brands were rather cheap blends of bulk wines bought haphazardly from dubious traders.

Stringent quality controls, the reliance on quality wine imports and the resignation of a series of Mogi clan managers in atonement (which facilitated generational succession) helped Kikkoman to rebuild its Mann's brand as a decent table wine over the years.

According to Kikkoman's current president and CEO, Yuzaburo Mogi, "Our new, vigorous management team is working to enhance our worldwide expansion through the establishment of new plants that will enable us to move our products more efficiently while seeking strategically located promising markets".

Kikkoman's approach was to seek to expand actively through recipe contests, cooking classes and editorial PR in food journals — the use of its sauces in non-traditional western dishes, like hamburgers, stews and salads. This strategy was tough, given the innate conservatism of culinary tastes, but it paid off.

Today growth of demand for Kikkoman soy sauces and teriyaki sauces is exclusively outside Japan (where competition is tougher and the population stagnating): in North America, Europe and in South-East Asia. Hence, Kikkoman plans to increase the output of its Wisconsin plant by 40% to some 130,000 kilolitres of soy sauce and teriyaki sauce, and of its Singapore and North Holland plants by 20% each to 12,000 and 9,000 kilolitres respectively.

In the field of seasonings, and supplies for fine dining globally and for decent wines and effective biotechnology in Japan, Kikkoman is thus well positioned.

The successful family management of the Mogis over ten generations certainly is a remarkable achievement over all human and historical odds.

Kikkoman follows the slogan "Flavors That Bring People Together", and the company is devoted to promoting international cultural exchange. It does so through involvement in educational and student exchange programs such as Youth for Understanding for high school students, and AIESEC, a work/ study program for university students. It also organises any amount of cooking classes worldwide.

Bibliography

Fruin, Mark W., *Kikkoman: Company, Clan and Community*, Cambridge, Mass: Harvard University Press, 1993.

Yates, Ronald E., *The Kikkoman Chronicles: A Global Company with a Japanese Soul*, New York: McGraw Hill, 1998.

Dow Jones, *DJO Japan's Kikkoman to Boost Overseas Soy Sauce Output*, 18 April 2003.

NFIA — Company Profiles: Kikkoman Corporation, http://www.nfia/html/company/c_kikkoman.hmtl

The World of Kikkoman, http://www.kikkoman.com/contents/company/comoverview.html

Ketchum, Case Study: Kikkoman International Inc., http://www.ketchum.com/displaywebpage/0,1003,797,00.html

K
I
K
K
O
M
A
N

Who Loves McDonald's?

The sheer mention of hamburgers will naturally bring an immediate association with the leading brand, McDonald's. Even though McDonald's is not the creator of the hamburger, nor is it the pioneer of fast-food restaurants, its revolutionary approach to franchising fast-food outlets and its successful corporate strategy enabled it to become a fast-food juggernaut that is recognizable throughout the entire planet. Perhaps that is not a hyperbole and in fact, McDonald's Corporation could be forgiven for boasting that "it is the world's leading food service retailer with more than 30,000 restaurants in 118 countries serving 46 million customers each day". Its success is further symbolized by the fact that "the corporation generates more than $40 billion in annual systemwide sales".

In order to understand the success of McDonald's, it is imperative to look back at the background of this fast-food restaurant. Throughout the years, there has been a popular argument over who the real founders of McDonald's are: Is it the McDonald brothers, or is it Ray Kroc? A satisfactory answer would be that while the McDonald brothers, Richard and

Maurice, were the founders of the first McDonald's restaurant in San Bernardino, Ray Kroc was the man who took the concept of the McDonald's fast-food restaurant, franchised it, and turned it into the money-spinning juggernaut it is right now. The McDonald brothers may have been portrayed as easily contented non-entrepreneurs by Ray Kroc in his semi-autobiography, *Grinding It Out*, but the fact that they were quick to capitalize on the success of drive-in restaurants in California in the 1940s, showed their entrepreneurial skills, which would be embodied in the McDonald's *esprit de corps*. Concerned with the negative image of female car-hops driving business away, the brothers revolutionized the concept of fast food. The menu was cut down to only nine items so that food could be produced in an assembly line-like manner. Hamburgers were priced at 15 cents so that the relatively low price did attract customers in droves. At the same time, despite producing food en masse and in quick time, the quality of the food served was among the best in the area; nobody fried French fries as crispy and delicious as the McDonald's restaurant in San Bernardino.

The success of the McDonald's restaurant in San Bernardino caught the attention of a Multimixer salesman, Ray Kroc, in 1954. Kroc was intrigued with the large amount of purchases made by the McDonalds of his Multimixers, which were used to make milk shakes. When he drove down to the desert town of San Bernardino, he was impressed by the restaurant. He felt that such a concept could generate a lot of attention if it was to be expanded nationwide. However, Kroc was surprised that the McDonalds would rather stay behind in San Bernardino than participate in the joint venture that he had proposed to them. Nevertheless, without the founders, Kroc's entrepreneurial spirit drove him to create McDonald's Corporation in 1955, where he would lease out franchising licenses to operators who would want to start a McDonald's of their own. Kroc himself was the first franchisee with his store in Des Plaines, Illinois, and the success of that restaurant was made as a model to other franchisees and a showcase for future operators.

At this point in time, it is important to note that when Kroc decided to enter the fray of fast-food restaurant operations, he thought less about the amount of money it would make, but more of making McDonald's a household name across the United States. He dreamt of seeing McDonald's restaurants in every city and suburb across America and it was his nature to go all out and win at all costs in his bid to make McDonald's a successful entity. In this endeavour, he was willing to be "ruthless" to the brothers by buying the rights to the name McDonald's as well as even denying them the right to use their own name McDonald's for their original store in San Bernardino. At times, he appeared very authoritarian.

Perhaps the early success of McDonald's from 1955 onwards to the end of that decade could be due to Kroc's single-handed, authoritarian-like, management. This was made possible since the McDonald's corporation started out in 1955 as a small company, with only Kroc's secretary at Prince Castle, June Martino, and the grillmen at the Des Plaines store on his company's payroll. Kroc himself was still drawing a salary from his job at Prince Castle, which also supplied McDonald's with its Multimixers. In 1956, Harry Sonneborn was appointed by Kroc as the financial wizard of McDonald's and joined the company. While Kroc may have been authoritarian in terms of setting out the rules and regimentation that every McDonald's franchise, restaurant and employee must follow to the letter, he gave Sonneborn full autonomy over the company's financial management since Kroc himself admitted that he was not a "money person". The McDonald's mechanism was not only fuelled by Kroc's vision, desire and meticulous planning, but also by Sonneborn's pragmatism to keep McDonald's financially afloat. These two contrasting personalities might be bound to clash every now and then, and Kroc himself admitted that he would often argue with Sonneborn over the future direction of McDonald's. It was up to June Martino, who was no longer a mere secretary to Kroc but a person directly influential in the development of McDonald's as a corporation, to mediate with empathy as she herself was the embodiment of the human element in the McDonald's corporate management mechanism. Martino was seen by Kroc as the person who gelled and synergized the different personalities together to work for the betterment of the McDonald's Corporation. She would also, in countless number of times, act as the mediator between Kroc and Sonneborn. Eventually Ms. Martino was to become the matriarch of the McDonald's Corporation.

By 1960, McDonald's had already grown into a corporation that took an almost family-like structure at the top. Kroc was the father. He was the patriarch who set out the tasks for his employees and franchisees, his "children", to follow. As a "father" to the company, Kroc was very charismatic and he inspired his employees to strive hard so that in the end, they could feel as a winner if McDonald's emerged triumphant in terms of meeting the objectives he had set. When Kroc promoted his McDonald's concept to potential franchisees, he would meticulously lay out plans and would be honest in informing them how much profits they could stand to make from their venture with McDonald's. Kroc believed that McDonald's Corporation must not profit at the expense of its franchisees but it must give full support to make its franchisees succeed. Full support came, and still comes, in the form of providing high quality food and equipment supplies at discounted rates, as well as providing thorough employee training to those working at the counters and kitchens, since quality food is vital to a McDonald's restaurant's success.

Only when its franchisees reaped profits from their venture, could McDonald's achieve any success from the joint venture.

Kroc was a strict conformist and would tolerate no nonsense and deviation from the plans he had drawn out for a standard McDonald's franchise. Kroc himself set equally demanding standards and work ethic for his employees at the McDonald's Corporation headquarters. However, to dub Kroc a dictator may be missing the mark, since he was very open to ideas from anyone, be it a high-ranking executive at the McDonald's HQ, or even the counterman at a McDonald's restaurant. This openness was vital to the eventual success of McDonald's. The most popular items on McDonald's menu was soon no longer the 15-cent hamburger that had been the trademark of the McDonald brothers since the 1950's, but new items in the likes of the Big Mac, the Filet-O-Fish and the Egg McMuffin. If Kroc had really insisted all franchises to sell hamburgers at 15 cents per piece and to follow strictly to his menu list, the franchises would have folded. Kroc allowed his franchisees to be creative so that they could serve their purposes well, and in turn, serve the corporation's interests well too. This enabled Lou Groen, a franchisee in Cincinnati, to introduce the Filet-O-Fish which helped his restaurant to rake up more sales. Herb Peterson would introduce the Egg McMuffin for the breakfast menu so that his McDonald's in Santa Barbara could open in the mornings to boost sales, while Jim Delligatti introduced the Big Mac, which would become the mandatory and most coveted item on every McDonald's menu lists. In terms of marketing the McDonald's name, Kroc also allowed its franchisees to use their creativity and the operators of the franchise in Washington, DC, John Gibson and Oscar Goldstein, scored big with the creation of Ronald McDonald to promote McDonald's among the young population.

Kroc emphasized commitment to McDonald's in each of his employees. In fact, Kroc himself embodied the spirit of commitment. It was a common sight to see Kroc working in his Chicago headquarters until late evening and when he ended, he would have to rush all the way to the subway station to catch the last train. This leading-by-example personality developed a strong loyalty among executives not only towards Kroc, but also towards McDonald's Corporation. This spirit is clearly shown in John F. Love's corporate biography, *McDonald's: Behind the Arches*, where he relates the story of a senior executive, Donald Smith, who left McDonald's after being promoted as its vice-president, to become the president of its arch-rival Burger King. Even though Smith would later return to Chicago as an executive in a different company, the other McDonald's executives did "not associate with him" for they would never forget nor forgive his betrayal.

During its early days in the 1950's, McDonald's would promote itself by serving an "All-American Meal". Eventually it would be exporting Americana and its "All-American Meal" to other parts of the world. The first international expansion began just across the border in British Columbia, Canada, where the first franchise was opened in 1967. The McDonald's International Division was created in 1969 and its first restaurant overseas was opened in the Netherlands. The franchise in the Netherlands followed the successful formula of McDonald's in the United States too closely that it did not take into account several crucial local factors that almost turned the venture into a disaster.

While the success of McDonald's in the United States came largely from the suburbs which were developing as more nuclear families set homes up there, the suburbs in the Netherlands were sparsely populated as its population remained more concentrated in the cities. Nevertheless, always eager to learn from mistakes, in 1971 McDonald's opened up its first franchise in Asia, with Japan as its chosen site. For this venture, McDonald's Corporation allowed the Japanese franchisee, Den Fujita, to experiment by introducing locally flavored items on the McDonald's menu. However Fujita also realized that McDonald's could never compete with the established sushi and family restaurants in Japan that served traditional dishes, so he decided to change the eating habits of the Japanese population. Hence, in order to achieve this aim, Japanese children were often the target of promotions and advertisements whereby they would pressure their parents to eat at McDonald's. This "Americanization" strategy did not only work in Japan but also in various other countries in Asia, including notably in Singapore. In Singapore, almost every McDonald's advertisement features the whole family, children included of course, dining out at McDonald's. McDonald's International has certainly made McDonald's an important feature in an Asian family regular dining-out-together session.

Americanization does not stop at McDonaldizing the family eating habits but also in terms of corporate management. Since the success of McDonald's in the United States is due to its American corporate culture, whereby the low power-distance between employers and employees enabled free exchange of ideas and creativity, the McDonald's corporate structure in Asian countries would naturally adopt the American corporate culture. Instead of adhering to the characteristically high power-distance of the Asian corporate culture, which may stifle creativity and the free exchange of ideas, the American corporate culture helps to instill creativity among the junior level employees, and also to ensure that the senior executives would not rest on their laurels and be free from criticism.

As long as people around the world are eating hamburgers, and as long as hamburgers are associated with McDonald's, the future of the corporation still looks bright. Despite the billions of dollars worth of profits made by McDonald's Corporation, the company makes a strong effort to portray itself not as an evil multi-national corporation, but as a company that contributes a lot to the welfare of the community, as shown by its Ronald McDonald Houses community program. The human element of a corporation is vital to the success of McDonald's and thus the Hamburger University was set up to provide training and career advancement to its employees. Thus, it is not an exaggeration to say that the success of McDonald's does not depend solely on profit-maximization but also on the desire of its executives to make McDonald's part of the family and the community at large.

Bibliography

Kroc, Ray, *Grinding It Out: The Making of McDonald's*, New York: St. Martin's Press, 1987.

Love, John F., *McDonald's: Behind the Arches*, New York: Bantam Books, 1995.

Watson, James L. (editor), *Golden Arches East: McDonald's In East Asia*, Stanford, California: Stanford University Press, 1997.

Wawro, Thaddeus, *Radicals and Visionaries*, Irvine, California: Entrepreneur Press, 2000.

"Welcome to McDonald's", official website, http://www.mcdonalds.com.

For God, America and the Real Thing: The Coke Story

A billion hours ago, human life appeared on earth. A billion minutes ago, Christianity emerged. A billion seconds ago, the Beatles changed music. A billion Coca-Colas ago was yesterday morning.

— Robert Goizueta
the late CEO of Coca-Cola, explaining in April 1997
that one billion Cokes are sold every two days worldwide[1]

Originally designed as a cure for the flu in 1886, Coca-Cola has turned into the world's largest manufacturer, marketer and distributor of non-alcoholic beverages. And in the process, it has indeed become an icon of globalization. Back in 1989, the Company sold $8.6 billion worth of beverages and by 1999 its

---

[1] For more on Goizueta's leadership role in the Coca-Cola Company, refer to "Goizueta and Juan Antonio Samaranch", in David Greising's *I'd Like the World to Buy a Coke: The life and leadership of Roberto Goizueta.* NY: John Wiley, 1998, pp. 251–257.

sales had more than doubled to $19.8 billion, for an annualized growth of 8.67%. (*Motley Fool*) To date The Coca-Cola Company has diversified its products to more than 300 brands whilst operating in over 200 countries worldwide.[2]

The "Good Ole" Days

In 1885, John Pemberton,[3] an Atlanta pharmacist, registered a trademark for "French Wine Cola — Ideal Nerve and Tonic Stimulant", a brew he had developed in a three-legged pot which he apparently stirred with an oar. The name was appropriate, since the stimulant is said to have contained cocaine, along with wine and a few other ingredients. After about a year, Pemberton decided to change the formula; he removed the wine and added caffeine and, for flavor, extract of kola nut.[4] At that point, his partner and bookkeeper, Frank Robinson, changed the name to Coca-Cola because he thought the two Cs, written in the Spencerian script, which was largely popular at that time, would look good in advertising. Coca-Cola, which joined the ranks of the many mysterious potions being peddled by traveling sales-men, was thus sold as a cure for both hangovers and headaches.

In a twist of events, Georgia businessman Asa Candler[5] bought the sole rights to Coca-Cola from John Pemberton in 1889. To expand the business Candler began to sell Coca-Cola syrup to

---

[2] Obtain latest press releases and financial statements of the Company vis-à-vis the Coca-Cola website.

http://www2.coca-cola.com/ourcompany/ourheritage.html

[3] "Dr. John S. Pemberton: Originator of Coca-Cola", *Pharmacy in History*, vol. 29 (1987), no. 2, pp. 85–89: Allen, *Secret Formula*, pp. 18–22.

[4] See "Use of the coca plant": in "Wonderful Coca", AC, June 21, 1985.

[5] Refer to Asa Candler, "Confidence in your Product", *1916 Bottlers Convention Booklet*, p. 76.

wholesalers, who in turn sold it to drugstores. In 1889, Benjamin F. Thomas and Joseph P. Whitehead of Tennessee approached Candler with a proposition to bottle Coca-Cola. They promptly sold regional bottling rights to other businessmen in the South and later to the rest of America, thus creating a network of independent bottlers numbering about one thousand by 1930. Each bottler had an exclusive right in perpetuity to bottle Coke in his area, and no one else except the soda fountains could sell Coke in the market. The bottlers[6] actually owned the Coca-Cola trademark in their territories and the company could not then refuse to sell them syrup (Oliver, 1986). This simple contract was to revolutionize the Coca-Cola business, giving birth to one of the world's most innovative and dynamic franchising systems in the world (Pendergrast, 2000).

Robert W. Woodruff "The Boss"

In 1919, Candler sold the company to Ernest Woodruff for a hefty $25 million. Subsequently in April 1923, Woodruff's son Robert became president of Coca-Cola. The boss, as he came to be called would soon make the name Coke virtually synonymous with that of America around the world. Yet this dominant figure worked behind the scenes in relative anonymity. He had even hired public relations personnel to keep his name out of the newspapers and told the publisher of *The Atlanta Constitution* that he did not want to see his name in that paper again unless he was convicted of rape. Interestingly, a plaque on his desk read, "There is no limit to what a man can do or where he can go if he doesn't mind who gets the credit", a saying that perhaps no other corporate president before or since has endorsed. With his

[6] Ralph B. Beach, "History of the Coca-Cola Bottler's Association", CC Bottler, April 1959, pp. 99–106.

fedora, and a cigar permanently jutting from his teeth, he led the company through the strength of his personality.[7]

Even to his closest associates, Robert Woodruff remained much of an enigma. Standing at an even six foot, his commanding presence made him seem much larger than life as he chewed on his ever-present cigar whilst silently assessing a room he had just entered. Without a doubt, Robert Woodruff had an indescribable presence, magnetism. For this reason, Coca-Cola men would do seemingly almost anything to win his favor and have since demonstrated fanatical loyalty over the years. Yet, on the surface, Woodruff was a singularly uninteresting man. Simply put, he didn't read.[8] Several of his intimates swore that he never finished a book in his life, and he refused to look at any correspondence that went beyond a single page, relying on aides to digest the material for him. He was also reputed to be unappreciative of culture, history, or art. When stuck in traffic only minutes from St. Peter's in Rome, he impatiently ordered his driver to turn around. "But Mr. Woodruff, we're only five minutes away!" his secretary exclaimed. "That's close enough", Woodruff snapped.

It is essential to note however that Robert Woodruff aptly inherited the corporate culture of Coca-Cola, a drink that already acquired a semi-mystical aura. In addition, he understood how to manipulate corporate structure in order to maximize profits, privacy, and control while minimizing taxes and governmental

---

[7] Woodruff prescribed a rigid Ichauway itinerary for his guests. "When you are with Bob Woodruff", remarked Freeman Gosden, the white actor who played Amos in Amos and Andy, "you are going to have a good time all right, but you are going to have it his way". (Elliot, Mr. Anonymous, p. 55)

[8] It has been speculated amongst scholars the possibility of Woodruff being dyslexic, amongst others such as George Patton, Woodrow Wilson, Thomas Edison and Nelson Rockefeller (Landmark College Correspondence).

scrutiny. In 1923, Robert Woodruff had expanded the former Information Department into the Statistical Department, which soon performed what would now be called the department for pioneering market research. During the decade's last three years, this department frenetically laid the foundation crucial for an enhanced scientific approach to selling more Coca-Cola (Pendergrast, 2000, p. 161).

Also, Woodruff began on an important mission to standardize the quality and output of Coca-Cola around the world. He did this by relating the message of a reward system to the bottlers: for if you abided by his rules, you were rewarded with more advertising support, more encouragement and more perks. If you choose otherwise, you would consequently find yourself with virtually no support, and possibly becoming ostracized by the many other members of the "Coca-Cola family." Woodruff found another solution for failing bottlers during the twenties as well, by simply buying them out of their crisis, which proved to be an effective economic move.

In addition, Woodruff also pioneered the Seeds of Foreign Conquest, applying his energy and organizational skills to birthing overseas markets. In 1922, with an expenditure of some $3 million, bottling franchises were started all over Europe, largely funded by Coca-Cola and run by locals in those selected regions (Pendergrast, 2000, pp. 164–166). In terms of advertising and publicity, the company has always believed in marketing its products well through aggressive advertising and the like, spending more than $4 billion annually on advertising and marketing worldwide. During World War Two, a different sort of advert rendered Coca-Cola's brand name famous worldwide. Coke supplied to the American GIs fighting overseas served as a powerful message and became iconic of American presence abroad. According to a returning war veteran, "Personally, I think that The Coca-Cola Company's cooperation with the Army in getting Coca-Cola to the men in the field is the best advertisement that Coca-Cola has ever had". Writing to his company boss exemplifying, "The things that are happening to these men now will stick with them for the rest of their life".[9]

And in the 1980s, in an attempt to compete with the preferred taste of Pepsi-Cola, Coke revamped its original recipe to one that boasts of superior taste to that of Pepsi and even the original Coke flavor. However that proved to be a marketing disaster as people were outraged with the insertion of a 'new' coke. As a result of the New Coke disaster, the original Coca-Cola garnered much more than $4 billion worth of publicity, rendering the Company's horrendous advertising irrelevant. The venerable cola roared back to claim its lead as the premier American soft drink. Unintentionally, Goizueta and Keough had converted the gigantic marketing blunder into a commercial coup (Allen, 1994).

Roberto Goizueta[10] who became Woodruff's successor, had always said that Coke products should be more popular than water. In terms of marketing Coke, the most powerful Coca-Cola appeal has not, ultimately, been sexual or physiological, but communal: if you drink Coke, the ads suggest, you will belong to a warm, loving, accepting family, singing in perfect harmony.

---

[9] In a poll of veterans in 1948 conducted by the *American Legion* Magazine, 63.67% specified Coca-Cola as their favorite soft drink, with Pepsi gaining only 7.78% of the total vote. In the same year, Coke's gross profit on sales reached a staggering $126 million, as compared to Pepsi's $25 million. As the Coca-Cola Company's unpublished history stated, the wartime advertisement "made friends and customers for home consumption of 11,000,000 GIs [and] did [a] sampling and expansion job abroad which would otherwise have taken 25 years and millions of dollars". See Pendergrast, *For God, Country and Coca-Cola,* London: The Orion Publishing Group, 2000, p. 212.

[10] Goizueta left an astonishing legacy, in Patricia Sellers, "Where Coke Goes from Here", *Fortune,* Oct. 13, 1997, p. 88.

Coke Nation Embodying Corporate Culture

At The Coca-Cola Company, employees are fervently attached to
their employer. "Everyone is very loyal to the company, they are
very proud of all of the accomplishments achieved there. There is
a certain amount of pride many of us take knowing that we have
helped get us to this point", according to one employee in a
conducted research poll.[11] Indeed, Coke is the very lifeblood of
the company, and its employees shunt the sainted liquid at their
peril. Says one former financial auditor who describes the
company's culture as quite strong where people are expected to
drink Coke.

The intense loyalty meshes with what is invariably described
as a "conservative" atmosphere, an ambience linked to the sheer
size of the company. Coke has a very conservative corporate
culture. Coke is an extensive company and has a seemingly
diverse and large company corporate culture. The company is
very proud of its heritage and integrity, and is fairly conservative
by nature. Coke people tend to be professional in dress and
nature, and are geared towards conservative behavior. This is not
to say that enthusiasm is not appreciated. In many cases, it is
often required.

The headquarters of The Coca-Cola Company is located in
downtown Atlanta, Georgia. According to an insider of the
corporate headquarters, "there is extreme security before you
even gain access into the Coke nation, and it continues
throughout the complex". The company actually has a Health
Management Department staffed with Health and Fitness
Specialists whose job is to reduce health care costs and encourage
healthy habits in the company. The company also subsidizes all of

---

[11] For the latest in details, refer to website http://www.vault.com/career/
The_Coca-Cola_Company_1999_Edition.html.

the services at its Coca-Cola's home campus, which include fitness centers and other amenities.

The Coca-Cola Company likes to propagandize that "Coca-Cola" is the second-best known expression in the world, next to "Ok." It is thus no wonder that The Coca-Cola Company credentials apparently stands out on a resume. Adding in the ubiquity of the product and the outstanding performance of its stock in the last few decades, the brand and business success culminates in an adage recipe for super-high prestige — especially in areas such as finance and marketing. It is reported that Coke has a great reputation everywhere in almost every area they are in. They like to believe that there is quality in everything they do, and they work very hard at maintaining that quality.

Insiders describe Coke's benefits package in glowing terms. Besides the benefits of the corporate campus, employees have the option to finance their car with the help of the company, have several healthcare plans to choose from, a tuition reimbursement, a stock-purchase, and can enjoy a 401(k) plan that has made many a Coke employee's retirement a golden one. There are also days off at Six Flags Atlanta, free ice-skating, Thanksgiving Dinners, and available concert tickets in the Coca-Cola section reserved in the front at almost any major venue in the country. And of course, there is the "all-you-can-drink" aspect of working at Coke, reportedly distributed through coolers, fountains, and vending machines rigged. So all you have to do is push the button and the Coke can drops.

Coke is not known for its outstanding record on diversity efforts, but if employees in Atlanta are to be believed, corporate headquarters is teaching the world to sing in perfect harmony, making Coca-Cola a truly international company by hiring people of all races, religions, and cultures. The diversity may be also drawn from the mixed backgrounds of management people and those working under them. At the helm is Coke's revered former

CEO, Roberto Goizueta, who was a Cuban immigrant himself, personifying the very aura of the Coca-Cola establishment, being the very self-made man that he is, a perfect symbol of the American dream rising to the pinnacle of success.

Criticism of Coca-Cola's Culture

It is not surprising that Coca-Cola finds itself in deep trouble in Europe. And this has to do with the company's corporate culture. If you think about it, Coca-Cola sells sugared water. That's all. Just sugared water. Yet it has managed to do it so skillfully for so long that it has taken on an almost mystical aura, even to its employees. Its success is due to a corporate culture that comprises superior marketing with that of aggressive legal enforcement. Coca-Cola lawyers are among the most aggressive in the world, enforcing the company's rules on how and where Coca-Cola is sold.

This combination of marketing and legal muscle has made the company extraordinarily successful, and perhaps left it feeling a tad omnipotent. However, entering the dust-up in Belgium and France over supposedly contaminated Coca-Cola products, we see that the company's culture didn't allow it to respond as quickly as it should have, and the result was a costly crisis. The culture is determined by how the CEO wants the company to run. Doug Ivester, Coca-Cola's CEO, is a good numbers man, but unimpressive in public relations thus resulting in this *mea culpa*.

The incident happened on June 8, 1999, where thirty-nine students in Bornem, Belgium, collecting bottle caps for a contest, complained of nausea and headaches and attributed it to the Cokes consumed. Clearly, the Coke brass was caught off-guard by how rapidly the crisis escalated. On June 16, two days after the Belgian government had placed a ban on all Coke products, Doug Ivester issued his first public statement, a bland bit of bureaucratese saying that the company was "taking all necessary steps" to ensure and safeguard its beverages' quality. But the following day, Ivester flew to Europe to exercise personal damage control. Penning an apology that ran in full-page ads in European newspapers, he appeared in a 90-second TV spot, and offered to buy every Belgian, 10 million of them a free coke! Finally, by June 24, both Belgium and France had rescinded their bans, although Coke still had to destroy its remaining stock before it could rejuvenate production. The massive recall cost the company and its major bottler over $100 million, but more damaging was its severely tarnished image, broadcasted over Europe extensively (Pendergrast, 2000).

Another obstacle to Coca-Cola's image and sales particularly in Europe is a general feeling of anti-Americanism. "There are many Europeans", commented one journalist, "who genuinely believed that the object held aloft by the Statue of Liberty is a Coke bottle".[12] Other criticisms include occasional concerns expressed over the alleged inclusion of cocaine in the Cola. However, cocaine is documented to have been removed from its formula since 1903. Of late, controversial debates of the drink as a health hazard in relation to its caffeine and phosphoric acid content have also risen sharply (Allen, 1994; Oliver, 1986).

Turning to the World (Global Strategy)

By the early seventies, investments in Japan had blossomed into the largest Coke market outside the United States. In 1973, Japan contributed 18 percent of Coca-Cola's entire corporate profit,

[12] See Richard Kuisel, *Seducing the French: The dilemma of Americanization*, Berkeley: University of California Press, 1993. Refering specifically to "Yankee Go home" which documents the Left, Coca-Cola, and the Cold War, pp. 37–69.

despite an increasingly militant consumer movement and various administrative import barriers. In 1972, Jimmy Carter revealed that he had ambitions beyond Georgia, asking Paul Austin for Coca-Cola's support if he ran for President. Austin agreed without contemplating that the nationally unknown Carter would actually succeed. Nonetheless, when the Georgian governor groomed himself by traveling overseas to Tokyo and Brussels, ostensibly to boost the nation's trade, but also garnering considerable international experience and exposure, Coca-Cola employees there squired him around the country, providing background information on local politics, culture, and economy. With Austin's sponsorship, Carter joined the prestigious Trilateral Commission set up by David Rockefeller and the East Coast establishment as a fellow member successfully.

In 1977, Paul Austin quietly flew to Cuba, where he held closed door secret meetings with Fidel Castro, presumably to negotiate the Company's return to the country, even though Coca-Cola officially held a $27.5 million claim against Cuba for confiscating its plants in 1961. His mission proved unsuccessful, except for some Havana cigars, which Castro had sent to Robert Woodruff by means of Austin. Having promised President Carter that he would report on his trip to Cuba, Austin then met with him briefly in the White House. When acid-penned columnist William Safire learned of the episode, he concluded that it was a nefarious scheme to obtain Cuban cane. "The Carter-Coke-Castro sugar diplomacy is not merely a potential conflict of interest," wrote Safire. "It's the real thing."[13]

Austin was more successful in negotiating for Coca-Cola's entry into Portugal, Egypt, Yemen, Sudan, the Soviet Union,

---

[13] It isn't surprising that Safire, a former Nixon speech-writer attacked the Carter/Coke connection (Louis & Yazijian, p. 93).

and China.[14] Though none of these coups could be attributed directly to Carter's intervention, the American President's well-publicized bias toward the soft drink undoubtedly provided essential leverage for its success. For instance, the long-awaited Portuguese permission coincided uncannily with the U.S. Treasury Department's approval of a badly needed $300 million loan.

Thus with the implicit Carter clout behind them, the Coca-Cola men triumphed in country after country — with the exception of India, where Coke departed in 1977 rather than reveal its formula to the government.[15] Their achievements, however, came only after years of patient negotiations that predated any presidential aid, as with Bob Broadwater's efforts in Moscow. Although Pepsi had an exclusive Soviet cola contract running through to 1984, Kosygin's men decided Coca-Cola could be served at special events. In 1978, Broadwater signed a contract to supply Coca-Cola to the Spartakiada, the East Block sports festival during the following year. That would serve as a warm-up for the 1980 Moscow Olympics, where Coke paid $10 million for exclusive rights to the event. Fanta Orange would successfully fizz not only during the sporting events, but also on a long-term basis throughout the Soviet Union (Pendergrast, 2000).

The real Austin plum, however, fell into his lap late in 1978, when Coke's executive Ian Wilson, holed up in a Beijing suite, hammered out an arrangement with the Chinese Communists only days before the U.S. State Department normalized relations.

[14] From 1949 until 1978, China banned Coke from its markets (*The New York Times Magazine*).

[15] In 1977, the nationalistic Indian government demanded that all of the soft drink be manufactured inside India, which meant revealing its secret formula. Coke refused, and the Company reluctantly withdrew, abandoning 22 bottling plants. "India may swallow Coke", *Time*, August 22, 1977, p. 44.

Now, despite Mao Tse-tung's pronouncement in his *Little Red Book* that Coca-Cola was "the opiate of the running dogs of revanchist capitalism", the highly popularized beverage has found its home on the Chinese mainland. And around the world, Coke pumped money into newly designated "anchor bottlers" — Coca-Cola Enterprises in the United States, Australia's Coca-Cola Amatil, Mexico's FEMSA, Mexico's PANAMCO, South Africa's SABCO, and Malaysia's Fraser & Neave — which since execute Coke strategy across geographical borders. That had to be its ultimate global networking strategy, a game plan consolidating its strongholds all over the world effectively.

Coca-Cola's Asian Strategy

Strategic moves made in Asia by The Coca-Cola Company have been driven by two key elements of its global strategy. These include implementing a worldwide 'anchor bottler' system and secondly, developing under-served markets wherever they are found around the world. One of the main driving forces of Coca-Cola's global strategy has been to re-align and strengthen its worldwide bottling system. The goal is to generate extensively increases in unit case volume, net revenues and profits at the bottler level and thereby generating increased shipments of Coca-Cola concentrate.

Traditionally, Coca-Cola often starts the process of strengthening its bottling system in a given region or country by buying out local bottlers and subsequently enhancing their production, distribution and marketing capabilities. Coca-Cola would then sell off the local bottler to one of its 'anchor bottlers', which becomes solely responsible to the Coca-Cola Company for the management of the bottling and distribution operation.

Anchor bottlers are essentially large and well-capitalized firms that share Coca-Cola's commitment to growth and have demonstrated to Coca-Cola that they have a strong management team and the capability to manage bottling operations in more than one country. The strategic alliance between Coca-Cola and the anchor bottler is structured to provide benefits for both partners. Coca-Cola provides the capital for financing the growth of the anchor bottler by taking equity in the firm. In return, Coca-Cola obtains membership on the board and the opportunity to participate in the strategic directions undertaken by the anchor bottler (Robert, 1998 and London: *Financial Times*, 1998).

In recent years Coca-Cola has established anchor bottlers in North and South America, Europe as well as Asia. In 1997, the company completed bottler transactions with a value exceeding US$8 billion, and it now has equity positions in bottlers responsible for more than 60 percent of its worldwide case volume production. Coca-Cola's anchor bottler system has been one of the main reasons for its widening global scheme, giving it a competitive edge over Pepsi-Cola. As the system gives Coca-Cola more direct control of its global business and enables it to deal with its worldwide operations regionally rather than on a more fragmented and less efficient country-by-country basis.

The Asian anchor bottlers of Coca-Cola are as follows:

◊ Coca-Cola Amatil (CCA), based in Sydney, which controls bottling and distribution in Indonesia, the Philippines and South Korea, and also has been one of Coca-Cola's European anchor bottlers;

◊ Fraser & Neave Coca-Cola of Singapore (F&N), which has Coca-Cola bottling operations in seven smaller countries in the region (Malaysia, Brunei, Cambodia, Nepal, Pakistan, Sri Lanka and Vietnam);

◊ Swire Beverages, which operates in Hong Kong, Taiwan and China, and Kerry Beverages, which shares bottling responsibilities with Swire in China.

Asia still accounts for only a relatively small percentage of Coca-Cola's global business. The region thus still offers opportunities for growth that far exceed prospects in its domestic market. From the global perspective of Coca-Cola, Asian markets are under-served, and represent prime targets for development. As demonstrated in calculated statistics, Coca-Cola sees significant opportunities in South Korea and China, where the population consumes much less of Coca-Cola products than in some other Asian countries. For example, India where 950 million people drink an average of only four servings of industrial soft drinks each year is seen as yet another vital market (Robert, 1998).

Global Culture

In the case of Coca-Cola, its corporate headquarters are based in Atlanta with a very dominant task-oriented role culture. After the subsequent death of the powerful and charismatic leader Robert Woodruff, the company has since lost some appeal of the power culture environment. Notably, the culture within is extremely strong with ties and loyalty to the product and company vision fervently attached. The goal of reaching the masses and making Coke more popular than water is a dream that is fast becoming commonplace. In light of its move to globalize, what the company did was to successfully invest heavily on Research and Development in meeting the needs of its customers worldwide.

With 80 percent of Coke's profits coming from sales outside the United States, Goizueta officially recognized the importance of the global nature of the business by reorganizing the Company's management structure. Previously, there had been two primary units namely classified under "North America" and "International". Now, he simply divided the world into five major groups, with North America being one of those partitions. "We not only *see* our business as global", he wrote, "but we *manage* it that way … We understand that, as a practical matter, our universe is *infinite*, and that we, ourselves, are the key variable in just how much of it we can capture". (Pendergrast, 2000, p. 448.)

Thus going by the dogma of "think globally, but act locally". This catch-phrase probably originated with Goizueta, though other CEOs snapped it up in the trendy 1980s and used it as their own mandate. Regardless of its provenance, Coca-Cola has demonstrated its wisdom, dipping into its own history for much guidance. In China and Indonesia, for instance, the first task involved building a strong infrastructure comprising concentrate factories, glass manufacturers, bottling plants, trucks, point-of-purchase signage — in American terms, this is time-warping back to 1905. On the other hand, in the former West Germany and Japan, the company has already a well-established business, but similar to the United States of the 1970s, there exist too many bottlers vying in small territories, rendering the task there of consolidation (Pendergrast, 2000, p. 468).

In terms of a 'globalized' common corporate culture, the Coke team remains largely American in running its businesses, aggressive in negotiating deals, tough in lawyering, engaging in powerful lawsuits for survival and self-protection. Based firmly upon American philosophy, the company has even been accused of cultural imperialism, particularly by the French. In Europe, Coca-Cola managers also try to keep its outlook and image American although shifty at times, thus resulting in the *mea culpa* such as the Belgium and French dust-up where the company was allegedly selling contaminated Coke. Failure to respond quickly and efficiently whilst adhering to the needs of the particular culture cost Coke millions of dollars and even more damaging was its loss of image and credibility.

In Asia, bottlers are given independence in managing the operations and its execution although the parent firm is the overall in charge of other marketing strategies and details. Depending heavily on advertising, the Coca-Cola Company sells Coke synonymously with America, thus branding them as largely American exports deemed to conquer the global markets. With regards to product diversification and variety, Coke tries to remain streamlined and has not since come up with an exceptional amount of localized versions after the failure of the "new Coke blunder" in the 1980s.

The way they allowed for change and flexibility probably lies in the fact that they allocate bottler rights and autonomy to run the factories provided that the quality and services are granted satisfactory by Coke personnel from its HQ. There is no direct localization of products to gain global reach, unlike in the case of MacDonald's and its franchises worldwide. There, autonomy is given with respect to product diversification and menus unique to locations are distinguished. For Coke, differentiation occurs in the event that firms operating in Indonesia probably have a bottler adapting to a culture quite different from one based in America.

The Pepsi Challenge

While Coca-Cola grabbed headlines around the world, the business back home was stagnating. Pepsi made inroads on the valuable take-home market, scooping Coke with one-and-a-half- and two-liter plastic bottles. As a symbol of Coke's loss of direction, *1600 Pennsylvania Avenue*, the Broadway production which had cost the company $800,000, folded after seven performances, as *The New York Times* critic Clive Barnes pronounced it as simply being "tedious and simplistic". Thus while Coca-Cola switched to the lackluster "Coke Adds Life" campaign in 1976, Pepsi bounced back with its new invocation to "Have a Pepsi Day." As usual, Coca-Cola undoubtedly maintained a product focus while its rival concentrated on life-styles.

Seemingly almost by accident, Pepsi launched a simultaneous strategy in direct contrast to its traditional approach. Pepsi man Dick Alven had been sent to Dallas with the almost hopeless mission of injecting life into the business there, where Pepsi claimed a miserable 4 percent of the soft drinks market. Alven convinced his boss that they needed drastic measures, so they petitioned Pepsi headquarters to allow them to use the local Stanford Agency instead of BBDO. Bob Stanford, who had discovered that Pepsi had beaten Coke in taste-tests while promoting a 7-Eleven generic cola, boldly suggested a daring assault on competitor Coca-Cola. In 1975, Dallas TV stations aired commercials urging viewers to "Take the Pepsi Challenge," showing candid shots of die-hard Coke consumers astonished to discover that they preferred Pepsi in such blind taste-tests. It seems that Pepsi had stooped to such an outrageous, virtually taboo approach, since comparative ads were considered unsportsmanlike. Nonetheless, the results were indisputable as within two years, Pepsi's Dallas market share jumped by 14 percent.[16]

While Coca-Cola's domestic market share remained relatively flat, Pepsi's steadily rose throughout the seventies. In 1977, Pepsi's advertising budget had actually surpassed Coca-Cola's for the first time, with each firm spending just over $24 million a year on their main brands. By the following summer, Nielsen market figures demonstrated that Pepsi had finally overtaken Coke in supermarket sales, dubbed the "free choice" arena. Defensive Coke men asserted that their drink still held an edge in the total retail outlets.

---

[16] See Timothy J. Muris, David T. Scheffman, and Pablo T. Spiller, *Strategy, Structure and Antitrust in the Carbonated Soft-Drink Industry*, Westport: Quorum Books, 1993.

In response, "they must use some strange numbers", speculated John Sculley, the combative young Pepsi-Cola president.

The world's most far-flung or globalized corporate empire was also poised for a world of trouble, rippling out from Asia. In Indonesia, the rupiah went into free fall in January 1998, and as unemployment soared, Coke sales plummeted. In counteracting this crisis, Doug Ivester urged managers to fight back rather than "to simply hunker down and ride out the storm". Reminding them that they're investing for long-term gains thus building along the way new capabilities to deal with *any* type of uncertainty. In obedience, Asian Coke managers tossed out their carefully articulated annual marketing plans and adjusted to new conditions, creating "market impact teams" to work at the street level, getting product to vendors as quickly and cheaply as possible.

To make matters worse for Coke, Roger Enrico was then leading a recharged Pepsico. In October 1997, Enrico successfully spun off Pepsi's restaurants, including Taco Bell, Kentucky Fried Chicken, and Pizza Hut, as Tricon Global Restaurants, allowing Pepsi to focus only on soft drinks and snack foods. Until then, Coke fountain salesmen could stymie Pepsi sales by dominating fast food chains. However, Pepsi soon struck new deals with Pizza Inn, Hard Rock Café, Planet Hollywood, and Warner Brothers theaters. Nonetheless, Coke owned 65 percent of the U.S. fountain business, compared with Pepsi's 22 percent. Coke countered by cementing a multi-year contract with Burger King and Wendy's adding to its other outlets (Pendergrast, 2000, p. 427).

In frustration and retaliating, Pepsi then sued Coke in 1998, alleging that Coca-Cola violated the Sherman Anti-Trust Act by threatening to cut off supplies to food-service distributors if they carried Pepsi, too.[17] Coke freely admitted dumping distributors

[17] Larry Light, "Litigation: The choice of a new generation", *Business Week*, May 25, 1998, p. 42.

that carried Pepsi. Indeed, its contracts specified that offering Pepsi was a "conflict of interest". But Coke asserted that its rival could always sell its soda directly to customers and that its distributors were fundamentally "an extension of Coca-Cola". The complex lawsuit would probably remain unresolved for years to come (Muris, 1993).

In 1998, as it celebrated its centennial, Pepsi also moved aggressively to offer and acquire new drinks. When acesulfame potassium, trade-named Sunett, a new sugar-free sweetener with a longer shelf-life than aspartame, was approved by the FDA, Pepsi came out with Pepsi One, a new one-calorie diet drink.[18] Pepsi's Mountain Dew continued to grab large segments of market share especially with teenagers. To counter Coke's highly successful Sprite, Pepsi now introduced Storm, its own caffeinated lemon-lime concoction. Finally, Pepsi bought over Tropicana for $3.3 billion, giving it the market-leading premium orange juice to aggressively counter Coke's Minute Maid.[19]

A World without End for Coca-Cola?

Despite Pepsi's new feistiness, Coke still continued to dominate Pepsi outside the United States by a 3.6-to-1 margin. Although it would take a miracle for Coke to reach its goal of garnering 50 percent of the U.S. market share by the year 2001, by 1999 it had snared 45 percent as compared to Pepsi's 31 percent. The Big Red Machine may have been slowed by global economic woes,

[18] Diet Coke was introduced way back in 1982 proving a huge hit with its consumers.

[19] "Pepsico buys Tropicana", *Advertising Age*, July 20, 1998, p. 25. "Beverage Wars intensify as PepsiCo Acquires Tropicana", *Chain Drug Review*, Aug. 10, 1998, p. 6.

but it still appeared unstoppable in the long run. Roberto Goizueta had always said that Coke products should be more popular than water. Was it then a "World without End" for the age-old soft drink company?

> *You can run from it, but you can't hide. Sooner or later, no matter how far you think you've ventured from the comforts and conveniences of the modern world, Coke will find you. Go to the foothills of the Himalayas, the hurricane pounded fishing islands off the coast of Nicaragua — go to the birthplace of civilization, if you like. Coca-Cola will be waiting for you.*
>
> — *The New York Times* editorial, 1991

As the world shrinks to a global village,[20] the appeal of Coke and Big Macs as "luxury" items are increasing, and some nutritionists express concern that these will soon gradually displace cheaper, traditional, healthier cuisine.

"When advertised in a culturally appropriate way with appealing symbols", writes an anthropologist, "the public consumption of such foods and soft drinks turns out to be a principal form of identification with Western lifestyles and power. Their long-term negative consequences are not fully assessed, but it is highly probable that they will progressively undermine the older [core diet] of poor agrarian societies," (Pendergrast, 2000, p. 445).

---

[20] See Americanization of the Global Village in Roger Rollin's *The Americanization of the Global Village: Essays in comparative popular culture,* Bowling Green, Ohio: Bowling Green State University Popular Press, 1989. Also, Jon Roper, "Encountering America: Altered States", in *Americanisation and the Transformation of World Cultures,* eds. Phil Melling and Jon Roper, Lewiston: Edwin Mellen Press, 1996, p. 1.

Similarly, although French critics initially called Euro Disneyland "a terrifying giant step toward world homogenization" and "a cultural Chernobyl", another Frenchman pointed out: "If French culture can be squashed by Mickey Mouse ... it would have to be disturbingly fragile" (Storti, 2001, p. 112). Nonetheless, Coke is now widely available in French cafes, but it is served almost as if it were an aperitif rather than a soft drink. "One might want to consider the 'Frenchification' of America", wrote Richard Kuisel in *Seducing the French*, "as well as the Americanization of France. If anything, we have learned that modern culture is eclectic and porous". In other words, we might regard the current cross-pollination of cultures as a kind of evolution rather than homogenization (Pells, 1997). "The differences among races, nations, cultures and their various histories are at least as profound and as durable as the similarities", wrote Australian essayist Robert Hughes, who predicted that the future belongs to "people who can think and act with informed grace across ethnic, cultural, linguistic lines", a seemingly perfect description of today's top Coca-Cola managers.

For the second year in a row, Fortune named The Coca-Cola Company the most admired American company. Its prospects seem bright despite caution from various economic gurus. With greater product diversification, innovations and acquisitions, Coca-Cola looks set to widen and deepen its markets worldwide. The overwhelmingly question remained however as to, "What must we do to make a billion Coca-Colas ago be this morning?" This adept question brings to mind in recollecting Coca-Cola's business strategies and philosophy. As Goizueta himself observed, "Working for The Coca-Cola Company is a calling. It's not a way to make a living. It's a religion", (Greising, 1998). Thus the global prospects of its legacy live on despite bleak economic downturns and hard knocks from its competitors as long as converts around the world believably remain loyal to the cult of Coca-Cola.

Bibliography

Allen, Frederick, *Secret Formula: How brilliant marketing and relentless salesmanship made Coca-Cola the best known product in the world*, New York: HarperCollins Publishers, 1994.

Brown, Robert and Washton, Ruth, *Leading Drinks Manufacturers in Asia: Corporate strategies in the face of crisis*, London: *Financial Times*, 1998.

Graham, Elizabeth Candler and Roberts, Ralph, *The Real Ones: Four Generations of the First Family of Coca-Cola*, NJ: Barricade Books, Inc., 1992.

Greising, David, *I'd Like to Buy the World a Coke*, NY: John Wiley, 1998.

Kuisel, Richard, *Seducing the French: The dilemma of Americanization*, Berkeley: University of California Press, 1993.

Melling, Phil and Roper, Jon (eds), *Americanisation and the Transformation of World Cultures: Melting pot or cultural Chernobyl?*, Lewiston, NY: Edwin Mellen Press, 1996.

Muris, Timothy J., Scheffman, David T. and Spiller, Pablo T., *Strategy, Structure and Antitrust in the Carbonated Soft-Drink Industry*, Westport: Quorum Books, 1993.

Oliver, Thomas, *The Real Coke, the Real Story*, London: The Chaucer Press, 1986.

Pells, Richard, *Not Like Us: How Europeans have loved, hated, and transformed American culture since World War II*, New York, NY: Basic Books, 1997.

Pendergrast, Mark, *For God, Country and Coca-Cola*, London: The Orion Publishing Group, 2000.

Pitts, Robert, *Strategic Management: Building and sustaining competitive advantage*, Cincinnati: South-Western College Publishers, 2000.

Rollin, Roger, *The Americanization of the Global Village: Essays in comparative popular culture*, Bowling Green, Ohio: Bowling Green State University Popular Press, 1989.

Storti, Craig, *Old World/New World*, Yarmouth, Maine: Intercultural Press, Inc., 2001.

Online Sources

http://www.vault.com/career/
The_Coca-Cola_Company_1999_Edition.html

http://www.coca-cola.com

http://www.mugu.com/pipermail/upstream-list/2000-November/
000888.html

http://www.diversitydtg.com/articles/cokeseries.htm

http://www.cokecce.com/srclib/index.html

Zubrowka Bison Vodka: The High Is the Limit

Screwdriver, Cosmopolitan, Black Russian and Bloody Mary ... what do these cocktails all have in common? Why, vodka, of course! Indeed, vodka is the focus of this chapter, which takes a look at the history and production of this world-famous spirit. More than just looking at its history though, this chapter also intends to examine the Polish vodka industry, paying particular attention to efforts to privatise the industry, while assessing the potential of the up and coming Zubrowka Bison Brand Vodka.

History of Vodka

Vodka, as we all know it, is a clear and potent drink, often used as a base for numerous long drinks and cocktails, and is typically associated with the Russians (think Stolichnaya). However, one should beware of accrediting the Russians with the discovery of the drink in the presence of the Poles, especially since the latter claim that it was their discovery, and not their eastern neighbour's. Regardless of who discovered this world-famous drink, it is certain that there are at least four predominant players in the vodka industry: Russia, Finland, Sweden and Poland. However, as earlier mentioned, it is the latter that takes centre stage in this paper.

The term "vodka", derived from "Zhiznennia voda" in Russian or "aqua vitae" in Latin, meaning water of life in English, is very much a part of the Polish culture and lifestyle. In Poland, vodka means "little water" (Eisenberg), but we all know how misleading that term is. Strong alcohol was first discovered in Poland in the 8th century and initially used only for medicinal purposes. The Russians seemed to have had methods of distilling vodka back in the 12th century, but according to Polish historians, vodka was discovered in Poland in 1405, only later reaching Russia (*The History of Vodka*). The origins of this spirit remain somewhat elusive, but suffice to say that in both countries, vodka is very much embedded into the people's lifestyles. In the 16th century, the production and sale of alcohol was permitted by the King of Poland, but such sales were restricted to the gentry, from which a 10% tax was extracted. With the establishment of a vodka industry of sorts, the concept of vodka as a national drink was introduced in the 17th century. It was also during this time that Poland began to export its vodka to the Northern European countries. By the 18th century, their distilling techniques had greatly improved and the triple distillation had been developed.

How Vodka is Produced

According to Gary Eisenberg, vodka is simple to make and the ingredients involved consist of almost anything that is fermentable. Often, vodka is produced from rye grain, wheat, barley, oats or potatoes, although the derivation of vodka from sugar cane and sugar beets is not unheard of.

The production of vodka has been refined over the centuries, with producers constantly looking for new ways to improve the quality of their vodka in order to give their products an edge in terms of flavour. The process of vodka production is not complicated. Simply put, the fermented product (i.e. rye, potatoes, wheat, etc.) is distilled and then filtered several times through charcoal (preferably birch charcoal), to get rid of impurities until a smooth, clear and odourless liquid is obtained (Tyler). Voila! Vodka is born!

The delicious experience of smooth Polish vodka is a result of strict standards imposed on producers who must at least triple-distill their vodkas. Some vodkas are filtered four times, and often at least two of those are through charcoal. This filtration process removes impurities, which can contribute towards some harshness in the vodka (Channels).

Vodka in Poland

In Poland the Polish word for vodka is "wodki", which refers to every kind of drink that has more than 20% alcohol content. The vodka that we refer to here, however, pertains to the clear vodka as is popular in the West and which is referred to in Poland as "czysta wodka" ("History of Vodka").

Poland is home to more than 20 different brands of vodka and produces a multitude of vodka varieties. Fortunately, Polish vodka can be divided into three general categories. These are "unflavoured vodkas", "flavoured vodkas" and "real traditional flavoured vodkas" (Deibel).

"Unflavoured vodkas" are generally believed to be pure vodkas, extremely clear and therefore of superior quality. This is a result of multiple filtrations that the vodka undergoes, removing impurities and resulting in an exquisite tasting spirit.

Impeccable in quality, these vodkas are often for mixing or drinking ice-cold.

The second category comprising "flavoured vodkas", are those easily found in convenience store coolers. They are considered extensions of already existing brands and are often flavoured peach, melon, cherry or a variety of other fruity flavours. These "flavoured vodkas" are produced in order to meet the consumption patterns of the masses. That means they probably do not pack as much punch as the pure stuff. This is because the dominant character of the drink is the fruity flavouring, while the vodka plays a secondary function in providing the alcohol content (Deibel).

The third type of vodka is one that is unique and rather interesting. Referred to as the "real traditional flavoured vodkas", these vodkas are special as they are created from time-honoured recipes, which call for all-natural ingredients to enhance the flavour of the brew. Using herbs and spices and other more unusual ingredients such as bison grass to flavour their vodka, brands such as Wisent, Krupnik and Zubrowka have found a place for themselves in this fascinating niche market. What makes these traditionally flavoured vodkas so special is that their recipes have been passed down over generations and represent a means for Poland to make a mark on the international vodka market with an innovative and distinct flavour, enjoyed thus far only by connoisseurs and locals in Poland (Deibel).

Zubrowka Bison Brand Vodka

One of the leaders in the latter category is a brand of traditionally flavoured vodka, called "Zubrowka Bison Brand Vodka". A rye grain vodka unusually flavoured with bison grass, Zubrowka has an original, one-of-a-kind flavour native to Poland. Attractively packaged, each bottle contains a blade of bison grass. As the Polish name for bison is "zubr", the vodka is aptly called "Zubrowka". The vodka has a faint green tinge unlike other vodkas and has a 40% alcohol content. This greenish tinge can be attributed to the fact that bison grass is infused into the vodka.

So what is this "bison grass"? Well, it is a sweet grass found abundantly in the Polish Bialowieska Forest that is eaten by the European bison. The bison is looked upon as a regal creature, great in size and majestic in appearance ("Zubrowka"). Perhaps it is these qualities that we are encouraged to associate Zubrowka with. Indeed, while some consider it a royal drink, others find that it has a more romantic appeal. Consider the following description found in a Somerset Maugham novel *The Razor's Edge*: The character Isabel says: "it smells of freshly mown hay and spring flowers, of thyme and lavender, and it's soft on the palate and so comfortable, it's like listening to music by moonlight". Sounds heavenly, doesn't it? Another character, Sophie describes its colour as "the green one sometimes sees in the heart of a white rose".

Zubrowka's romantic appeal is also emphasised by the fact that some believe bison grass to possess aphrodisiacal qualities (*Bison Brand Vodka — The Legend*). Perhaps this association came about when the European bison, which eat the bison grass, came back from the brink of extinction to repopulate and live in various protected areas in Poland. Regardless of the reason for its appeal, Zubrowka is one of the top-selling vodkas in Poland and the world, thus causing some conflicts with regard to ownership of its distribution rights.

The Polish Alcohol Industry and Privatisation[1]

With the liberation of Poland from the communism and the need to modernise the economic landscape of the nation, Poland's leaders embarked on a massive project to privatise the economy in order to make it more competitive. A variety of various industries made this transition and in the early 90s, the Polish Spirits Monopoly was broken up into 25 autonomous firms (PVWS, 1999). This, however, raised the problem of allocating rights to produce the bigger Polish brands, because each had assumed themselves co-owners of the near 200 brands that the Polmos state monopoly had had.

The solution was an auction at which the individual Polmos companies could bid for the brands of their choice with points they had been allocated upon appraisal. At the end of the auction, the top two vodkas, Wyborowa and Zubrowka went to Polmos Poznan and Polmos Bialystok, respectively. These Polmoses now had the right to produce these spirits exclusively. Unfortunately, they still did not have the right to export these spirits as that right belonged to Agros Holdings S.A., a former state-owned foreign trade agency (Business News from Poland, 2001) and one of the largest companies in the food and beverage sector in Poland. With a 350-million euros turnover, its main functions include production and distribution through leading brands in the market. ("On 17 April", 2001) In fact, Agros held the monopoly to export and the rights from foreign registration of about 20 trademarks for almost 40 years (Ratajczyk & Styczek, 2000).

[1] This section can also be found in an Academic Exercise entitled 'Poland's Industrial Policy in Preparation for European Union Accession' (2002/2003), which was prepared in partial fulfillment of a B.A. (Hons.) degree at the National University of Singapore.

In 1991, the Polmoses began to demand the return of those rights and although understandably reluctant, the firm came up with a compromise in which they would relinquish their rights to all but two of the brands, Wyborowa and Zubrowka, as well as supplement it with a cash settlement. This did not go down well with the Polmoses and a claim was filed against Agros that was later dismissed by the Warsaw Provincial Court (PVWS, 1999).

Progress however, has been made with regard to the ownership of these export/distribution rights. Agros and Pernod Ricard, a world leader in the spirits and wine markets ("On 17 April", 2001), concluded a joint venture agreement in 1999, where 37% of the capital share in Agros Holding S.A and 74% voting rights were transferred to Pernod Ricard. (*Pernod Ricard in France and Agros*, 1999) Following this, a compromise was reached regarding the ownership of trademark rights. Agros agreed to give the trademark rights of almost all brands of Polish vodka to their respective producers. (Business News from Poland, 2001) At the same time, Pernod Ricard was in the process of negotiating the purchase of Polmos Poznan, the producer of the top quality vodka, Wyborowa. The purchase was completed in 2001 with the acquisition of 80% of the capital of Polmos Poznan for 300 million zlotys (approximately 82 million euros). This purchase tied in with Poland's privatisation plan and helped to inject much-needed capital investment (*Business Wire*, 2001).

In addition to this, Pernod Ricard also signed a five-year renewable agreement with Polmos Bialystok regarding the distribution of Zubrowka in Europe, but which excludes Russia and Poland (*Business Wire*, 2001). Having made a breakthrough in the Polish spirits market, and being one of the top operators in spirits and wine: being number 1 in the Euro zone, number 2 in Asia Pacific as well as in Central and South America and number 6 in North America, Pernod Ricard has indeed much to be proud of. How then does this company achieve what it sets out to do?

Pernod Ricard

With the merger of two French companies, Pernod Ricard was founded in 1975 and has since then developed one of the richest portfolios in the industry through internal growth and clever acquisitions like that of Polmos Poznan, producer of Poland's top vodka, Wyborowa. The key to its success lies in its corporate strategy, which ensures that it only goes after the big fish and that means looking only at big brands. It also pays attention to developing strong local or regional brands as well as wholly owned distribution networks in major markets. This means that there is great emphasis given to being the best in the market. Furthermore, it allows employees to be independent in a highly decentralised organisation ("Pernod Ricard: Company Strategy").

Pernod Ricard prides itself on dealing with products with strong cultural roots (think Zubrowka). It is why its decentralised organisation is so advantageous. It allows decisions to be made according to what is most suited to the market. Such specific decision-making also allows problems to be dealt with more efficiently. At Pernod Ricard, the holding company develops overall strategy, while the subsidiaries deal with specific everyday affairs ("Pernod Ricard: Company Organisation").

The company has certain values that it feels are important for its success. It believes these common values form the backbone for the progress of the company, which is so diverse in its culture, products and traditions. Pernod Ricard believes in sociability as it encourages the sharing of ideas and thoughts. It also encourages friendships, which can make the workplace a more enjoyable place to be in. It also helps that sociability is related to the nature of their products.

At Pernod Ricard, a passion for entrepreneurship is appreciated as it supports their decentralised organisation. Entrepreneurship implies initiative and that is important in learning about and acting upon consumer preferences and the marketplace.

The existence of a decentralised organisation also calls for one to value integrity. This means that conducting business in an open and ethical way is appreciated. With fewer tendencies towards corruption, a company should run into fewer problems and inspires trust among their customers, employees and the general public, thus allowing for greater success.

Pernod Ricard certainly sets great store by the passion for excellence. Representing only leading brands, Pernod Ricard is set on delivering only the best quality products, placing emphasis on innovation and progress ("Pernod Ricard: Company Ethics — Values"). Only the best is good enough at Pernod Ricard.

It is therefore no surprise that Pernod Ricard does its best to attract and retain its culturally diverse employees. How does it do so? Well, it encourages empowerment through its decentralised organisation, which allows one to use initiative, so as to achieve professional fulfilment and exercise personal responsibility within a common code of conduct. This calls for some measure of autonomy so as to allow subsidiaries to cater to local desires.

Another employee-friendly measure is profit sharing. Many of the Group's subsidiaries possess an employee compensation plan that coincides with personal or company performance so as to encourage employees to give their best. Executive compensation consists of stock options related to the companies they manage, so again hard work and dedication is encouraged. The measures must work because dedication certainly is evident in the fact that average seniority is more than 10 years in general and more than fifteen in France, resulting in a higher level of experience and expertise that certainly improves the overall well being of the company ("Pernod Ricard: Company Ethics — People"). This well-being is further preserved with training programmes for employees that are set up by each subsidiary.

Corporate Challenges

Zubrowka might not be directly controlled by Pernod Ricard, but the fact that its distribution rests in the hands of the illustrious spirits company implies that certain standards must be maintained, and that in turn entails in all likelihood, changes that must be implemented and challenges that must be surmounted so as to ensure that Zubrowka does not lose its current position as a unique and much sought after vodka.

Zubrowka's association with Pernod Ricard must therefore compel its producer Polmos Bialystok to improve its professionalism and ensure that Zubrowka's quality retains the excellence and quality of flavour that first brought it to the attention of Pernod Ricard, which deemed it worthy to be included among its other lofty and notable brands of spirits (e.g., Chivas and Martell). This will allow Zubrowka to benefit greatly from the marketing endeavours of Pernod Ricard, which works conscientiously to thrust its products up into the ranks of world-renowned must-haves.

In a bid to guarantee that product quality is of impeccable standards, stringent quality controls are necessary, and presumably both Wyborowa and Zubrowka are subjected to such measures to improve their international marketability, which will in turn help to increase their profitability. This is indeed a marked difference from the past where a number of distilleries would produce Wyborowa and Zubrowka vodkas without a thought as to any uniformity or quality in production.

With Zubrowka now being marketed on an international scale by Pernod Ricard, where once it was predominantly a domestic product, one can expect to see increased sales and profits. Certainly, with Pernod Ricard now in the picture, the Polish vodka industry and more specifically Zubrowka Bison Brand

Vodka can look forward to a brighter future where one can also reasonably assume improved quality and management.

Conclusion

We have thus seen how the Polish vodka industry has developed over the last few years. The process has been trying, what with the long drawn out battle between Agros and the Polmoses regarding export rights. The privatisation process has not been easy, but the efforts to do so have reaped some rewards. Certainly, such efforts will go a long way in establishing a good reputation for Poland's vodka, which has much promise, especially if we consider brands like Zubrowka as the standard of the exemplary quality we hope to experience in the future.

Pernod Ricard has certainly set the privatisation of the spirits industry in Poland on its way and with measures such as those discussed above; it is no wonder that Pernod Ricard is such a lucrative company. Their strategy of finding the right people to contribute their talents to the company, while adhering to a common set of values, combined with a strategy aimed at excellence inspires confidence in the future of the two brands they have taken under their wing, Wyborowa and Zubrowka. Indeed, with their steadfast efforts in introducing the two brands into the international market, it seems like the privatisation of the Polish spirits industry is off to a great start.

However, caution is advisable with regard to the continuation of the vodka industry's privatisation process. While Polmos Poznan represents an encouraging success story, problems should not be discounted, especially considering the Polish government's recent efforts to sell off an 80% stake in Polmos Bialystok, the producer of Zubrowka. A number of firms including Pernod Ricard have expressed interest, but doubts regarding the viability

ZUBROWKA BISON VODKA

of Pernod's offer have risen amidst concerns of Poland's competition regulations. One must also take into consideration that the domestic vodka industry faces the additional trials of cheaper, illegal competition from home brewers and neighbouring countries, not to mention a weak local market that makes sales difficult.

As if this were not enough, the government seems to be fixed on selling off all of its remaining distilleries at the same time. This could make redundant existing efforts in the quest towards privatisation, especially since it is believed that only about six of the more than 200 brands of spirits are viable in the long run (*BBC News Online*, 2001). The future of Zubrowka and the Polish vodka industry thus hangs in the balance, as efforts continue to be made in a bid to privatise Poland's vodka industry. With great care and determined commitment, anything is possible and Zubrowka just might take the world by storm.

Bibliography

"Poland's Top Vodka Brand for Sale", *BBC News Online*, July 27, 2001.

"Bison Brand Vodka — The Legend", (n.d.),
http://www.bisongrassvodka.com/the_legend.htm

Business News from Poland, "Agros Agrees to Give Trademark Rights of Polish Vodka to Their Producers", April 7, 2001.

"Privatisation in Poland: Pernod Ricard Acquires 80% of the Capital of Polmos Poznan–Wyborowa — and secures the distribution of Zubrowka in Europe", *Business Wire*, July 17, 2001.

Channels, Bill (n.d.), "The New Face of Vodka",
http://www.polishvodkas.com/new_face_of_vodka.html.

Deibel, Juergen (n.d.), "Polish Vodka — Which Way to Go?",
http://www.polishvodka.com.pl/juergen.html.

Eisenberg, Gary (n.d.), "Vodka Dreaming in Poland", http://www.polishvodkas.com/miscelany/voddream/.

"History of Vodka: Its Origin, Name and Distilling in Poland, Varieties", (n.d.), http://www.polishvodkas.com/history-vodka/fs_consumption.htm.

"On 17 April, the Securities and Exchange Commission Complied with Pernod Ricard", (April 14, 2001), http://www.agros.com.pl/english/html/aktual/pres.php.

"Pernod Ricard: Company Ethics — People", (n.d.), http://www.pernod-ricard.com/.

"Pernod Ricard: Company Ethics — Values", (n.d.), http://www.pernod-ricard.com/.

"Pernod Ricard: Company Organisation", (n.d.), http://www.pernod-ricard.com/.

"Pernod Ricard: Company Strategy", (n.d.), http://www.pernod-ricard.com/.

"Pernod Ricard in France and Agros in Poland Announce Joint Venture", (April 16, 1999), http://www.pernod-ricard.com/.

"PVWS Team", (July 30, 1999), "Polmos Trademarks Sold", http://www.polishvodkas.com/news/Polmos_T_Sold.html.

Ratajczyk, Andrzej and Dariusz Styczek (2000), "Agros Holdings vs. the Polmoses", *The Warsaw Voice*, No. 23, June.

"The History of Vodka", (n.d.), http://www.ivodka.com/history.html.

Tyler, Simon (n.d.), "Vodka", http://www.viewpub.co.uk/drink_feat_vodka.asp.

"Zubrowka", (n.d.), http://www. polishvodkas.com/fr_zubrowka.htm.

ZUBROWKA BISON VODKA

Ikea: The Småland Way Goes Global

IKEA as the route to nirvana, people believing they'll find spiritual freedom through home furnishings.

— Actor Edward Norton[1]

What is the secret to IKEA's success such that it captures the imagination of people in thirty-one countries over five continents? Why is IKEA's annual catalogue, with 110 million copies published in 34 languages, one of the world's biggest press runs? What makes IKEA tick? To answer these questions, its origins must be traced.

Origins of IKEA

IKEA is the acronym for Ingvar, Kamprad, Elmtaryd and Agunnaryd. Ingvar Kamprad is the founder of IKEA, Elmtaryd

---

[1] Quote taken from *Life!*, 16 April 2002.

was his farmhouse and Agunnaryd is his home county in Småland, Sweden. Perhaps due to influence from his maternal grandfather, who had owned a very successful local store, Kamprad started doing business from a very tender age. One of his first business deals started when he bought one hundred boxes of matches at eighty-eight öre and sold them between two and five öre each. Kamprad was an enterprising boy who sold Christmas cards, fish he caught himself and even garden seeds. He sold whatever he thought there was a demand for and from which money could be made. As his father constantly lamented the lack of money to fulfil his many plans, Kamprad decided to start his own firm to help resolve his father's cash-flow problems. Kamprad was only seventeen when Ikéa Agunnaryd was founded in 1943.

Ikéa Agunnaryd initially sold pens, cigarette lighters and whatever Kamprad found a need for and which he could sell at a reduced price. These products were later sold through mail-order when Kamprad was no longer able to make individual sales due to booming business. He later switched to furniture retailing as it was more profitable and the close proximity to furniture makers from where he lived made the switch even easier. He advertised his furniture in a brochure — Ikéa News — which he published and sent to customers. This was the precursor for his future IKEA catalogue. Kamprad also gave names to furniture because it was tough to remember order numbers. Note that giving names to furniture had the effect of giving each of them a personality and a life of their own. This innovative act appealed to customers because they could select furniture which corresponded to their actual or idealised lifestyles. Moreover, furniture with names were so much easier to remember than long order numbers, making it easier for customers to order. This far-sighted business decision certainly endeared IKEA further to customers as they saw IKEA to be customer-oriented. The first furniture to be christened was Ruth, an armless chair.

Kamprad changed strategy as a result of the cutthroat mail-order business. Rather than competing with his main competitor on price, which would invariably affect the quality of his wares, he decided to compete on the basis of quality. There should therefore be a permanent display of the furniture he was retailing so that people could see and judge for themselves the quality of the furniture he was selling. Customers would then be convinced of the superiority of his wares, of which a higher price would be justified. It would be a win–win situation because he could continue being in business while earning and maintaining his customers' trust.

His first furniture showroom was displayed in a second-hand building at Älmhult, Sweden, which was bought over from an old associate. Based on his decision to buy over a second-hand building, one can discern Kamprad's frugality and a belief that there should be no waste. All things had a second life. Despite being born with a silver spoon, virtues such as thrift and frugality can be observed in the man himself. Perhaps these virtues were found in many a Swede, but it was Kamprad who instituted them as fundamental pillars of his company's culture. These values were later to affect the development of his furniture empire. Possibly believing that his store was to have an aesthetic value and to differentiate it from the nondescript buildings in the area, Kamprad's showroom was built based on New York's Guggenheim Museum. It was to be built circularly to save space and to provide optimal exposure for the displayed items. Furthermore, coffee and buns were to be provided on the opening day because Kamprad believes that "no good business should be done on an empty stomach". When Kamprad became a furniture dealer, he was only twenty-two and he changed the name of his firm to IKEA to emphasis his switch to furniture-retailing.

The Early Years

The showroom, which opened in 1953, was a resounding success. Even before the doors were opened, there were already one thousand people waiting to enter the store. What was significant was that many people actually made the trek to Älmhult even though it was located in a remote part of Sweden. The use of his catalogue as a means of temptation was a success. Besides, the IKEA logo, which was printed on his brochure covers, was in the colours of the Swedish national flag. This sought to convey that IKEA's products were reliable and clean and to emphasise IKEA's Swedish identity as it achieves global recognition. The idea of allowing customers to walk around and touch the furniture they were interested in was revolutionary at that time. People loved the idea for it meant giving them a wide selection of furniture to choose from as they were further allowed to test the items they wanted to buy. In a way, this empowered the ordinary customer. He was no longer hostage to tyrannical furniture retailers. Traditionally customers were to pay astronomical prices for furniture they were not allowed to try out before purchase. Kamprad's radical but ingenious ideas laid the basis of the modern IKEA concept.

It was also during this time that Sweden modernised rapidly, leading to an exodus of people from the countryside to the towns. These people needed to furnish their homes as cheaply as possible. In 1954, the Swedish government published the *Good Housing* publication that set regulations for minimum space and stipulated that every room was to serve a specific purpose. In addition, certain furniture was to be essential in every household.

IKEA's appearance on the scene around that time coincided with the rapid changes the Swedish society was undergoing. IKEA's furniture was affordable, of good quality and aesthetically beautiful and it was no surprise that IKEA was quickly embraced by the general public with little resistance.

Despite IKEA's success, there were lingering doubts, especially by competitors, that low prices often corresponded to products of dubious quality. They sought to discredit IKEA but tests conducted by the esteemed furniture magazine *Allt i Hemmet* in 1964 put to rest those doubts. In the price test, a living room was furnished in two parts: one part solely with IKEA furniture; the other with similar furniture but from other suppliers. The price difference between IKEA's room and that of the most expensive competitor was a whopping Skr6000 ($750). The price difference meant a lot to Swedes who were setting up homes for the first time in the towns and in the suburbs. Choosing IKEA's furniture meant substantial savings on their tight budgets. This is why IKEA appeals to many students, young couples and small families now for the same reason: quality furniture at affordable prices.

To critics, the assurance that quality and durability could not be guaranteed because of IKEA's low prices. The quality tests conducted by the same furniture magazine however vindicated IKEA's claims. Test results gleaned from a Swedish design lab showed that IKEA's furniture was more durable than its more expensive versions. Despite 55,000 tippings in a machine, IKEA's Ögla chair (which was retailing for Skr33 then) was still intact, but the more expensive Thonet model (which retailed for Skr168) was not. It was a vindication for IKEA for it showed the hollowness of claims made by jealous competitors that cheap products were synonymous with inferior quality. The results of the tests and the implicit endorsement of the eminent furniture magazine further propelled the acceptance of IKEA in Swedish society, even in middle-class homes. It also led to an acceptance in countries worldwide when IKEA branched out overseas.

The principal reason why IKEA could offer such low prices was because it cut out the middlemen. Further, IKEA does not produce the products it designs. To Kamprad, low prices are essential to avail a wide range of quality home furnishings to as many people as possible. Gillis Lundgren, a designer with IKEA then, hit upon the idea of self-assembled furniture when he realised he could pack the legs of table under the tabletop. In this way, shipping costs would be greatly reduced and these savings could be passed on to customers. Furthermore, customers were also encouraged to pick up their purchases themselves from the warehouse. Savings gained from self-service would be passed on to customers.

The Man Himself

Every employee or "Ikean" has to be well-versed in *A Furniture Dealer's Testament* that was written by Kamprad himself. This framework of ideas was written with the hope that Ikeans would continue to adhere to this concept that had served IKEA well for the past fifty years. It is also hoped that it would keep IKEA uniquely Swedish in outlook even after Kamprad has faded away from the scene. Then who is Ingvar Kamprad? What is he like and how have his views shaped his company?

Ingvar Kamprad is "the furniture king who does not look like a capitalist". Despite his wealth (he is reported to be worth $27 billion and according to *Forbes*, is the world's 17th richest person), he flies economy, travels railway second-class, frequents discount outlets and buys groceries just before closing time when prices are lowest. It also did not matter to him if he were to stay in a hotel room that was infested with cockroaches and that the water supply would be cut off in the middle of a shower. To him, having a place to stay is sufficient, despite the shabbiness. Because of the example he set, subordinates do not enjoy better benefits. He professes that if he were to change to a more luxurious lifestyle, his empire would collapse as IKEA remains based on his low-cost concept. Practising what he preaches for Kamprad is an act of good leadership. It is also a way of telling his employees and the public that he is an ordinary guy just like them.

A shrewd business acumen surely is one of Kamprad's attributes. He believes it is essential to have a restaurant in his store ("no one does good business on an empty stomach") and a child care facility consisting of a playroom with a pool of coloured balls for children to dive into ("who can do vital shopping with the kids yelling around their feet?"). Toilets are necessary because "a full bladder must not be what decides the customer on buying or not buying something" and a bistro must be situated beyond the checkout so as to have a "calming effect" on the customer after her purchases. He also hit on the idea of selling hotdogs in the bistro based on the "five kronor" principle. This meant that one Ikea hot dog could be bought just by using a single coin. In Switzerland, a hot dog costs one Swiss franc, in Germany one Euro, in Singapore S$1.50 and so on. This reflected Kamprad's keen business acumen and in how he wanted shopping at IKEA to be pleasurable and stress-free. To him, making a profit, regardless of the amount, would still be a profit. The customer's satisfaction matters most.

In many companies, the power distance between superiors and subordinates could be rather wide. This is not so in IKEA. Kamprad treats his business associates and subordinates like intimate friends. He knew all his employees' names when IKEA started out. As a way of bonding with people, when speaking to people, Kamprad would move closer to them, look into their eyes and hug them when the conversation ended. He would also share hotel rooms and talk into the middle of the night about everything with his subordinates. Or if only a bed was available, he would even sleep head to toe with his partner. This might seem to others a sign of parsimony but to Kamprad, it is a way of strengthening personal bonds and like the South Europeans, a way of establishing trust. His way of treating people like family certainly endeared him to his business associates. Two Polish directors loved his East European way of showing emotions and they reminisced the time they spent with him in his room, sitting around, holding hands, singing folksongs and making speeches. His subordinates try to behave in a similar way. This has fostered the Ikean spirit of fellowship, of belonging to a family. Clearly, Kamprad's frugal and hearty way of doing things has been imposed on the company.

The Culture Within

Like Japanese firms, IKEA prefers to recruit employees straight from school, or those who have not already been immersed in another corporate culture. IKEA, like the Japanese, would rather train them for the company, by the company and in the company's methods. Young employees would not only keep wage levels down in this cost-sensitive organisation but could also be trained in the company's ways of *ödmjukhet*, of being humble, modest and respectful towards their co-workers. In addition, young employees usually are more ambitious and enthusiastic when they first step into the corporate world. They would also be more eager to learn and accept greater responsibilities. This complemented IKEA's culture of virility and enthusiasm. More importantly, internal training coupled with internal rotation through different jobs would maximise a common understanding of the organisation. As a result of IKEA's hiring policy, the average age of a store manager is only thirty-four. This implies that new blood is constantly injected into the organisation, making the organisation very young in outlook. A constant infusion of new blood also means that the organisation is quick to react to changes. Finally, it also suggests that bold decisions can be made more willingly and quickly.

From the outside, IKEA is thought to have a power culture where power is rested in the hands of one person, the founder. Before his subordinates were to proceed on any piece of work, they would often ask, "What will Ingvar say?", "Do you think Ingvar would…?" or "Ingvar said that…". They always take into consideration what Kamprad would think or feel and often, his words would become law by default. IKEA stores used to close at 6 pm in Sweden, but they close at 8 pm now after he commented on the futility of operating a store if it were to close just minutes after people got off from work. Like many family businesses, Kamprad resisted listing IKEA on the stock exchange, justifying his stand that IKEA would have had to make short-term shareholder decisions that could conflict with long-term planning. He fears that too many foreign shareholders would influence the way IKEA operates should IKEA go public. Moreover, going public is expensive as public companies would have had to distribute at least a third of their profits to their shareholders. As such, it would not allow IKEA to build up reserves to take bold decisions, like the one when IKEA decided to lose money for ten years just to enter the Russian market. Clearly Kamprad has an overwhelming influence in his company.

The culture within IKEA is akin to that of a family. Whenever Kamprad talks to his employees, it is like a father speaking to his children and grandchildren. He would always begin with "Dear IKEA family, a great hug to you all" in his annual Christmas message. Kamprad never fails to throw a Christmas party for his employees. What had started off as a party for his initial thirty employees has now ballooned. In the Christmas party of 1998, 1000 out of 1600 employees in Älmhult turned up for a dinner of Christmas rice, milk, coffee and ginger biscuits. Then Kamprad addressed his audience, exhorting Ikeans to continue adhering to IKEA's philosophy and so on. Upon the conclusion of his address, he then shook everyone's hands and presented them with a Christmas gift. Through his meticulous efforts, he successfully built up his firm based on a family concept where fellow employees treated each other as part of a large, extended family. This came about because his family were his first customers and had helped him when his firm grew. For instance, his father would help keep the accounts while his mother helped with the packing. It surprised no one when he regarded his growing firm as his family. Employee loyalty to the firm was severely tested when Kamprad in 1994 faced a series of insinuations, alleging that he had been a Nazi sympathiser some fifty years ago. Naturally Kamprad denied the allegations. But as a sign of loyalty to Kamprad then IKEA of Sweden (IOS) sent him a note together with hundreds of signatures of his employees, reading:

> "Ingvar,
> We are here whenever you need us
> The IKEA Family IOS"

This showed in times of need Kamprad's successful attempts and efforts to mould his company to that of a big family where loyalty is valued.

The culture within IKEA is Swedish and more so Smålandish in outlook even though the company is now a multinational corporation. Kamprad is of the view that the Smålandish values of thrift and cost-consciousness that have assisted the company in its nascient stage should be kept and maintained and to remain integral to IKEA's management policy. To Kamprad, expensive solutions are signs of mediocrity and it is a mortal sin to waste resources. As such, management personnel travels economy-class like he does, share hotel rooms and so forth. There is even an IKEA guidebook, informing employees where they can get budget hotels and cheap airfares when they go on business trips. Even though urgent appointments have to be kept, it should not be an excuse for first-class travel, as one executive found out. Kamprad refused to accede to his request, instead "recommending" that the executive should travel by car as an alternative. This reflected that even in times of urgency, it was no reason for expensive solutions in this cost-sensitive organisation.

There is also an emphasis on all things Småland that Smålandish specialities like sausages with potatoes in white sauce and meatballs with lingon berries are sold in IKEA restaurants worldwide. This not only serves to acquaint customers with IKEA's Swedish roots but indirectly, to perpetually remind employees of the Swedish work ethic.

IKEA subscribes to a "dress-down" policy. Kamprad's standard business attire are open-necked denim shirts, and slacks and a blazer for important occasions. Employees dress in a similar way because in Kamprad's considered view too much time would be wasted if they always think of what to wear. The environment within is very informal and egalitarian because both management and the rank-and file are dressed similarly. This prevents any form of elitism should employees be discriminated based on their dressing.

Since the culture within promotes egalitarianism, "antibureaucrat weeks" are organised, requiring all managers to work in store showrooms and warehouses for at least one week every year. This is intended to ensure that managers remain firmly rooted to the ground and do not detach too much from their subordinates. Moreover, by working together with employees on the shop floor, managers continue to have a pulse on their subordinates' feelings and do not introduce policies that could generate worker dissent.

More pertinently, managers working with their subordinates in the stores together sent a message: that the managers are "one" with the rank-and-file.

Perhaps the people working for IKEA feel as if they are working for the well-being of society and they like it also because the company suits their way of life. They believe to be altruistic is to bring affordable and quality furniture to as many people as possible. Hence staff is not particularly motivated by high salaries. In fact, salaries particularly at management levels are "peanuts" compared to their counterparts elsewhere. Staffers joined IKEA because it suited their way of life without having to think of status and fame and that "they have now become more in harmony with themselves". Like in Swedish society, an informal *du* culture is also prevalent within the company, flattening the hierarchy. As a model worthy of emulation, Kamprad has the habit of walking around in his stores, hugging and clasping his employees. He even requests them to address him by his first name. This further cemented employee loyalty to IKEA because they feel they are treated as equals and are valued within the organisation.

European Business Culture

The European business culture is similar throughout Europe despite regional variations. It is of no surprise that IKEA expanded successfully into continental Europe first. Part of it was the result of ingenious marketing strategies. In Germany, the elk symbol was used whenever IKEA was launched. It was so successful that it competed strongly with the brand name. In another move, if there were more than one store opening, one Swedish clog would be given out to customers as a sign of IKEA's gratitude. If customers were interested in getting the other half, they would have to go to the other new store. This resulted in an explosion of sales in Europe However, it took IKEA a period of

22 years before being able to announce that all 20 stores in the U.S. were generating profits.

The American Business Culture

Initially IKEA did not realise that doing business in the U.S. was a different ballgame. It expanded too rapidly without fully understanding the American buying culture. This even threatened at one point, to sink its flagship store in Älmhult.

First, the brand IKEA was not sufficiently introduced to the Americans. Even though 9 out of 10 Americans had heard of IKEA, only 3 of them knew that IKEA was in the furniture business. There was thus insufficient publicity to announce IKEA's arrival in the U.S. The complacency was blamed on the group of store managers who were managing the U.S. stores. They thought since IKEA was already a household name in Europe, it would automatically become one in the U.S. based on the strength of the brand. Part of the blame also rested on the management back home. The management had given a lot of autonomy to the managers to set up and run the stores but they did not realise that some control was needed. Both parties also did not take into account the differences in American and European buying habits and their corresponding lifestyles.

A case usually cited was when an American lady walked into the IKEA store in Houston. She liked the bed she was looking at, but did not understand what 160 cm meant. In Sweden, a 160 cm bed meant a double bed but this did not make sense to the American mindset. All the lady (or the American public) wanted to know was if the bed was king- or queen-sized. As a result, a sale was lost for she walked away without buying the bed. Other examples to show a clash of cultures was when dinner tables had to be redesigned to be huge enough for an overstuffed Thanksgiving turkey, with space for crockery on both sides. Or couches had to be overstuffed because Americans prefer sofas they can sink into rather than to sit on them like the Europeans. Because of these new demands, product ranges had to be modified to cater to the American market. This contravened the IKEA concept where uniformity was demanded, be it in terms of store design or the same items being retailed, throughout the stores worldwide. A little tweaking of the concept was nevertheless justifiable, especially if IKEA wanted to break into the American market. By 1998, all 20 stores in the U.S. were making money after products were redesigned for the American market.

Despite a clash of cultures, positive benefits were reaped. In the U.S., the managers lowered the turnover rate of employees drastically and increased loyalty . They did so by mandating that sales from one Saturday a year were to go in full to the employees. Each employee would receive a percentage of sales corresponding to their length of employment. So even the last one hired gets something. This inculcated a sense of belonging to the IKEA family as they were rewarded for their hard work. They felt a stake in the continuing success of IKEA in return. This resembles one of the central tenets of Confucianism: reciprocity, which refers to the fact that employees would be rewarded in return for their loyalty to the organisation. This system of rewards nonetheless upped motivation levels and as such, was lauded and adopted in IKEA stores worldwide thereafter.

The success of the IKEA concept has also spawned a number of American copycats. STØR was founded to give the impression of a Scandinavian firm and was copying IKEA in almost everything. Firms like Home Depot and Crate and Barrel too have jumped onto the bandwagon and have followed IKEA's concept of providing as much as possible at low prices under one roof. Unfazed by the competition and believing in the strength of its concept, IKEA fought back and now offers apartment types like "single-mum with infant" to the American public rather than the traditional single-room setting. A flexibility to change and the ability to adapt quickly were noticed.

The Empire

Fearful of being in debt and worried about the survival of IKEA after his death, Kamprad divided his empire into three holding entities: The IKEA Group, The Inter IKEA Group and The IKANO Group.

The IKEA Group is owned by a Dutch foundation, the Stichting INGKA Foundation/Stichting IKEA Foundation. It owns the stores, except the franchises, worldwide, and everything related to retailing. Inter IKEA owns the concept of the IKEA brand and the group's intellectual property. It also gives approval to open and run the store — either for IKEA's own stores or for an outsider as the franchise permit to use the IKEA concept under extremely well-specified conditions. If a store manager wishes to deviate from the laid-down concept, be it to eliminating the playroom or to designing narrower aisles, he has to seek prior approval from the Group. If rules are broken by the franchisee, Inter IKEA has the power and the right to take away the IKEA signboard and to discontinue all supplies. Both groups have large, hidden reserves to help fund expansion and create a cushion for economic downturns. Kamprad's sons can "control" Inter IKEA by appointing the board of the group but they cannot own it. This is to prevent any inheritance fights. More importantly, it is to bring about financial stability and to prevent his family from being taxed too heavily by the Swedish authorities. It is also to ensure that IKEA will endure in his image after his demise.

The only group that the Kamprad family owns is the IKANO Group. It controls Habitat, a home-furnishing chain and IKANO has investments in financial service, real estate, insurance and banking. It is also an umbrella-name for all Kamprad-owned companies not under the control of the INGKA Foundation. A precursor of these three groups occurred when Kamprad set up a series of companies in the 1950s to circumvent the threat of a supply boycott by furniture suppliers that were bent on crushing this young upstart who was undercutting their prices. The complex collection of these holding companies therefore, was to ensure the survival of IKEA and that it can never be dismantled. It was also to forestall the empire from breaking up or being sold off because of succession disputes.

Prospects

Kamprad is always seen as the spiritual leader of IKEA. However, there is no one at present who has the charisma and flair to take on his position. Like Virgin's Richard Branson, IKEA is basically driven by the personality and leadership of its founder, Ingvar Kamprad. Would IKEA continue to survive after Kamprad's demise is a question that remains open. IKEA's senior management remains predominantly Scandinavian and although IKEA's former president, Anders Moberg, was quoted as saying that a good grasp of the Swedish language was imperative in career advancement, there are justifiable fears and worries that as IKEA expands globally, non-Swedish managers would be recruited to make it difficult or impossible for IKEA to retain its Swedish roots. Already a Canadian is now responsible for all the stores in Sweden and an American advertising manager now manages the catalogue business. Whether they will be able to assimilate into the Swedish culture or the Smålandish psyche, which demands management to be simple, people-oriented and non-hierarchical, or whether they will reject it and instead impose their own cultural imprint onto IKEA will be seen only in the future.

Bibliography

Bartlett, Christopher A. and Ghoshal, Sumantra, *Transnational Management*, Singapore: McGraw-Hill, 2000.

Lewis, Richard D, *When Cultures Collide: Managing Successfully across Cultures*, London: Nicholas Brealey, 1999.

Torekull, Bertil, *Leading by Design: The IKEA Story*, New York: HarperBusiness, 1999.

Brown-Humes, Christopher, "The Bolt that Holds the IKEA Empire Together", *Financial Times* (12 August 2002), p. 7.

Ebeling, Ashlea, "Size Matters". <http://www.forbes.com/global/2000/0807/0315036s2.html>, 7 August 2000.

Heller, Richard. "The Billionaire Next Door", <http://www.forbes.com/global/2000/0807/0315036a.html>, 7 August 2000.

Heller, Richard, "Hidden Wealth", <http://www.forbes.com/global/2000/0807/0315036s1.html>, 8 July 2000.

Heller, Richard, "IKEA's Founder Concerned about Rapid Expansion", <www.nordicbusinessreport.com>, 6 January 2003.

The Rise and Fall of the
Seibu-Saison Empire

It normally takes the 3rd generation to ruin a business empire. The Tsutsumi brothers managed to do that in the 2nd. In fact, Seiji Tsutsumi's Saison-Seibu enterprise as part and parcel of Japan's bubble economy of asset inflation in the 1980s, was built up and collapsed during a few decades of his own business activities alone with him as probably the most spectacular protagonist and ultimately also victim of the profligate years. After a decade of failed rehabilitation attempts, Seiyo, his real estate arm, went down in July 2000 with $5 billion of debts, with Seiji Tsutsumi being forced to divest most of his remaining Saison Group Holdings. His struggling erstwhile avant-garde Seibu Department Store chain had to be merged in 2003 with the equally bankrupt Sogo chain in a desperate attempt by the bankers to somehow rehabilitate both, and to avoid the stigma of bankruptcy which would destroy the remaining brand value of the previously up-market department stores. The Seiyu supermarkets have been swallowed by Wal-Mart since.

Seiji's half brother, Yoshiaki Tsutsumi, who inherited most of their father's railroad and hotel empire, and who most famously more or less bought for himself the Nagano Winter Olympics of 1998, lost similar amounts, but as one of the world's richest men back in 1990 with a then net worth of $16 billion, he could take a $13 billion crash to stay in the black with a more modest net worth of $2.8 billion (2001) according to Forbes.

Central to the Seibu saga is the founding father and patriarch Yasujiro Tsutsumi (1889–1965), his three wives and countless mistresses. As a farmer's son, he lost his parents early and grew up in rural Shiga prefecture. After elementary school and military academy he mortgaged his grandfather's heritage to study at Tokyo's Waseda University as a young family man already.

A couple of speculative deals usefully multiplied his meagre funds. His interests at the egalitarian Waseda, which then was a breeding ground of nationalist-minded reformers, were however less scholarly. Yasujiro became Secretary to Shigenobu Okuma who later was to become Prime Minister of Japan. In the politico-economic interface so typical of many Japanese developers, he then used his personal and political contacts for his budding business ends. Already in his student days he bought up cheap wasteland and pastures near the popular elite mountain resort of Karuizawa, which he subsequently developed with vacation houses, leisure facilities and the necessary infrastructure. By the end of World War I, he had laid the foundations of his future post-industrial leisure empire.

Having set up his own construction companies, Yasujiro was able to profit from the building and reconstruction boom following the Kanto earthquake of 1923. One year later, he was elected to Parliament to fill a seat in his home prefecture of Shiga which, except for the purge years during the U.S. occupation (1945–51), Yasujiro should hold until his death in 1965. As a member of the war-advocating Democratic Party, he already in 1932/4 rose to the position of a parliamentary vice minister. Yet he remained disinterested in ideology and continued to use his political work almost exclusively for business purposes: to purchase early land earmarked for future development, to take over competing railway lines in the west of Tokyo (the Musashino and Seibu lines), and to furnish the logistics to supply ammunition to the military.

His fear to be expropriated by the victorious Americans as a war profiteer remained unfounded. Instead Yasujiro bought up cheaply bombed-out land around his Tokyo railway terminals. He also bought out impoverished aristocrats, who could no longer afford to pay inheritance taxes. He demolished their residences and put up hotels of his cheekily-named Prince Chain. He also pioneered three new towns along his West Tokyo railways, which subsequently turned into fashionable pricey suburbs.

As a highlight of his political career from 1953 to 1955, Yasujiro Tsutsumi was elected president of Japan's Lower House, a position that was the most tangible recognition of his elevated status amongst Japan's post-war *nouveau riches*.

His open display of polygamy and despotic leadership style — nicknamed 'Pistol' for his gunslinging business methods and his speed to fire non-complying subordinates — were public knowledge but did not hurt. He also survived a fairly well documented vote-buying scandal and after his sudden death in 1965, he was buried with all honours at a cemetery, which he himself had typically developed profitably earlier.

His business empire was divided unequally between his two unequal sons. Seiji, the older son, was born to a poetess whom Yasujiro had briefly married. He was a cultured intellectual, who in the postwar years for a while flirted with a communist student group. Disinherited by his father, he was excluded from the CP for leftist deviance and promptly returned to the fold to serve his father, then President of Parliament, as a political secretary. Of his father's business, Seiji was to inherit only a run-down department store at a Tokyo railroad terminal at Ikebukuro.

The vastly more valuable railway lines, hotels, real estate holdings and resorts went to his half-brother, Yoshiaki, who as the son of Yasujiro's favourite mistress had inherited his father's ruthless business acumen and autocratic ways. Similar to Yasujiro, he used his student days to develop privately-financed swimming pools and ice stadiums. Within two decades he built his father's inheritance into Japan's leading hotel, ski resort and golf course operator and developer. This helped to smoothen political connections, notably with the then ruling LDP's powerful construction business oriented Takeshita faction. Yasujiro's electoral district was inherited by a close affiliate, Ganri Yamashita, who later became Minister of Defence.

Resort development in Japan's typically mountainous and fragile environment is usually done in the most ruthless ways. Unspoiled rural areas would be brought up cheaply, the forests chopped up and the landscape bulldozed to make way for golf courses, ski slopes, parking lots and hotel complexes. Yoshiaki, in addition, made sure that the necessary infrastructure was provided free from public funds.

He also applied this pattern blatantly when purchasing the 1998 Nagano Winter Olympics as President of Japan's Olympic Committee and Vice President of the Nagano Organising Committee from IOC President Juan Samaranch.

Yoshiaki's Seibu Group (later renamed Kokudo Group) then already owned most of Nagano's hotels, shopping arcades and ski slopes. The Olympics brought publicly funded highways and a Shinkansen line, which shortened the distance from Tokyo to Nagano to 90 minutes, thus assuring a steady supply of day skiers into this volatile Alpine region ever thereafter. Widely criticized, the construction destroyed rare habitats of endangered species in protected National Parks, turned natural rivers into cemented canals and changed unspoiled forests and farm plots into wastelands of clear cuts and concrete. The Olympics helped to channel an ever larger share of Japan's $8 billion annual skiing business into the balance sheets of the Kokudo Group, but it also generated unwelcome international attention to Yoshiaki's business methods. Not only issues of unethical environmental practices and political collusion came to the fore, his idiosyncratic management style was also scrutinized. As the *Japan Times* at the time put it:

"He is obsessed with frugality and apart from supporting political friends, loathes donating money to anyone or anything. He roams the country in his helicopter, inspecting his empire of hotels, barking orders, keeping his staff on their toes ('I don't need employees with fancy college education', he once said. 'I want people who can do what I tell them') and making sure that nothing is wasted. Towels in his hotels are used for an extra year, after which they are used as rags in Yoshiaki's offices".

Obviously recycling old towels has not helped to stem the evaporation of Yoshiaki's real estate values and corporate wealth. Still he remains a major player in the Japanese hotel (Prince), railways (Seibu), resort and golf course scene. As owner of the leading Seibu Lions professional baseball and of an ice hockey team, Yoshiaki still plays a major public role.

His rival half brother, Seiji has retreated from public view after the collapse of his Seiyo development corporation. He now spends his time writing poetry and runs a small non-profit foundation to support the performing arts. In charge of his father's neglected department store in Ikebukuro, then a run-down neighbourhood in the 1950s, he had introduced the products of then unknown young designers like Yves Saint Laurent and Issey Miyake to his Seibu department store. His modernised stores became early symbols of a status and glitter oriented consumer culture, which affluent youngsters embraced once the hardships of the postwar years were overcome. Almost singlehandedly, Seiji anticipated future trends of consumer tastes. In 1963, he started the later immensely profitable Seiyu supermarket chain. In 1968, with his new flagship Seibu Shibuya, he founded a trend-setting consumer palace for the baby boom generation, followed by the trendy Parco shop-in-shop boutique concept for fashionable affluent teenagers. In the 'golden age' of Japan's consumer boom in the 1980s, Seiji unfolded a firework of new business ideas, most of which were novel to Japan: the Seibu Card (1982) — as solid Japanese banks would never credit finance flippant teenagers' consumer fads , department store based sales of financial services, like the Seibu All State Life Insurance, exclusive sales licenses with up-market western brand producers, and a chain of convenience stores ("Family Mart") which stay open for 24 hours.

Seibu depaatos were celebrated for art exhibitions, operating trendy in-store restaurants, coffee shops, theatres, concert halls and cinemas. In the 1970s and 1980s, Seibu and Parco were the most profitable and avant-garde amongst Japan's otherwise conservative and over-priced department stores. As a sponsor of avant-garde theatre, including difficult pieces by playwrights like Kobo Abe, and of contemporary art (exhibited in the Seibu Museum of Art) Seiji cultivated an image of liberal intellectual modernity, which not only contrasted well with the gruffly greed of his unloved half-brother, but more importantly harmonized well with the message of a luxury oriented civilisation of Japan's newfound wealth opened by his up-market stores catering to the new bubble boom rich and those living on credit card facility.

Like most of his customers' lifestyle, Seiji's own rapidly expanding empire was built on credit. The high turnover of his store resulted in only smallish profits and debt service ate up most of the cash flow. In the asset inflation of the 1980s, when debt could easily be turned into equity, this posed no problem.

So Seiji expanded and diversified further, declaring in the fuzzy logic of the bubble's heydays: his group should service "every facet of living". Seiji's Seiyo real estate subsidiary hence began to venture into his brother's business territory by developing up-market shopping complexes, leisure facilities, hotels and condominiums.

In a spontaneous decision, Seiji in 1983 bought the then 98-hotel strong global InterContinental chain from Grand Metropolitan for $2.2 billion. He expanded it quickly to 187 hotels, adding also a super luxury hotel at the Ginza, which catered to Elizabeth Taylor and the likes. The economics of this entirely credit financed frenzy was doubtful. But surely brother Yoshiaki's pedestrian 56-hotel strong Prince chain was duly dwarfed.

Seiji's Seibu Group did not collapse overnight. But his message of eternal lifestyle consumerism and over-priced spending excitements looked quickly out of place in a recession ridden Japan where people soon rediscovered the virtues of their traditional frugality.

While his retail operations might have survived on their own, the credit financed capital wasted on real estate developments, like for resorts and 15 golf courses for which there was no longer any demand, heavily weighted down the group.

In 1991, Seiji formally resigned. As it was he who had called the shots, the group drifted. Half-hearted restructuring showed little results. Occasional divestments equally had little overall impact.

In July 2000, Seiyo Corporation, Seibu-Saison's real estate arm, went bottom up, forcing Seiji to sell most of his remaining shareholdings. Intercontinental Hotels were sold in 2003 to Bass, a British brewer, for $2.9 billion, all of which went for debt servicing. Forced by the main creditor, Mizuho Bank, the remaining Seibu Department Stores had to dismiss 40% of their 9000 strong staff. In return for these restructuring measures, Mizuho Bank (under pressure from the Ministry of Finance) was ready to forgive yen 230 billion ($1.9 billion) of Seibu's debts and accept a yen 10 billion worth of debt for equity swap.

As Seibu's Tokyo locations remain somewhat profitable, inspite of being no longer the avant-garde of anything, they were merged with the equally bankrupt but undistinguished Sogo department stores. The rest of Seiji's empire (Seiyu supermarkets, Family mart, Parco stores, etc.) are about to be gradually disposed.

Today, four decades after its auspicious beginning, the Seibu-Saison party is definitely over.

Bibliography

Downer, Lesley, *Die Brüder Tsutsumi: Die Geschichte der reichsten Familie Japans*, München: Heyne Verlag, 1997.

Havens, Thomas R., *Architects of Affluence: The Tsutsumi Family and the Seibu-Saison Enterprises in Twentieth-Century Japan*, Cambridge, Mass.: Harvard University Press, 1994.

Macintyre, Donald, "Learning to Let Go", *Time Asia*, 31 July 2000.

"Bubble-era expansion still tormenting Saison Group", *Asahi Shimbun*, 1.2.2003.

"Computer statt Piste", *Die Zeit*, 50/1999.

"Seiyo goes bankrupt with 550 billion yen debt", *The Japan Times*, 19.7.2000.

"Developer's business likely to win gold from Nagano Games", *AP*, 21.2.1998.

"Seibu set to receive ¥230 billion rescue package", *Financial Times*, 15.1.2003.

"Sales will be real test of Seibu, Sogo Merger", *Asahi Evening News*, 28.2.2003.

"The Tsutsumi Family: Brotherly Hate", *The Economist*, 8.10.1988.

"The Nagano Olympics and the destruction of nature", http://nolimpiadi.8m.com/enolim01.html.

United, the Benetton Way

There are only very few family-owned enterprises which managed to develop world brands. Benetton, an Italian, family-owned enterprise is one such case. It belongs to a family of four siblings, Luciano, Giuliana (both of whom were the initial founders of the company), Gilberto and Carlo Benetton. The company's roots are intricately entwined in the family's history.

The Benetton children lost their father, Leone Benetton in 1945 during the Second World War when all of them were just mere adolescents. Luciano, the eldest, was only ten years old when his childhood ended. He became the de-facto breadwinner of the family, selling newspapers and panini (sandwiches) at the train station near their house in the morning and bars of soap after school on a door-to-door basis just to make ends meet. Giuliana, the only Benetton daughter and the second eldest had learnt to knit from children's comics when she was young. She quit school to work in a garment sweat shop to help support the family income. When Luciano grew older, he worked for several years as a retail salesman in the Dellasiegas' clothing store in Treviso where he lived. As time passed, he began to realise that he and his sister were capable of producing and selling jumpers on their own instead of selling them on commission for other people.

Luciano's enterprise was based on a simple notion: making and selling colourful knit-wear which was of a commendable quality and which could be bought at a cheap and affordable price, targeted specifically at a previously untapped youth market. In 1955, some jumpers were designed and produced by Giuliana with a home sewing machine in their house. They were given the brand name "Très Jolie". Luciano consequently managed to persuade his employers, the Dellasiegas' brothers, to sell the jumpers and this proved an astonishing success. What made them saleable was as much the quality of the jumpers as the fact that they were unique in design. Giuliana had produced jumpers that were unseen of at that time. Colours that ranged from red to blue to yellow were produced. Consumers greedily drank up all the colours and the jumpers became so popular that queues were often formed outside the stores. The reason for their popularity was that customers were tired of the somber dark colors like black and grey which were typical of the post-war era. Subsequently, Giuliana would design the woollen models (when the current trend was for acrylic pullovers) and be in charge of fabrication, while her brother would handle the marketing side, acting as commercial representative. It was then too that Luciano succeeded in his efforts to improve the quality of the wool that was used to produce the jumpers by travelling to Scotland to learn how the Scots manufacture the wool to remove the 'itch' caused from wearing it. He also managed, together with the help of Adalgerico 'Ado' Montana, a dyeing specialist, to invent a method of dyeing a whole jumper after it was finished rather than dyeing it in parts as it was more cost-efficient to do so. (The original method was to dye the jumpers in its constituents rather than as a whole since dyeing it whole would cause the jumper to shrink.)

In 1955, there was just Luciano, Giuliana and a sewing machine. Ten years later, the company had a hundred and fifty employees with all four Benetton siblings working full time in the company: Luciano was in charge of sales and advertising, Giuliana was responsible for clothing designs and the coordination of preparations for productions, Gilberto was in charge of administration and Carlo was the head of the manufacturing process.

The first store that sold exclusively Benetton knits was opened in Belluno in the quietest part of town. It was a 50/50 venture with a friend named Piero Marchiorello. The shop was named 'My Market' so as not to expose the real brand name of Très Jolie to market failure. The store became a tremendous hit with the youth of Belluno. After opening a few more stores, Luciano Benetton decided that it was possible to build up a network of retail stores manned by potential partners selling exclusively Benetton products. He introduced the franchising system similar to that of McDonald's and Coca-Cola's. Young potential entrepreneurs who were eager to cash in on Benetton's success could do so. This is where Luciano's 'gentleman's agreement" (Mantle, p. 241) came in. Despite using a franchising system so closely associated with American companies, Luciano's franchising system was unique in the sense that unlike the American style of franchising which were based on a voluminous amount of documentation, agreements with store owners were signed with a simple handshake with an absence of a written contract and this agreement was based on mutual trust; similar to the first agreement that the Benettons made with Marchiorello in the beginning. Also, the franchisees had an added advantage. They need not pay any royalties to Benetton if they made profits or used the brand name. However, it was done on condition that the stores sold exclusively Benetton products with a no-return policy and they had to buy the store equipment designed by the Benettons's architect, Tobia Scarpa. Moreover, it was Luciano who ultimately made the decision to approve the store location and he had the right to periodically supervise the store.

By the early seventies, the company had opened stores all over Italy. The whole decade showed a tremendous increase in turnover: revenues in 1971 amounted to a total of 1.1 billion lire which subsequently skyrocketed to a value of 100.4 billion. Net income passed from 0.3 million lire in 1971 to 3.1 billion in 1979. In order to increase production efficiency and meet the increasing consumer demand for the clothes, Luciano devised a system of subcontracting the manufacture of the clothes to small family-owned workshops which employed no more than twenty workers who were paid on the basis of the number of garments they produced. Benetton provided the raw material, the design and the manufacturing plan which left the subcontractor responsible for bringing in the equipment and the workforce. In 1973, nearly eighty subcontractors worked for Benetton which minimized the company's investments in capacity. As sales volume increased subcontractors were coordinated by a series of small factories partially owned by the Benetton family.

Retail stores also increased in numbers. To better coordinate and keep an eye on retail stores, Benetton decided to build a chain of stores hierarchically coordinated by agents. These agents were personally selected by Luciano himself and were responsible for sourcing more young entrepreneurs keen on opening a Benetton shop. They were also in charge of organizing the presentations of new collections to retailers, taking down their orders for "flash", that is, unplanned (Mantle, p. 122) collections (which actually revealed Benetton's ability to respond to adrupt changes in consumer demand) apart from the usual ones and relating all these information to the Benetton headquarters in Ponzano.

In the eighties, the Benetton's main strategy was that of internationalization and diversification. This was done to capture a larger share of the consumer market which was coherent with Luciano's strategy of empire-building. The former "McDonald's of the jumper" (Mantle, p. 126) now not only produced knitwear, but also casual wear, jeans, and menswear. The stores operated under the names of Benetton, My Market, Sisley, Jean West and Tomato. Sisley, for example, was acquired in 1978 to create an independent collection to target a market segment higher than that of Jean West (also another jeans producing brand under Benetton). Further diversification had brought about the creation of other forms of Benetton merchandise like maternity wear for women, clothes catering to children ranging from three to twelve years of age under the brand 012 which was introduced in 1978, casual men's and women's wear as well as a broad selection of accessories like cosmetics, perfumes and shoes, offering a full range and wide selection of Benetton style and quality that catered specifically at almost all age groups.

Today, the company has Benetton outlets in about 120 countries around the world with an international retail network of 5,000 stores. Further diversification of the products had resulted in the evolution of subsidiary brands like The Hip Site, Sisley for teenagers and the sportswear brands of Playlife and Killer Loop.

Also, as business expanded overseas, the notion of franchising arose. Benetton subsidiaries in respective countries were managed by local entrepreneurs who became the franchisees. Apart from overseas expansion, Benetton also began diversifying its products as it extended its business abroad. Brands like Sisley and Killer Loop were specifically targeted at the youth market. There is also a clothing line for pregnant women. Also, innovation in logistics resulted due to Benetton's desire to increase efficiency and reduce product wastage which occurred when a sales order required the manufacture of Benetton products. Despite internationalization and diversification strategies and attempts at innovation, Luciano Benetton is still the head of the company with the Benetton family still fully controlling the business.

Advertising Campaigns

"All over the world Benetton stands for colorful sportswear, multiculturalism, world peace, racial harmony, and now, a progressive approach towards serious issues" (Giroux, p. 6).

Luciano Benetton was constantly attuned to the changing needs and attitudes of consumers. Unlike the consumers of before, present consumers were more aware of their social environment and were also more environmentally or socially proactive. He realized that consumers were no longer buying a product simply for its uses but buying a product for what it represented and what attributes of a product also appealed to their sense of an individual identity. He wanted to project the image of Benetton as more than just a manufacturer of products. Benetton had to symbolise a lifestyle and a worldview to stay in tune with consumer needs. Moreover, a global image was of utmost importance to Luciano since 70% of the profits were derived from the international markets. There had to be a common global image for product identification that linked all Benetton shops together for business to increase. In 1972, Benetton conferred its advertising campaigns to the Eldorado agency, which decided on a poster campaign. Hence in 1982, photographer Oliviero Toscani from the Eldorado agency started working with Benetton, and before long the label had acquired a certain notoriety.

Benetton adopted the "multi-racial" theme since it was in tandem with the theme of colour in Benetton clothes. At first, the posters focused on depicting a celebratory mix of kids and adults of various races dressed in colourful ethnic clothing with a sense of simplicity and happiness with the slogan "Benetton: All the colors in the world!" attached.

The posters changed and became increasingly provocative. These posters under Toscani's artistic direction became extremely controversial and generated a huge amount of publicity for Benetton. Some examples of Benetton's posters were: a picture of a dead Aids victim surrounded by his family with a Christ-like aura, a poster of a priest and nun kissing and a poster of a blood-stained shirt and army fatigue-pants of a dead unknown soldier. The list goes on, but although this might have generated a lot of negative publicity for the company, it had achieved its purpose. Sales almost always increased when Toscani's controversial posters were advertised. It was known to decrease when tamer advertisements were used instead.

To put it negatively, Benetton's advertising launch was an attempt to commodify culture, to boost sales by trying to revive the dried up image of the company in the eighties. This was based on the growing notion that consumers now did not buy the product but rather bought what the product aesthetically represented. Put positively, Benetton Group's advertising campaigns were meant not only as a means of communication but also an expression of our time. The advertisements contained a diverse range of universal themes of racial integration, protection of the environment and Aids. Through their universal impact, they have succeeded in attracting the attention of the public and stood out amidst the current clutter of images. The campaigns have gathered awards and international acclaim. Likewise, they have provoked strong reactions, sometimes vicious, other times plain curiosity, confirming once again that they are always a focal point of discussion and of confrontation of ideas.

However, critics have attacked Benetton's advertisements as blatant exploitation of people in horrifying situations. One American critic, Henry Giroux in his book *Disturbing Pleasures* called it hyper-ventilating realism which basically equates to a realism of sensationalism, shock and spectacle, commenting that the advertisements simply register rather than challenge the dominant social relations reproduced in the photographs. Two racially marked ads which sparked sharp criticisms and attacks on Benetton were used by him to substantiate these claims.

The first depicts a black woman and a white baby. The black woman is shown wearing a crimson cable knit cardigan pulled over her shoulders which exposes her right breast. Her hands reveal traces of scar tissue and her nails are trimmed short with the baby shown suckling on the black woman's breast. Given the legacy of colonialism and racism of blacks in America, it was inevitable that the photo was interpreted as an imperialist coding as it privileged an offensive reading of an ingrained racial stereotype of the black-slave wet nurse. Though this advertisement was pulled from billboards in the United States, it ironically won Benetton many awards across Europe including Le Grand Prix de L'Affichage in France.

The second ad portrayed two hands, one white and the other black being handcuffed together. Critics had not removed the possibility that the poster depicted a false and calculated sense of equality. In reality, it only served to reinforce, at least at the level of consciousness that crime, turmoil and lawlessness were fundamentally a black problem.

Benetton's Company Culture

Since Benetton is an Italian-owned company, much of Benetton's style of management is similar to the approach that the Italians take to business. Benetton, being family-owned reflects the relative importance of family to business and life in general. There is a strong sense of familism within the family with personal loyalties given to the immediate and extended family. Trust with outsiders is not easily built and this is the reason why personal networking is of the utmost importance in Italian business circles. Luciano himself "was an indefatigable world-class networker, known from the White House to the Kremlin" (Mantle, p. 205). People who became franchisees of Benetton in the international arena were mostly of Italian descent and were usually friends of friends who personally knew the Benettons. Indeed there seemed "an impression of favoritism towards friends and friends of friends" (Mantle, p. 127). This method of networking within trusted circles and forming business partnerships only with people whom Benetton trusted was exemplified when Luciano tapped into the American market by approaching the Italian Chamber of Commerce and enlisting the help of an American-Italian individual named Sal Salibello. Also, the first Benetton shop to open in Prague was attributed to the help of "friends who found [them] a path through the bureaucracy" (Mantle, p. 137). An Anglo-Italian businessman close to the Benetton family once said in response to rumours that Benetton was linked to the mafia.

There is a culture which goes very deep in Italy, and which the likes of American investment banks don't always understand. It is a culture of who you know, and of using this knowledge. It may appear crooked, in the sense that it depends on who you know, but it is also a defence against far greater crookedness (Mantle, pp. 270–1).

The issue of trust is again highlighted when it is found that the family had maintained a full hundred percent control of the company through Edizione Holdings. Twenty-five percent of shares were placed in flotation in the Milan stock exchange. This strategy was adopted to transform Benetton from a family-owned company into a mature corporate enterprise. However, ultimate control of Benetton Group Spa belonged to Edizione Holdings (the parent company). Unsurprisingly, the nexus of power lay in the hands of the four siblings who were the directors of Edizione and no outsider could gain access to that power: "Benetton was and is like a mountain whose summit was above the clouds. At the top, which was effectively invisible, this was and always will be purely a family company" (Mantle, p. 119).

An amount of patronage evident in Italian businesses can also be found in Benetton. Indeed Italians in authority feel a sense of obligation to employees and even non-employees who belong to their personal network. Luciano, for example, employed his childhood friend Nico Luciani as the director of the Benetton Foundation, even though they had been estranged from each other for twenty-five years. The notion of friendship which accompanied business relations was also evident when the Scarpas, long-time family friends of the Benettons who were their main architects, broke off all personal and business relations with Luciano and family when Luciano separated from his wife, Teresa, and married another.

Luciano also adopted a personal approach to the management of Benetton, which is a common trait of Italian business culture. He saw Benetton as more than just a company, to him, it exemplified the principle of entrepreneurship, hard work and initiative and as a symbol of how far the family had come. This personal pride in the organisation was shown when Villa Minelli, a mansion that Luciano had dreamt of living in during his childhood was bought and converted into the headquarters of Benetton. His hands-on approach in the business was also well-known. He was committed in the active role he took in locating the stores and supervising the shops personally from time to time, often being away from the headquarters in Italy to inspect the shops. He would know where to locate the stores since he spent a lot of time observing people and their shopping habits.

According to *Management Worldwide*, "the [Italian] captains of industry are powerful, privileged individualists, whose reputations colour their organizations" and they also like to focus "on those aspects of the business which interest them and which they judge to be important, and leaving the rest to others" (Hickson & Pugh, p. 81). This was definitely true of Luciano Benetton. Certainly, Luciano was and is the most famous Benetton in the Benetton company and he made himself in charge of sales and marketing while leaving the other departments to the other siblings to handle.

Luciano was known for detesting the structures of bureaucracy. In 1981, Aldo Palmeri, a former Bank of Italy officer became the chief executive officer of Benetton. This was an apparent move to keep investors happy since they wanted greater transparency within the company and were wary of the Benetton "quartpartite" control of the company. The arrival of Palmeri resulted in the growth of a bureaucratic style which overlapped and sometimes conflicted with the dominating entrepreneurial and informal Benetton culture. The strong involvement of not only Luciano but all the Benetton siblings in operations contributed to the maintenance of styles. This informal and personal style which was also physically manifested in Luciano's casual attire for business is a characteristic of the low power distance typical of a familial Italian business culture.

Luciano encouraged the entrepreneurial spirit in his employees. He personally saw to the employment of subcontractors and distribution agents. The original selection criteria of selecting subcontractors which Luciano adhered to was to see if there was any presence of an independent entrepreneurial spirit in the subcontractors. He also looked to see if there was any potential in the person for growth and whether the person possessed an in-depth knowledge in manufacturing. In this Luciano seemed to be almost always accurate as he seemed to possess this innate ability to see if a person had untapped potential. The sub-contractors were given relative freedom in their operations of employing the workforce and buying equipment. In choosing distribution agents acceptance criteria demanded a thorough understanding of the company style of management, a sense of mutual understanding between the management and the subordinate agent, his in-depth knowledge of the market, a dedication to the business idea, entrepreneurial spirit and a sense of loyalty.

Indeed, since Luciano also gave a relatively large amount of freedom to his employees to take their own initiatives and realize their creativities, they often felt empowered enough to be motivated. Motivation was also enhanced by the implementation of reward schemes for the employees. As such Benetton employees often possessed a strong level of loyalty and commitment to the company. However, herein lay a paradox: although entrepreneurship and initiative were seemingly-valued qualities in an employee, Luciano often conducted "cleaning the network" sessions on retail shops around the world. It was a process in which "agents and shops were regularly observed and, where necessary, their performance [was] adjusted". This was accomplished with "a ruthless clarity of vision that was at odds with the image of the 'gentleman's agreement' that Luciano still liked to imply was unchanged since the early days of the business" (Mantle, p. 241). Certainly, the informal "gentleman's agreement" could have allowed Luciano Benetton to attain greater control of the distribution-end of production.

Despite this, Alessandro Sinatra in *Corporate Transformation* wrote that there are several reasons for the formidable success of Benetton. The first was the idea of using creativity to try to be innovative in the face of the scarcity of cash. In the beginning, the constant lack of financial capital led to the implementation of the most important design principles and resulted in original solutions. This idea of using creativity when cash was scarce became one of the tenets of Benetton's philosophy and is evident in the employment of subcontractors in manufacturing, the franchise agreements in retail, the advance made in the dyeing process, and subsequently the highly-advanced information and logistics systems. The continuous emphasis on cost-efficient methods is also due to the influence of the locals in agricultural Treviso on the importance of frugality and cost-efficiency methods. The last reason is due to the foresight of Luciano who saw the potential in the retail market, and took the initiative to seize the opportunity. He came up with the business idea and saw it through till the end.

Bibliography

Giroux, Henry A., *Disturbing Pleasures: Learning Popular Culture*, New York and London: Routledge, 1994.

Hickson, J. David and Pugh, S. Derek, *Management Worldwide*, London: Penguin Books, 1995.

Mantle, Jonathan, *Benetton; The Family, the Business and the Brand*, London: Little Brown and Company, 2000.

Sinatra, Alessandro, *Corporate Transformation*, Norwell, Massachusetts: Kluwer Academic Publishers, 1997.

Nike Just Did It

If you have a body, you are an athlete...
And as long as there are athletes, there will be Nike.

Company History

In 1962, a young business student by the name of Phil Knight was inspired to write a school paper after overhearing staff from the *Oregon Journal* debate whether Japanese Nikon cameras would one day replace the expensive, German-made Leicas. A middle-distance runner for the University of Oregon, Knight argued that if low-cost Japanese producers could manufacture good quality running shoes, the price differential would open up a new market, undercutting European manufacturers like Adidas and Puma. Though Knight graduated and went on to work as an accountant, he set out on a summer trip in 1963 and travelled to Japan, where he met the managers of the Onitsuka Company which produced Tiger running shoes. Stirred by the sight of the cheap, lightweight shoes, which were decent imitations of their European counterparts, Knight was motivated to purchase samples which he brought home to show his old track and field coach, Bill Bowerman. The legendary Oregon coach was impressed enough to agree to invest $500 in a partnership and the two contracted with Onitsuka and bought 1000 pairs of Tiger shoes under the name of Blue Ribbon Sports (BRS) (Katz, 1944). Retailing the shoes out of the trunk of his car at sports meets, Knight sold $8000 worth of shoes in just a year and immediately quit his job and ordered more stock. Knight hired a small team of salespeople, who were like-minded competitive runners, and BRS gave them the opportunity to hold a job, make a decent living and enjoy running.

In 1966, Bowerman, who was always experimenting with new ways of making lighter shoes, shipped Onitsuka one of his own designs that consisted of a soft, nylon upper, instead of a leather one. The resulting shoe, the Cortez, was a huge hit in track and field circles despite the taunts and laughs from Adidas representatives. By 1969, BRS had sold a million dollars worth of shoes, however, its overly-dependant relationship with Onitsuka had become shaky and Knight's fears were validated when the Japanese began to look for bigger distributors and threatened to pull out of the business affiliation. Knight was forced to either sell his stake of the company and face legal action or find another way to produce the shoes. Thus, along with his small team of employees, who had begun to design and innovate a separate line of shoes, Knight decided it was time to take a big risk and strike out alone. After severing ties with Onitsuka for breach of contract and locating a local factory in Exeter, Knight joined forces with the Japanese trading company, Nissho Iwai (which provided them with credit) and began to sell the shoes under a new name and trademark. During a particularly restless dream, the image of the Greek goddess of victory came to Johnson and the name Nike was quickly adopted. With the help of local student Caroline Davidson, who was paid $35 for her design, a fat checkmark was also incorporated as the new logo. The logo was initially disliked because unlike Adidas' stripes which supported the arch and Puma's which supported the ball of the foot, the checkmark was only purely decorative. However, the "Swoosh", as it was nicknamed, would later become one of the world's most recognized symbols and prove to be vital to Nike's phenomenal success.

Early Competition in the Athletic Footwear Industry: Adidas — Letting Market Advantage Slip Away

Based in Herzogenaurach, Germany, Rudolf and Adolf Dassler designed and marketed their Adidas brand of shoes under the Adidas Company. An established footwear manufacturer, its breakthrough came during the 1936 Olympics when the famous medallist, Jesse Owens, agreed to wear Adidas shoes. This initiated a marketing strategy that associated running shoes with famous athletes, thereby setting a precedent for other athletic shoe manufacturers. However, in 1949 the brothers fell out and went their separate ways. Adolf stayed with the Adidas line while Rudolf set up the Puma Company, which became the world's second largest manufacturer. Adolf continued to innovate and develop a variety of shoes, including the spiked soccer boots that were instrumental in Germany's World Cup win over Hungary in 1954. Adidas dominated international sports meets with its great variety of superior products. For example, 82.8% of medallists at the Montreal games in 1976 were equipped with Adidas, giving the company tremendous publicity. Adidas' lead seemed insurmountable, diversifying into athletic apparel, sports bags, tennis racquets, swimwear and even ski equipment.

During the 1970's, the American athletic footwear industry experienced exceptional change and growth, fuelled in part by the

1972 Munich Olympics and increasing concerns with physical fitness. The publication of scientific studies such as Dr. Kenneth Cooper's *Aerobics* and James Fixx's *The Complete Book of Running*, endorsed the physical benefits of jogging and became monumental bestsellers. The footwear industry was then largely dominated by Adidas and Puma. However, by the end of the decade, the little upstart company that was Nike had outstripped all its competitors, including Reebok, L.A Gear, Converse and New Balance. How did Nike surpass Adidas which stood on the threshold of dominating the entire market and more importantly, what were the ingredients of Nike's success in these initial years?

In a classic case of miscalculation, Adidas had underestimated the entry and aggressiveness of competitors in the U.S. market and lost out on the recreational boom of the century. As an experienced manufacturer, it dismissed its new rivals as weak opportunists and complacently believed that they would not pose any serious threat to the market leader. It also underestimated the growth of the market for running shoes which it had dominated for four decades. During that period, the market had only seen slow, stable growth and Adidas was sceptical of the durability of the boom. However, with the preponderance of magazine articles and television programmes promoting a healthy lifestyle, the notion of exercise became an activity one did for fun and self-discovery. Adidas was not the only player to be caught offguard. Other U.S. firms that were traditionally strong in the industry also misjudged the market opportunity, notably Converse and Uniroyal's Keds. While Adidas strayed into other product lines, Nike remained focused at the forefront of the industry, with major commitment to research and development, so as to introduce the most technologically advanced shoes on the market. Nike took full advantage of the industry's favourable primary demand and offered an even wider product line than Adidas. By offering a wide variety of styles at different prices,

Nike appealed to all kinds of runners. It was able to convey the image of a comprehensive shoe manufacturer with a readily recognizable trademark. Most of its manufacturing process was contracted out to Asian firms, allowing flexible, short product runs at low-cost. Consequently, Nike did not have to establish a large infrastructure with high fixed costs, leaving it resistant to changes in demand (Hartley, 1998). These techniques were not unique to Nike for it imitated Adidas rather than becoming a revolutionary innovator. However, it simply did it better than its competitors and true to its early Japanese influence; it became a case of the imitator outdoing the original.

Nike's Growth and Development

During the early 1980's, Nike sales grew from $270 million and exceeded $1 billion by the fiscal year-end of 1988 (Hartley, 1998), boosted by the creation of a patented 'waffle sole' and a cushioning system known as Nike Air. These technological developments attest to Nike's early commitment to research and product development. Demand for Nike's soared to a point where distributors could place orders up to six months in advance under the Nike 'Futures' system that cut inventory costs and guaranteed delivery. In the 1982 Forbes Annual Report on American Industry, Nike ranked as the most profitable firm in the past five years. At the same time, the company went public, making Knight an instant millionaire with a net worth of almost $300 million. However, the 1980's also saw Reebok emerging as Nike's greatest competitor. Part of the reason was that Nike was slow to respond to the fast-growing market for women's aerobic shoes, choosing instead to focus on male-dominated basketball. This failure to appreciate new trends in the industry and lack of perception concerning women's fitness needs caused sales and profits to sink by 18% and over 40% respectively, between 1986 and 1987. Yet, unlike Adidas, which never managed to regain its lead, Nike fought to remain the dominant player.

While Nike's core business was traditionally made up of running shoes, it also began to diversify into other areas. Under its footwear segment, basketball shoes accounted for nearly a third of all sales by virtue of its universal appeal and popularity amongst male teenagers. However, Nike expanded its range to pursue the market for soccer boots, children's footwear, cross-trainers, tennis, aerobics and even golf shoes. Nike also successfully forayed into the outdoor footwear category, with its own line of hiking boots, sandals and 'All Conditions Gear' (ACG's). Nike also began to promote its line of athletic apparel which included men's and women's clothing, warm-up suits, team-licensed attire and more recently, outfits for women's yoga classes. Nike also entered the market for casual wear with its purchase of Cole Haan Holdings Inc. in 1988. Cole Haan now produces high quality, casual luxury footwear and accessories. In addition, Nike also produces its own line of eyewear, time pieces and heart monitors. The company's acquisitions include Tetra Plastics Inc. which manufactures the plastic compound used in Nike's Air cushioning system. In addition, Bauer Nike Hockey, based in Montreal, Quebec, is the world's leading manufacturer of hockey equipment and a wholly owned subsidiary of Nike. The company's research, design, and development centre, as well as manufacturers, are based in St. Jerome, Quebec. Nike has also partnered with Hurley International, a premium teen lifestyle brand based in California in its efforts to truly consolidate its position in the sports industry. Hurley sells $70 million worth of T-shirts, cargo pants and surf shorts annually, capitalizing on a craze for surf and skateboard gear. According to Matt Powell, a consultant to athletic shoe retailers at Princeton Retail Analysis, Nike wasn't considered authentic in the skate and surf crowd, thus this move has been applauded.

Corporate Culture

Nike's belief is that every individual is an athlete and that includes its own employees. In order to be a 'Nike guy', one has to 'get it', which can mean anything from having an aggressive attitude to an unquenchable thirst to win. Nike's corporate culture tends to project masculinity, with its emphasis on assertiveness and individuality. Its male dominated management could also be the reason why it has not traditionally done well in the women's market, unlike Reebok. At its headquarters in Beaverton, Oregon, the buildings surrounding a seven acre artificial lake are named in honour of influential athletes such as Michael Jordan, Bo Jackson and Steve Prefontaine. Posters and sports paraphernalia adorn the interior, making it seem more like a college campus than a corporate headquarters. Nike's workforce is made up of fit, healthy and surprisingly youthful employees attired in informal wear rather than business suits. Many are former professional athletes, collegiate competitors and even former Olympians who still continue to pursue recreational sports. Corporate videos describe the working environment as "a factory for fun" and "being in a playground". The corporate "we" is regularly and sincerely used and new recruits receive a catalogue of Nike's values: use structure to promote innovation, stay flexible and adaptive and challenge the status quo. Smoking is prohibited on the grounds and employees are rewarded and encouraged to ride bicycles to work instead of driving. The sheer athleticism and competitive mindset that characterizes its corporate culture has even permeated the administrative vocabulary of employees, who use terms such as "quarterbacking" a committee. Sports metaphors are also prevalent elsewhere, with employees regarding work weeks and fiscal quarters as countdowns on a game clock or a seasonal game. A career with Nike has effectively become an extended sports moment for some.

In return, Nike provides its employees with state-of-the-art facilities, including hairdressers, massage parlours, fully equipped gyms and a comprehensive day-care centre (Katz, 1994). The isolation of the headquarters has led to it being nicknamed the "berm", outside of which lies the real world.

The Nike attitude and the anti-establishment image it conveys comes from its roots as the entrepreneurial underdog that snapped at heels of a bureaucratic and sober Adidas. Its corporate heritage includes a shared determination to work for the company cause without taking oneself too seriously. This has sometimes been interpreted as corporate arrogance, with critics claiming that sports and business should remain separate entities. Along with its meteoric rise to the top of the industry, Nike also had to deal with the anti-Nike establishment. It has been denigrated as a cult organization that holds too much power over the athletes that it endorses, thereby spoiling the game. During the 1992 Olympics held in Barcelona for example, the Dream Team which included basketball heavyweights such as Jordan and Barkley, refused to take to the medal stand as the American anthem played. The reason behind the players' defiance was that the official awards ceremony jacket had the Reebok emblem on it. The stand-off, which was wrongly perceived to be a carefully orchestrated corporate strategy, caused immense public controversy as the athletes had placed corporate loyalty before patriotism. Although the incident arose entirely out of the players' own initiative, Nike executives later commented that "Michael Jordan holds us to our values", attesting to the company's ability to inspire loyalty. Attitude surveys held by the James H. Joerger firm confirm this by ranking Nike as having the highest level of corporate loyalty and acceptance of company policy ever recorded. A similar Business Week survey rated Nike thirteenth for most improved productivity out of all the Standard and Poor 500 companies.

Organizational Structure

Nike's top management today includes Knight, one of the original founders of the company. Bowerman passed away in 1999 after his retirement, leaving Knight as the company's CEO. A sports enthusiast and the epitome of a sports fan, he has an unconventional management style, hating negotiations and preferring informal discussions and meetings. Yet, it is obvious that he is well qualified to run the company, given his passion and determination for sports and his educational background, which boasts an MBA from Stanford. Reputed to be a recluse who rarely entertains interviewers, Knight lends his enigmatic aura to the rest of the company. Other notable executives include Mark Parker, President of Nike Brand, Tinker Hatfield, Vice President of Special Projects and Dennis Colard, Vice President of Global Operations.

Nike employs 22,000 people worldwide, from its Nike World Headquarters in Oregon and Nike European Headquarters in Hilversum, The Netherlands, to almost every region around the globe, including Asia Pacific, the Americas, Europe, the Middle East and Africa. Including manufacturers, shippers, retailers and service providers, nearly one million people help bring Nike products to consumers everywhere. Of the 11,000 Nike employees located in the U.S. about 5,000 work in Oregon at the World Headquarters, Wilsonville Distribution Center, and numerous retail venues. The original Nike European Headquarters opened in Amsterdam in 1980. The current European headquarters, a state-of-the-art complex designed by William McDonough & Partners, opened in 1999 in Hilversum, The Netherlands. Nike Partners is the subsidiary in charge of dealing with local distributors located in Eastern Europe and Middle East, including Israel. Nike's latest addition, Africa, came under the administration of the European region in the middle of 2000. Eleven offices are located in the Asia Pacific region, including Australia, China, Hong Kong, Japan, Korea, and Singapore.

Nike's organizational structure has been described as a matrix, mixing its entrepreneurial past with its current status as a global corporation. It does not fall into any recognized, standard organizational structure, and seems to be more of an Oriental hybrid, given its association with Japanese firms. Although it is generally streamlined in order to foster autonomy, it retains a formalized management structure so as to facilitate accountability and responsibility. Nike's mission is to design, develop and merchandise its products and is a market-driven company. Its focus is on research and development to produce high-tech shoes and other equipment to meet future trends. Research and testing takes place in the Nike Sports Research Lab (NSRL) where accomplished scientists study athletes in motion and the ways in which they are affected by various shoe, apparel and equipment design during specific activities. Key areas of ongoing research include the biomechanics and physiology of performance enhancement and injury prevention. The NSRL also accommodates the Environmental Chamber, which can imitate various conditions that athletes face in order to improve the design of fabrics. A notable feature in Nike's operations is that it does not see it self as a manufacturer. Instead, Nike outsources all its production to contract manufacturers in Asia. This has resulted in it being labelled a "hollow corporation", as it is essentially nothing more substantial than a design company that depends on other firms for production.

Manufacturing and Labour Pains

Manufacturing overseas has been a familiar practise for Nike. Almost all of its footwear is produced in Asian factories based in

Taiwan, China, Indonesia and Thailand because of lower labour costs, less union involvement and fewer government regulations. These management contracts are critical to Nike's operations as they ensure a reliable supply to all retail outlets under its Futures program. The independent contractors provide several advantages, namely; greater flexibility to control inventories, lower capital requirements and more accurate sales forecasts. However, this dependency on foreign contractors also means that Nike is vulnerable to political instability, exchange rate fluctuations and criticism of its treatment of employees. In recent years, Nike has faced accusations of unfair labour practices. Human rights groups and labour unions claimed that Nike has profited from child labour and paid its employees below the minimum wage. In 1998, negative publicity generated by the "discovery" of Pakistani children, stitching Nike soccer balls for 6 cents an hour further tainted Nike's corporate image. Workers in Asian factories were allegedly exposed to harmful chemicals, physically abused by supervisors for not meeting production targets and were not paid for overtime. In addition, their living quarters were cramped, dirty and they were apparently paid less than $1 daily. These accusations were true to a certain extent in some factories; however, such criticisms had a tendency to focus on perceived malpractices of a wealthy multinational corporation instead of the broader social and global context.

Although wages were meagre by Western standards, workers earned a steady income that was much higher than subsistence agriculture, which remains the main form of employment in developing countries. It would be fallacious to insist that the minimum wage in a Third World country be comparable to that of a developed nation. In fact, these very shoe factories were responsible for dramatically lowering poverty and unemployment levels and paving the way for industrialization. Jobs at shoe factories were actually considered desirable because they provided additional benefits such as meal and transport allowances and there were never shortages of applicants. Furthermore, the heavy reliance on female workers brought about a social transformation in some Asian societies by empowering women with the ability to earn their own income. The factories that Nike contracted were often run by ethnic Chinese, who dominated the business communities in Asia (Litvin, 2003). Their Confucian management styles often conflicted with workers of non-Chinese origin, for example, Indonesian workers would often complain of verbal abuse from aggressive Chinese bosses. However, this was a cultural issue which stemmed from historic tensions and miscommunication, rather than Nike's management style.

It can be argued that Nike was not even responsible for these issues because it had no ownership of the factories, nor did it dictate the terms of employment or set wage limits. Government policies in developing nations encouraged and even provided incentives for such factories because of the billions of dollars worth of investments and revenue that were generated. However, because of Nike's high profile and its huge profit margins, the company, rather than the respective governments and officials, was singled out for condemnation (Litvin, 2003). These same factories also produced shoes for Reebok and Adidas, yet the media sought to highlight only Nike's involvement in what has been termed a contortion of corporate responsibility. Nike bashing was thought to be a means of justifying opposition to successful multinationals and the company took the blame for the entire industry. Some human rights groups even obscured the fact that their motives stemmed from a protectionist desire to save their own jobs which were threatened by cheap, foreign labour. Yet, Nike accepted these responsibilities in its stride and introduced its Code of Conduct. The Code stipulates the maximum working hours per week, provides compensation for overtime, prohibits the employment of children under the age of 16 and ensures the general health and safety of workers. All Nike contractors are also required to sign a Memorandum of Understanding requiring compliance with local government regulations. Factories are also open to inspection by independent organizations and schemes for free education and business loans to workers are also available. While significant improvements have been made, there is no global consensus on labour standards, leaving Nike open to continued criticism and an ethical dilemma. Yet, this situation also serves to illustrate Nike's powerful ability to effect positive change along a broad spectrum of society.

Interestingly, just as Nike's geographical distance from its manufacturing plants could not protect it from the labour controversy; it has also meant that Nike is not immune to other conditions that affect Asia. Most recently, the outbreak of the SARS virus in China and other parts of Asia has had a significant impact on the company's production. Orders have been rescheduled, on-site visits have been replaced by communication via e-mail and the entire manufacturing process has effectively slowed down. This incident only serves to again highlight Nike's heavy reliance and dependency on these Asian factories and how significant they are to its business.

Ingredients for Success

In a world where image is everything, the Nike "Swoosh" is one of the most recognizable symbols in the world. It is integral to understanding Nike's success and corporate culture because it is a commercial symbol that has given the Nike brand global omnipresence. The "Swoosh" has become so familiar to the public that Nike signs its advertisements only with its icon because they are so confident that it will be recognized without any text. It has become a cultural icon that Nike relies on to increase its brand value, recognition and status. No other athletics company has achieved this level of brand identification. In order to illustrate this point, ask anybody what the name of Reebok's logo is and they will probably draw a blank. In fact Reebok's logo is named the vector, only it is not as readily recognized or desired by consumers. Nike, along with its advertising agency Wieden & Kennedy, now focuses on keeping the logo highly visible in its advertisements. The company's advertising and promotions budget has been estimated to be 10% of its annual revenue in order to firmly lodge the symbol in public consciousness.

So why is the Swoosh so important to our understanding of Nike's business culture? The reason is that it goes hand in hand with the good old American philosophy: "Just Do It". Nike does not simply sell running shoes; it sells consumers a way of life and this is the core of its success. The inspiration that the swoosh stands for, along with the motivation and determination behind its philosophy is something that everyone can relate to, whether you are an athlete or not. Nike uses the language of empowerment in order to motivate its consumers. No matter who you are, what colour your hair or skin is, what physical or social limitations you are confronted with, Nike convinces consumers that it is possible to achieve. It tells people to get up, take control of their lives and act. The simple, yet highly effective logo and mantra have come to represent athletic excellence, achievement and hip authenticity. Behind the "Just Do It" slogan lies a very American ideology; yet with globalization, what was once an American ideology has become a universal aspiration. The idea of a level playing field that allows you to compete not only in sports, but in every aspect of life goes back to the early American pioneer spirit and desire for success. The expression sells to the world the great American dream and promotes its work ethic by telling consumers that if you are motivated and competitive enough, you will excel and conquer.

In this way, Nike has created a personality and an attitude for itself by encapsulating a very human desire to achieve. By cleverly using a very simple tagline and logo, it has managed to turn a lifestyle into a commodity.

In today's athletic industry, companies no longer gain a significant advantage from the actual manufacturing process. Therefore, in order to stay competitive, one must focus on selling an image in order to gain value. As we have seen, Nike is not a manufacturing firm but a company that concentrates on developing and marketing its products. One of its most successful marketing strategies is the use of celebrity endorsements to promote its products. The most famous of all was Michael Jordan, who was enlisted as a spokesperson in Nike's basketball advertisements. These television commercials conveyed a theme of human transcendence by capturing Jordan in mid-flight. They also provided Nike with an identity and enticed viewers with the tagline "it's gotta be the shoes". The creation of a superhero image and its association with Nike was crucial to propelling both Jordan and Nike to the top of the industry. The Air Jordan line of basketball shoes became one of Nike's most popular and lucrative innovations, selling over $100 million in its first year alone. Jordan himself became an instant role model for youths and inspired them to follow the American Dream. This reinforced Nike's image of performance and achievement, while at the same time imbuing it with a personality that consumers could relate to. Nike's shoes stood for fame, success and reaching the impossible: if you wore Nike's, just maybe you would be empowered with the ability to fly like Jordan. This psychological and emotional connection was a powerful marketing tool that translated into billions of dollars worth of sales. Nike has also been consistently advertised by a stable of talented, top athletes, including Andre Agassi for tennis, Bo Jackson for baseball and Tiger Woods for golf, thus appealing to a broad spectrum of consumers who want to emulate their heroes. Nike has also harnessed popular culture, in particular music, to promote its products. Catchy tunes such as Monty Python's 'Always look on the bright side of life', accompanied images of athletes such as Ronaldo in various stages of distress and injury, reinforcing the notion that there is no gain without pain. Keen to avoid its earlier mistakes, Nike has also tailored commercials to capture the women's fitness market. Instead of using sexually exploitative advertising or stereotyping, Nike has sought to represent the empowerment of women. Commercials have a more narrative style and use motivational discourse to convey inspiration. The use of female celebrities, such as soccer player Mia Hamm, represents Nike as an advocate of gender equality in sports.

Current Competition

According to the Sporting Goods Intelligence newsletter, it is estimated that at the end of 2002, Nike had 39.1% of the U.S. athletic shoe business, Reebok had 12%, New Balance had 11.6%, and Adidas-Salomon AG, had 9.6%. While Nike continues to rule the footwear industry, analysts say Reebok has a good chance of at least doubling its share in the next few years and thus poses the biggest threat to Nike's business. Since Paul Fireman regained control in November 1999, Reebok has increased sales, its capital and its exposure in the marketplace. In the fourth quarter of 2002, Reebok's total sales gained an unprecedented 14.8%, reaching $763 million. Apparel sales in the U.S. grew 48.1% to $145 million. According to a Lehman Brothers report in February 2003, Reebok has had 11 consecutive quarters of sales increases. In December 2000, Reebok and the National Football League announced the formation of an exclusive partnership with the NFL's restructured consumer products business. The NFL granted a 10 year exclusive license to Reebok beginning in the 2002 NFL season to manufacture, market and sell NFL licensed merchandise for all 32 NFL teams. The agreement also gives Reebok exclusive rights to develop a new line of NFL fitness equipment. In August 2001, Reebok formed a 10-year strategic partnership with the National Basketball Association under which Reebok will design, manufacture, sell and market licensed merchandise for the NBA, the Women's National Basketball Association and the National Basketball Development League. Beginning in the 2004 season, Reebok will have the exclusive rights to supply and market all on-court apparel, including uniforms, shooting shirts, warm-ups, authentic and replica jerseys and practice gear for all NBA, WNBA and NBDL teams, thereby encroaching on Nike's traditional basketball and football territory.

At present, Reebok is hurrying to fill the empty shelves in more than 2,500 U.S. branches of Foot Locker Inc., a gap opened up by a rift between Nike and Foot Locker, the largest athletic footwear chain in the world. In February 2002, Foot Locker told Nike the store wanted to reduce the number of Nike's Air Jordans, Shox and Air Force Ones that sell for more than $100. The move, which reflected reluctance amongst teenagers to buy expensive basketball shoes, came at Nike's expense. Foot Locker told Nike it wanted to reduce its marquee shoes from 12% of the chain's business to 6%, and cancelled $150 million in Nike orders. Nike later denied that it had pulled back on existing orders or punished Foot Locker with late shipments, as had been reported. However, the relationship with Foot Locker has been testy since the beginning of 2004, and Nike has already been busy finding alternative chains. Foot Locker is no longer a primary distribution for Nike's marquee and launch products. Nike's Hall of Hoops displays in Foot Locker stores were replaced by Reebok's Above the Rim, featuring RBK shoes endorsed by Reebok's Allen Iverson. Reebok has also filled the vacuum with more of its Classic line, part of the "retro" look that has been successful for sneaker brands such as Converse and Puma, responding to the American market's need for nostalgia.

Although Nike has always been historically able to reinvent itself and surprise industry watchers, its competitors are catching up fast. Despite the refusal of competitors such as New Balance to cash in on marketable celebrities, other companies like Reebok and Adidas have copied Nike's lead and recruited their own athletes for endorsements. Watching the television these days, it is hard to differentiate between an Adidas commercial and a Nike commercial as they both use generic inspirational imagery, slogans, music and athletes. Adidas sponsors Zinedine to endorse its soccer boots while Nike sponsors Ronaldo. Adidas' latest A3 running shoe boasts technology that cushions the foot and maximizes energy use just like Nikes latest Shox technology. And to top it all, Reebok's corporate website shares the same grey, black and orange colour scheme as Nike's, further blurring the distinction between the two! A global homogenization of consumption means that there is very little substance or technological advantage that differentiates a Nike product from that of a rival. Thus marketing, image and the 'cool factor' remain very important when targeting consumer groups, especially the youth segment. It appears that in an industry that seems to have reached market saturation, the only real difference is whether a customer prefers to be seen in a Swoosh, vector or three stripes.

Bibliography

Books

Goldman, Robert and Papson, Stephen, *Nike Culture: The Sign of the Swoosh*, Thousand Oaks, California: SAGE Publications, 1998.

Katz, Donald, *Just Do It: The Nike Spirit in the Corporate World*, Holbrook, Mass.: Adams Pub., 1994.

Strasser, J. B. and Becklund, Laurie, *Swoosh: The Story of Nike and the Men Who Played There*, New York: Harcourt Brace Jovanovich, 1991.

Chapters in Books

Aaker, David A. and Joachimsthaler, Erich, *Adidas and Nike — Lessons in Building Brands: Brand Leadership*, New York: Free Press, 2000.

Grigsby, David W., Gaertner, Susan and Roach, Karen, "Nike, Inc.", in Grigsby, David W. and Stahl, Michael J. (editors), *Cases in Strategic Management*, Oxford: Blackwell Business, 1997.

Hartley, Robert F, *Nike: Riding High with a Great Image, Marketing Mistakes and Successes*, New York: John Wiley & Sons, 1998.

Litvin, Daniel B., "The contortions of corporate responsibility: Nike and its Third-World factories", in *Empires of Profit: Commerce, Conquest and Corporate Responsibility*, New York and London: Texere, 2003.

Sonia El Kahal, *Nike: Ethical Dilemmas of FDI in Asia Pacific Business in Asia Pacific: Texts and Cases*, New York: Oxford University Press, 2001.

White, Randall K., "Nike, Inc.", in Peter, J. Paul and Donnelly, James H. (editors), *Marketing Management: Knowledge and Skills*, Boston, Mass.: Irwin/McGraw-Hill, 2001.

Articles from Websites

"2003 to see major tech strides in US athletic shoes", *Market News Express*, http://www.tdctrade.com/mne/footwear/footwear019.htm

Rozhon, Tracie, "Former sneaker king making a comeback", *International Herald Tribune Online*, http://www.iht.com/articles/88965.html. March 7, 2003.

Horrow, Rick, "If the shoe fits: sneaker wars heating up", *CBS Sports Online*, http://cbs.sportsline.com/general/story/6211588

Dukcevich, Davide, "Nike's Got Global Game", *Forbes Online*, http://www.forbes.com/2002/09/18/0918nike.html

Back, Brian J., "Nike campaign pointing toward a future with football", *The Business Journal*, Portland, May 17, 2002. http://portland.bizjournals.com/portland/stories/2002/05/20/story2.html

"How Nike got its game back", *Business Week Online*, November 4, 2002, http://www.businessweek.com/magazine/content/02_44/b3806118.htm

"When to run with Nike", *Business Week Online*, April 18, 2003, http://www.businessweek.com/technology/content/apr2003/tc20030418_2274_PG2_tc109.htm

Kitchens, Susan, "Footwear in Flight", *Forbes Online*, April 15, 2002, http://www.forbes.com/global/2002/0415/061.html

Online Sources

www.nike.com
www.reebok.com
www.adidas.com
www.newbalance.com

Nokia: Connecting People through a Disconnected Past

Until the 1980s, Nokia was a Finnish company, in the 1980s Nokia was a Nordic company and in the beginning of 1990s a European company. Now, we are a global company.

— Jorma Ollila
President and CEO, Nokia (1997)

Nokia's rise to global prominence is nothing short of astonishing. From its humble origins in Finland, Nokia has grown into a global company and a brand greatly admired by companies and employees all over the world. Yet Nokia's runaway success was not an overnight miracle but one that has been borne out of numerous failures and successes, trials and errors before becoming what it is today.

Today, Nokia is the world's leader in mobile phones and the leading supplier of mobile and fixed broadband, and Internet Protocol (IP) networks. Equally impressive is Nokia's net sales which totaled €30 billion in 2001 and has some 17 production facilities in 9 countries, R&D centres in 14 countries and employs nearly 52,000 people worldwide

In order to understand in depth how far Nokia has come, we need to trace Nokia's origins and history. We will also focus on the two prominent leader figures, Kari Kairamo and Jorma Ollila, who have both shaped Nokia with their own unique brand of management. As Nokia is synonymous with design and technology, we will also look into the aspects of design, marketing and telecommunications technology of Nokia. As Nokia's success is driven by Nokia's employees, this chapter will not be complete without examining the work ethics and attitudes of 'Nokians' and the company's policies towards its employees.

Origins of Nokia

For many years, the world outside Scandinavia was misled by the Nokia name into thinking that it was a Japanese company. Many people today find it hard to believe that Nokia used to produce toilet paper and rubber galoshes. And some will be astonished to learn that Nokia is not a 'new economy' company but one that can boast of a 138-year history. Nokia was originally started in 1865 with the founding of *Nokia Aktiebolag* (Nokia Forest and Power) by Fredrik Idestam, a 25-year-old mining engineer. He imported the pioneering groundwood techniques from Saxony into Finland and revolutionized the making of paper. Since Finland is blessed with lush forests and water-power resources, Idestam seized the opportunity to set up his wood pulp plant along the river Nokia, which had actually derived its name from a dark, furry weasel known as a nokia.

However, the current Nokia Group was only officially formed after the merger of Finnish Rubber Works (*Suomen Gummitehdas Oy*), the Finnish Cable Works (Kaapelitehas Oy) and Nokia Forest and Power in 1966. Although Nokia has become a substantially large company, there was little value added from the merger in 1966. Instead, much effort and management time was consumed having to coordinate the newly enlarged operations.

The 1960s was an equally interesting period for Nokia because it was Nokia's first venture into electronics. Although Nokia treaded slowly into the electronics industry, it laid the foundation for Nokia's modern day success in digitalization. Despite the entry into electronics, cable products to the former Soviet Union remained a major contributor to Nokia's earnings. Unknown to many outside Finland, Nokia began to import computers into Finland and it also manufactured electronic equipment for the modest Finnish defense industry. In the 1970s, Nokia produced the popular office computer, Mikro Mikko and it grew to become one of Nokia's major divisions in the 1980s. Another important, far-reaching decision was to produce digital telephone exchanges. It was a bold move because it pitted Nokia in direct competition with the more established Ericsson's core business.

While the growth of Nokia's electronics business was attributed to clear and sound objectives, it owed its success partially to the domestic industrial policies in Finland. A new wave of deregulation and internationalization was sweeping across the world. The ripple was first started in Europe by former British Prime Minister, Margaret Thatcher in her crusade for free competition. This notion gradually spread to other countries including Finland. Although the deregulation of the financial markets in Finland resulted in an economic boom in the 1980s, this was followed by in deep recession in the late 1980s.

The Cold War period proved particularly challenging for Finland as it has to straddle between trading with the Western democracies and the Soviet Union. Finland committed itself to economic cooperation and integration within Europe through the European Free Trade Agreement (EFTA) and later (since 1995) the European Union, while supplying products to the former Soviet Union. It has managed to maintain that image of 'neutrality' so remarkably well that Finland has never been regarded by the West as pro-communist.

The Kairamo Era

Two individuals were instrumental to the success of Nokia — Kari Kairamo and Jorma Ollila. Kairamo was Ollila's predecessor and it was he who single-handedly steered Nokia's transformation from a purely traditional company to an electronics company from the 1970s to 1980s. Kairamo first joined Nokia in 1970 as vice president of Nokia's international affairs division. He was a charismatic and inspirational leader who subscribed to the virtues of hard work and constant learning. As the 1970s to 1980s were a transitional period for Nokia, it offered the golden opportunity for Kairamo's trailblazing streak to emerge. Unlike his predecessors, Kairamo forsaw Nokia's future beyond the shores of Finland and the need to conquer new markets to ensure Nokia's survival. When he became managing director and CEO of Nokia in 1977, Kairamo introduced reforms to allow Nokia to compete on the world market. Traditional formalities and processes gave way to speed and immediacy. Change and flexibility soon became important attributes of Nokia.

Kairamo pushed Nokia onto the path of competitive advantage. He wanted Nokia to be more productive, efficient, innovative and to manage its resources carefully in order to gain a competitive advantage. Kairamo's vision of transforming Nokia into a competitive company was unprecedented at a time when the notion of comparative advantage held sway. Until the mid-1980s, internationalization was dominated by the idea of comparative advantage, in which labour, natural resources and financial capital were regarded as the most important factors in determining a company's continuous success.

At the beginning of the 1980s, Nokia set out to expand its consumer electronics and telecommunications business with renewed vigour. Part of Kairamo's grand plans for Nokia was the acquisition of companies as a way of rapidly expanding Nokia. Kairamo wanted to turn Nokia into a Japanese-like conglomerate with a presence in a diversity of industries. Kairamo believed that time and money will be saved if they acquire established companies instead of spending time investing and cultivating new companies. More significantly, Kairamo identified the electronics business as a core business and invested heavily into buying key electronics companies. With that objective in mind, Kairamo acquired Mobira, Salora, Televa and Luxor of Sweden, and Nokia soon became a major producer in TV sets, monitors, and computers. Between 1983 and 1984, Nokia was transformed from a diversified industrial conglomerate into an electronics company.

Unfortunately the acquisitions in the 1980s proved costly for Nokia. When Nokia bought two television set manufacturers in central Europe in 1987, it sank Nokia further in the red. By 1988, things seemed to be going terribly wrong. Profits were trickling away. The rapid buying spree seemed to have exhausted management resources. The strain became evident when the management including Kairamo began to make misjudgments and Nokia had to grapple with unprofitable electronics divisions. The management also became split internally and decision-making sometimes reached an impasse. On 11 December 1988, Kairamo committed suicide. Although the motive for his suicide was not fully explained, it was quite clear that the losses Nokia was making, an overworked schedule and dashed hopes contributed to his death.

Kairamo left Nokia with a dual image. While he led Nokia into its major losses and mistakes, it is undeniably due to his inspiration and focus on internationalization that has paved the way for Nokia's bold ventures into telecommunications and mobile phones, and its subsequent conquest of the global market.

Restructuring Nokia

After Kairamo's death, Simo Vuorilehto was appointed chairman and CEO of Nokia. He embarked on the streamlining of Nokia's businesses and dismantled the internal Board, replacing it with an Executive Board. Overall management was further streamlined by placing each member of the new internal Executive Board as head of a business division. Between 1988 and 1989, Nokia shifted its activities from aggressive buying to selling. Vuorilehto sold off Nokia's basic industrial units but did not sell or divest those businesses he considered strategic, in particular consumer electronics, data communications, mobile phones and telecommunications. However, Nokia failed to turn around amidst the sea of tumultuous changes in the world between 1988 and 1991. The Soviet economy collapsed and the overheated Finnish economy plunged Finland into a deep recession.

The New Visionary: Ollila takes the helm

While Kairamo has been ambitious in diversifying Nokia, Jorma Ollila has been bold in divestiture. Jorma Ollila took over the helm from Vuorilehto in spring 1992. He was then the President of Nokia Mobile Phones (NMP) before being appointed CEO.

At 41 years, Ollila was a youthful, energetic leader and he was responsible for shedding Nokia's non-core information technology and basic industry operations to focus on telecommunications.

Before Ollila joined Nokia in 1984 as vice president of international operations, he served as a member of the board in Citibank Oy, the bank's Finnish subsidiary. In 1986, he became Chief Financial Officer at Nokia and in 1990, he led Nokia Mobile Phones (NMP) unit.

Restructuring at Nokia did not start with Ollila. It began soon after Vuorilehto became CEO in 1988 but Ollila continued and completed this phase. Ollila understood the strategic importance of NMP and he also knew that mere restructuring would not suffice; Nokia has to refocus.

On 1 July 1991, Finland became the first country in the world to introduce the wireless digital GSM network which could carry data in addition to high quality voice. But it was not unexpected. Nokia had prior experiences with analog telephones. The Mobira Talkman were the first car phones made by Nokia. The first handheld phone was also produced by Nokia. Since then, the telecommunications and mobile phones divisions have been growing.

The Scandinavian countries provided the preliminary testing ground for Nokia's telecommunications technology before they were released to the rest of the world. In 1981, the world's first cellular mobile telephone network, the Nordic Mobile Telephone networks (NMT), was introduced in Scandinavia. The introduction of NMT was important for Nokia because its immediate consequence was to create a market for Nokia to test its telecommunications products. By the late 1980s, Nokia has become the largest Scandinavian information technology company through the acquisition of Ericsson's data systems division.

The rapid growth in the mid-1990s presented a cash-flow problem for Nokia. It was in 1994 that Nokia was listed on the New York Stock Exchange. This helped to finance the tremendous growth of Nokia. It also meant that Nokia's share ownership moved overseas, mainly to US investors during the 1990s. This is a dramatic departure from the past when Nokia was owned by Finnish commercial banks such as the Union Bank of Finland and *Kansallis-Osake-Pankki* (National Bank, KOP). This means that Nokia is now answerable to a wider distribution of share holders instead of having to consult the major banks on management level decisions. This freed Nokia from potential conflicts between management and the commercial banks.

By 1994, Nokia had grown so rapidly that it needed to address the question of profitability and growth. Alarm bells started ringing when profits fell below budget in 1995-1996. Yet Ollila and his team looked for solutions quickly — improving the production chain. The improvements were achieved through a more efficient inventory control and the old centralized inventory system was replaced by a new Regional Demand/Supply Process. Nokia called the new, leaner worldwide logistics system the Integrated Supply Chain. Another important improvement was the move to outsource mobile phone parts to suppliers.

Nokia's Strategic Intent

No politics, a lot of trust, realism with equality between people, titles are not important — teamwork with openness is. There is a Finnish word, nöyryys, *which means humility, humbleness that you take pride in the past but don't project it into the future.*

— Dr Matti Alahuhta
President, Nokia Mobile Phones

Ollila's vision was extraordinary. By the end of the 1990s, Nokia's brand was synonymous with product innovation, flexibility, and rapid responsiveness. For Nokia, the key to all strategic considerations was simple — to listen to the customer. Yet Ollila knew right from the beginning that the customer is a moving target.

Between 1986 and 1991, Nokia created a foothold in key European markets by relentlessly pursuing emerging and deregulated markets. Unlike the mobile subsidiaries of Ericsson, Siemens and Motorola, Nokia's mobile unit was considered mid-size. But for what it lacked in scale and scope, it gained in speed and timing.

Nokia emulated Japanese companies; it is constantly on the lookout for new markets in telecommunications and internet technology advantage. So far, Nokia has built strategic alliances with new wireless technology companies to deliver cutting edge mobile phone platforms such as Symbian and WAP. Ollila's new focus is on integrated wireless and internet products — 'combining mobility and the Internet and stimulating the creation of new services' became Nokia's new direction.

Ollila also shuffled his senior management and moved them out from their comfort zones. He believes in cross fertilization and helps learning across the companies. In turn, Nokia's senior management believed that an elitist management hierarchy could disenfranchise the organization.

Nokia's persistent determination to focus on the cellular business has distinguished the company from its rivals since the 1990s. But Ollila was not alone in crafting the strategic direction; he discussed and debated strategic issues with a small circle of veteran Nokians and the group executive board, whose teamwork served as a model for other teams within Nokia. One of Ollila's strengths is not to monopolize power and decision-making, but to delegate his authority.

The New Nokians

The objective (at Nokia) is to always have decisions made by the people who have the best knowledge.

— Dr Matti Alahuhta
President, Nokia Mobile Phones

Nokia has a youthful workforce with an average age of 32. It has nearly 52,000 employees worldwide. Almost 41% are located in Finland; 24% in other European countries and 16% in the Asia-Pacific. Attaching and retaining the best and brightest talent is vital in Nokia — employees are paid above-average wages and receive a 5% bonus if annual profits achieve 35%. And about 5000 executives are given stock options.

As a result of the Finnish penchant for an egalitarian, flat organization structure, Nokia is similarly not only less hierarchical than most large corporations, but decidedly anti-hierarchical. The practice of meritocracy management nurtured an environment of creativity, entrepreneurship and personal responsibility.

Kairamo and Ollila believed in continuous training and learning. To this end, Kairamo devoted himself to education issues and promoted them vigorously. Ollila channeled large amounts of funds into Nokia Research Centres (NRC) and training for employees. He valued his employees and viewed them as assets to Nokia. In 1981, Kairamo said:

Finland has quite a few resources. Briefly put, there are 2 of them: the people and the trees. Exports are obligatory in the future as well. Things must be sold abroad, so that living conditions will remain good domestically. This, in turn, requires that we have extensive experiences in international business.

Human resource issues are treated as strategic issues. Strong corporate culture and values are entrenched in the Nokia Way — a brochure distributed to all old and new employees. The Nokia Way played a critical role in communicating the company's vision, strategy and values. It also gave rise to the slogan "Connecting People". Contemporary Nokia was built on Kairamo's dictum that people should replace trees.

Nokia has encouraged an environment that nurtures creativity and the collective realization of individual ideas. Despite its rapid growth, Nokia has continued to stress on a corporate culture more typical of an independent, innovative and creative start-up. The objective has been to maintain this culture no matter how large the company has become. The values were also important to impart a sense of cohesiveness to Nokia offices around the world. These values include:

◊ A drive to achieve customer satisfaction.
◊ Respect for the individual.
◊ Willingness to achieve and belief in continuous learning.
◊ Encouraging sharing (information and responsibility) and openness (to each other and to new ideas).

These values are extended consistently worldwide with some local differences. Additionally, Nokia recognizes 3 fundamental principles: serving the society in which the company works; protecting the environment and working according to strict, ethical principles.

When Ollila promoted Nokia in the late 1980s to 1990s, his maxim has been to focus on the telecommunications and mobile phones. Has the corporate culture of Nokia changed? Yes, but the change is not drastic. Today, Nokia is still advocating designing phones with the consumers in mind (human technology) and making it fun and accessible. Nokia phones are selling well today because of their functionality and user-friendly interface.

The corporate culture is still dominated by the visionary Ollila. He still seeks out new markets to conquer by customizing phones according to consumer needs in different markets. Nokia has also spearheaded or initiated pioneering research into 3G technology and aggressively persuading countries to adopt the 3G technology.

Nokia still remains rooted in the anti-hierarchical, relatively flat structure in which ideas are valued. However, with enlarging markets and growing number of employees, it is expected that this flat hierarchy may not be as attractive to talented individuals seeking promotion and status. The Finnish egalitarian culture pervades Nokia — although it creates a sense of equality and loyalty, it may not be as attractive for ambitious employees. But Nokia has recognized this problem and reacted by allocating stock options.

Not only is the power distance in Nokia low, it is a fairly feminine culture which is concerned with the working environment, conditions and welfare of the employees. Although slightly less aggressive in marketing nowadays after having established a large global market share, it still continues to spend a substantial amount on marketing annually. Nokia continues to make us of wide-ranging media from TB to print.

On the research and development side, Nokia has joint ventures and partnerships in developing new telecommunications standards and it spends quite a lot on training its employees.

However, one major problem for Nokia is competing technologies like the CDMA in South Korea and a different standard in Japan. Moreover, several strong competitors such as Sony Ericsson, Matsushita and Mitsubishi Electric are also spending a lot on joint research and marketing to stake out a larger market share.

Having paid much for the 3G licenses, there are concerns as to whether the 3G technology will take off. There may be a risk of being parochial and over-focusing on the 3G technology instead of exploring viable alternative technologies.

Furthermore, Nokia appears to be battling for more countries to adopt the 3G technology so that they will be compatible with Nokia mobile phones. Nokia is still concentrating on its mobile phones and networks, without any intention to diversify. As to whether Nokia can continue to maintain or exceed its current foothold in the mobile phone industry will depend how dynamic and efficient it is in adjusting itself to market conditions and consumer expectations.

Nokia Research Centre

Nokia's R&D unit has played a central role in the company's new product development efforts. By the end of 1999, almost one-third of Nokians worked in R&D. Nokia did its utmost to integrate R&D into the whole corporate process. It actively participated in works of standardization bodies and various internationalization projects in cooperation with universities, research institutes and other telecommunications and mobile companies. Nokia established R&D centres worldwide in order to tap the knowledge there and to commercialize the products for those markets quickly.

The roots of Nokia Research Centre (NRC) date back to 1979. Since then, it has developed several programs such as an electronic mail system called NoteX. However, in the 1990s the NRC's role increased substantially under Ollila.

By 1999, R&D investments grew to FIM 10.6 billion. Nokia's R&D strategy was to develop generic platforms that could be quickly adapted to different standards. Even in R&D, Nokia focused on software development because software is the principal component that adds value to the handset. This approach fitted well with Nokia's overall strategy of speed to market with innovative products that covered multiple standards.

Nokia also recruits its new employees from student trainees working at Nokia. In the late 1990s, some 1,000 students annually prepared their theses while working at Nokia.

While rivals like Motorola and Ericsson pursued and developed new technologies (upstream innovation), Nokia focused on listening to its customers (downstream innovation). Listening to customers became the sole distinctive characteristic of Nokia's R&D. For example, Nokia purchases semiconductors from suppliers instead of pouring R&D investments into them so that it can concentrate on other areas such as network standardization and technology alliances.

Upstream Innovation

Around 1992, Nokia's team of 25 researchers, scientists and managers embarked on a secret project code named Responder. The purpose: to combine Internet, computer and telephone technologies to produce a portable machine that converge all 3 capabilities. The final result was the Nokia 9110 Communicator launched in 1996 — the world's first pocket-sized mobile office which allows users to send e-mails, receive and send faxes, conduct conference calls and surf the Internet. Although the Communicator was not a runaway commercial success, it anchored Nokia's image as an innovative company.

By 2000, the competitive environment of mobile phones was increasingly global and highly volatile. New product and process development had become the focal point of competition. To ensure its continual leadership in cellular technology, Ollila urges Nokia into key technological coalitions. Nokia's process chains remains highly focused. It consists of 3 basic categories: R&D, upstream innovation (platforms/standards, logistics), and downstream innovation (branding, segmentation, design).

Branding and Marketing to Niche Markets

By the end of the 1990s, the mobile market was rapidly expanding and many people were buying their first phones or upgrading their old ones. Nokia introduced colourful snap-on covers in the mid-1990s. Today they come in an assortment of colours with snazzy names like zircon green and electric purple to reflect different moods and lifestyles. Following the colours was graphic design. Nokia hired emerging young artists from Europe and America to design the snap-ons. Yet the market is segmented. While some consumers base their purchase decisions on the snap-on covers, business users prefer functionality.

Nokia excelled in market segmentation. Throughout the Kairamo era, Nokia relied on decentralized marketing for its exports but the direction was ambiguous. But Ollila focused Nokia on global consumer segmentation. Nokia cleverly segmented the markets according to different consumer lifestyles. The advantage for Nokia is that it can now tailor its phones to suit and complement the needs of a particular niche. As the reliability of Nokia phones became established, consumers began to base their choice of phones on the designs and user interface over technical capabilities.

Marketing plays a crucial role in Nokia. Design has always been important at Nokia. Back in the 1960s, Nokia produced brightly coloured rubber boots for the hip, fashion-conscious consumers. Today, Nokia's interchangeable clip-on phone facias come in a variety of designs and colours. The design of Nokia mobile phones was given a clear direction when Ollila decided to set up the Nokia Design Centre in Los Angeles in 1995. Nokia hired Frank Nuovo as its chief designer and vice president. Nuovo designed the Classic 2100 cell phone which was to become the breakthrough phone for Nokia. Nuovo has worked with major brands including BMW before and has myriad experience designing for a wide array of products — furniture, consumer electronics, car interior, medical equipment and even instrument panels for power stations and computers.

Nuovo hired young designers form art schools in order to keep in touch with the latest trends. The designers are encouraged to form work teams to produce well-thought out designs. Nuovo also recognized the aesthetic appeal in simple Scandinavian designs and incorporated them into many Nokia designs. Finnish designer Marimekko and Sony were among Nuovo's inspirations for design. The result is the creation of highly appealing and attractive phones. With the lower costs of owning a mobile phone and making a call from mobile phones, Nokia phones no longer became solely used for business. It has become a mass-market product like a Swatch wristwatch.

Nokia leads in the market because its product cycles have decreased over the years. Nokia introduces about 20 new products each year. In April 2000, Nokia's 8860 arrived in Hollywood with a glamorous marketing blitz — the elegant phone was spotted on celebrities from Nicole Kidman to Christie Turlington. Overnight, owning a Nokia phone became hip and fashionable not only in the United States but all over the world.

In 1905, Nokia evoked a river in Finland. By the 1990s, Nokia became a global brand name coupled with its slogan "Connecting People". It has not always been the case in the past. Today, it stands alongside Coca-Cola and Nike as an instant globally recognized and highly valued brand. Nokia's most intensive brand-building efforts were between 1993 and 1995. Nokia employed all possible channels and tools for its global branding strategy. In addition to print advertising, Nokia invested heavily in television advertisements and sponsored MTV and the Science and Technology program on CNN.

Conclusion

By combining high-end technology and trendy, forward-looking design in mobile phones, Nokia has managed to corner a huge global market share in the telecommunication industry. However, the other phone manufacturers are catching up in these aspects. In order to stay ahead of the competition, any mobile phone manufacturer has to re-invent itself and take bold risks in revolutionizing how future forms of telecommunications will be. Such thinking has always been Nokia's maxim. Nokia's vision of 'putting the internet into everybody's pocket' was one such maxim. But it's not just placing the Internet within the everyday reaches of the common man, but to make it relevant and consumer friendly to the end user. By combining mobility and communication, Nokia has managed to stimulate the creation of new services and products, thus revolutionizing how people communicate and do business. Digital convergence is the new buzzword in Nokia.

From rudimentary prehistoric cave-wall paintings which were the first signs of human communication in a non-technological age, to the MMS technology pioneered by Nokia, we seem to have come full circle in our exploration of how we choose to relate to our fellow humans. A simple picture paints a thousand words. Perhaps by keeping communication in its simplest form, Nokia has managed to stay in the forefront of the telecommunication industry.

A key aspect of Nokia's success is its uncanny ability and willingness to 'listen to the customer'. This capability has been perfected into an art form — through excellent strategy, structure and maximizing human resource allocation.

Nokia's future is as bright as the Finnish midnight sun. Its future direction is presently dependent on the 3G standardization in the world. It faces steep competition from other mobile phone manufacturers like Japan's NTT DoCoMo, Panasonic, Sony, and South Korea's Samsung. But this future is only possible if 3G standardization is adopted in most, if not all countries. At present, 3G standardization is still at its infancy, although interest in it has been expressed in most parts of the developed world. As long as Nokia stays focused with its winning formula of combining user-friendly technology and sleek design, there is no doubt that Nokia's star will continue to shine.

Bibliography

Nokia website, 2003. Available from <http://www.nokia.com>.

Häikiö, Martti (2001), *Nokia: The Inside Story*. United Kingdom: Pearson Education.

Kulkki, Seiji and Mikko Kosonen (2001), "How tacit knowledge explains organizational renewal and growth: The case of Nokia", in *Managing Industrial Knowledge: Creation, Transfer and Utilization*. edited by I. Nonaka and D. J. Teece, London: Sage, pp. 244–269.

Steinbock, Dan (2001), *The Nokia Revolution: The Story of an Extraordinary Company that Transformed an Industry*. New York: AMACOM, 2001.

Vikkula, Kaisa (1998), "Nokia: Two directed issues, one private placement and one euroequity issue", in *Corporate Strategies to Internationalize the Cost of Capital*. edited by L. Oxelheim *et al.*, Middleton, WI: Copenhagen Business School Press, pp. 199–213.

Sony: Made by Morita

The story of Sony's postwar success does not quite follow the popular "rags to riches" pattern. In 1944, the future founding fathers, Masaru Ibuka, a civil engineering contractor, and Akio Morita, a Navy lieutenant with an engineering degree from Osaka University, met in a task force charged to develop a heat-seeking missile for the Japanese Navy. Their work was too late to change the course of war, but the duo turned out to be the perfect complement: Ibuka, an impulsive tinkerer and technical explorer, and Morita, a marketing genius with a keen business acumen and a drive for recognition and success.

Both came from well off and well connected families. Ibuka's father-in-law was governor of Niigata prefecture, and Morita as Akio Kyuzaemon Morita the 15th, was to be head of the household of a prosperous sake brewing family from Nagoya, which also produced miso (fermented soy bean paste) soup base and soy sauce. Morita grew up in affluence in pre-war Japan and throughout his life as an absentee chief (his brother managed the family business), his word was law as a traditional household head.

When Ikeda and Morita set up their Tokyo Tsushin Kogyo (Tokyo telecommunications company) in the ruins of Tokyo in 1946, Morita's father contributed most of the capital, and the company's Board of Advisors was packed with influential people with good financial connections. Hence placing stock and obtaining credit was never a problem (Nathan, p. 24). The fledging company started out with radio repair and by producing Ibuka's invention of a voltmeter driven by vacuum tubes. In the visionary exuberance in a survivors atmosphere, Ibuka then decreed as the corporate philosophy the principles of an engineer's company (valid in Sony until today): "to create an ideal work place, free, dynamic and joyous where dedicated engineers will be able to realise their craft and skills at the highest possible level". As a rare gift, Ibuka in fact managed to kindle and to harness the innovative spirit in his engineers. They soon produced magnetic tapes and tape recorders, which were invented by Grundig and Telefunken during the war in Germany. When in 1952, the company wanted to move to transistors, MITI temporarily blocked the move by vetoing the payment of $25,000 as licensing fee. In 1957, the first pocket-sized transistor radio appeared, which with 1.5 million units sold made Sony soon a market leader in this modest segment.

Morita made his first visit to the U.S. in 1953, which for him was an overwhelming experience. Catching up, acceptance and success in the U.S. became a lifelong obsession. In the mid 1950s, he changed the corporate name to a mixture of 'sonus' (sound) and 'Sunny', thus arriving at Sony.

In 1963, Sony produced its first colour TV Chromatron under licence purchased from Paramount. As it had difficulties to master the new technology, high losses resulted. In 1966, they discovered RCA's improved system which in 1968 Sony adapted to its 'Trinitron Colour TV' and after agonising years moved on to Betamax technology. Ultimately in 1978/80, Sony lost the

Betamax battle in the home video market against Matsushita's VHS, which was lower priced and longer playing. Morita's advocacy of the Walkman and of the 8-millimeter video camera, both huge commercial successes, rescued the company.

In 1963, Morita and his family had moved for one year to New York. While he resided at the exclusive Upper East side he wanted to observe the all important U.S. market first hand and to build up Sony's U.S. subsidiary. Unlike other Japanese companies who managed their overseas subsidiaries with expatriate Japanese managers by remote control from headquarters, Sony hired mostly local managers (based on a 'man's word', not on detailed contracts), and insisted mainly on building up business, not on showing earnings. For advisory and management functions, Morita curiously hired exclusively American Jews. One of them is quoted as saying "He (Morita) seems to have felt that Jews were smart, imaginable and very compatible with the Japanese in temperament" (Nathan, p. 61). Nathan correctly sees this as "naive stereotyping" (p. 62), suspecting that Morita felt the need for tough allies and hired hands for Sony to survive in the U.S. business jungle. Often after a while these hands however, would turn against him, having raided his accounts, switched sides or made extravagant renumeration requests.

In 1976, Ibuka de facto retired and as an honorary chairman wrote bestsellers on technical education for children. Many of the new technologies like laser (for compact discs) and parallel signal crossing (for computers and integrated circuits) were no longer accessible to him. Sony in the 1980s was in fact run by Morita as a Chairman since 1976 in an autocratic one-man show with little checks.

As the story of Sony's U.S. subsidiary with its periodic management purges shows, Morita as an autocrat was able to delegate, but he never abdicated. In 1982, Morita appointed his handpicked successor Norio Ohga, a Tokyo and Berlin trained accomplished musician as his successor. Ohga who had entered Sony in 1959 at bucho (director) level, created the shallow 'cutie pie boom' for teenagers rather than promoting European classics or Japanese enka ballads.

Reputed tyrannical and aloof, his focus was on modern marketing and stylish design, the "Sony look" with premium placement and a polished look of the logo. When Morita had achieved the Walkman, it was Ohga who pushed for the digital age with the compact disc and forced his engineers to use the general action laser. Since 1982 Ohga did most of the operational decisions (including moving Sony Europe's HQ famously to Potsdamer Platz in reunited Berlin), subject to final approval by Morita.

Since the Betamax disaster, Morita had insisted on acquiring the music and cinematographic software to complement Sony's traditional hardware (had they had both at the time, in his view, the calamity would not have happened). Hence, Sony USA in 1987 purchased CBS records (with performers like Michael Jackson, Bruce Springsteen and Barbara Streisand); and in 1989 bought Columbia Pictures, Columbia Pictures TV, Tristar Films and the Loews Theatre chain for $3.2 billion plus $1.6 billion in assumed debts.

To Sony's surprise, this then largest purchase of a U.S. company by the Japanese created a lot of public resentment, which was already fuelled by the takeover of vast tracks of prime real estate in Florida, California, Hawaii, the acquisitions of Firestone Tyre, the Rockefeller Centre etc. by Japanese investors aided by the strong Yen of 1985–90.

It quickly transpired that Columbia had been purchased at a level almost twice the original share price. Sony was seen by U.S. sellers as "hungry, cash rich and naïve about the movie business" (Nathan, p. 187). It is unclear (and doubtful) whether due diligence was undertaken prior to the purchase. As chairman,

Morita was known to believe in the synergy of music, films and Sony hardware. His dream of owing a Hollywood studio and of sharing its glamour made Sony pay the asking price (much as Seibu Season would buy Intercontinental Hotels, and like many other big ticket ill-fated Japanese foreign acquisitions of the bubble years). Sony's board, which was packed with 30 Sony directors, duly rubber-stamped the deal with no awkward questions being asked.

Colombia was subsequently renamed as Sony Pictures Entertainment and a five year history of costly troubles ensued, which was greatly enjoyed by the U.S. public. Sony USA paid the best salaries for its top executives, and given the high turnover of its quarrelsome senior staff, also faced the highest severance payments. It had twice the overhead costs of other studios and through overspending and lack of commercial successes by 1993, lost at the rate of $250 million p.a. Yet as Sony was keen that the studio was seen to be run by Americans, the Japanese continued their hands off approach, while U.S. senior staff continued to milk this generous entity with apparently little scruples (Nathan, p. 278) or incentives to succeed.

Sony USA ventured into a range of new businesses like the Viva music channel, Sony & Warner, which syndicated music programmes to radio stations, Sony Signatures which did merchandising with Sony stars, and created a series of Sony multiplex theatres from San Francisco to Berlin. Only when losses mounted with the need to write off debts of $3.4 billion in 1994 was Sony USA's chief, Michael Schulhof finally fired.

Already in the 1970s and 1980s, Morita had coveted top positions in international fora like the U.S.-Japan Economic Relations group, the Trilateral Commission etc. and was proud to be on the international advisory boards of Pan American, IBM, Morgan Guarantee Trust, etc. He enjoyed hobnobbing with famous has-beens on the international policy and party circuit and to be seen and photographed with Henry Kissinger, Mike Mansfield, Otto Graf Lambsdorff, etc. As one of the few Japanese executives, who could argue their case well abroad, Morita was liked and respected. In spite of lots of socializing with celebrities, artists, politicians and businessmen at home in Shibuya and in New York, Nathan observes an "illusion of familiarity" (Nathan, p. 81), as Morita felt obliged "to act as the most international understanding businessman in Japan", while in reality he was rather a conservative autocrat of the traditional mold, who insisted on primogeniture (favoring his first born son Hideo), had his share of polygamous adventures, and generally entertained a nationalist world outlook. Morita's vision for Sony Japan was to control electronics manufacturing and development, while Sony International in New York should handle marketing and software. In his last active years, Keidanren's private economic diplomacy with Europe and the U.S., and the advocacy of Japan's national business interests were his main concerns. The objective was to become elected as Keidanren's chairman, a position, which so far had been reserved for chairmen of Japan's established Keiretsu companies, not for recent post-war upstarts like Sony.

After tireless efforts, tragically Morita was felled by a stroke in 1993 (one year after this had incapacitated his old partner Ibuka) just the day prior to his foregone election to Keidanren's prestigious chairmanship. Without regaining his physical functions, Morita died on 3 October 1999.

Ohga, his chosen successor, turned over the chairmanship of Sony, by now a $45 billion operator, to Noboyuki Idei in 1995. Idei, a Waseda economics graduate with extensive marketing experience in Western Europe dating back to the late 1960s, today insists that Sony remains driven by the vision of its founders, but that its management should become professional instead of being guided by personal friendship. There is no longer any sign of an inferiority complex towards foreigners, which Morita displayed, nor of the self-indulgence and showiness which both Morita and Ohga liked.

Sony has moved into the age of corporate normalcy. But will its Japanese management mainstream (which had since able to produce a couple of new playstations) deliver strokes of a genius like the transistor radio, the Walkman, the handycam or the CD player?

Sony was always an eager provider of corporate visions, not all of which were sound. Since 2002 Chairman Idei pursues the vision to integrate ("network") its electronics, media and software business in order to exploit the convergence of television, mobile phones and the internet. Sony would cease to be a classical audio-visual appliance manufacturer and entertainment provider and move towards internet linked audio-visual devices, games and computer equipment. PCs, TVs, camcorders and mobile phones are all supposed to be transformed into "gateways to networks". TVs are being reborn as centres of broadband entertainment. Sony's Vaio computers already function also as TVs and can play compact discs as well.

The big price question remains: How to make money on the contents side? The Playstation was a closed system. Everything had to be bought, but the net by definition is for free.

A massive reorganisation followed. Audio-visual and IT divisions, hardware and software providers were to be integrated. In what Idei termed "localised globalisation" Sony will organise its 168,000 employees into three regional hubs: Tokyo/Shanghai, London/Berlin and New York. Sony Europe, for instance, aims to ensure closer cooperation of its electronics, music, film, games and mobile com (Sony Ericsson) departments through a top management committee. Sony Pictures Entertainment and Sony Music (promoting Bruce Springsteen, Jennifer Lopez, Shakira) were merged to "Sony Music Entertainment", forming the world's third largest music company. Its chief music mogul Tommy Mottola was promptly forced out.

The regional hub concept is supposed to overcome the fragmented country organisation by "regional empowerment" (Idei). This is also meant to attract and to keep the best of the younger local staff and to avoid them getting frustrated by Japanese corporate bureaucrats.

Since 2002, Sony's profit margins hovering around 2.5% have been far below expectations. The company faces multiple pressures: the commoditisation of computers, mobile telephones and of home entertainment as well as piracy and copyright protection problems for its music business. Canon and Samsung have moved into Sony's neglected Camcorder business. Market shares are being lost in its core electronics sector. Also on the Chinese market for premium electronics the Koreans have been quicker. In the new synergised fields, there will be competition from established operators from all sides: electronics, media, software. Currently nobody makes decent profits in these once glamorous areas.

Earnings from films and cable TV are notoriously volatile. Successes like "Spiderman" and "Man in Black" need sequels. A large chunk of Sony's operating profits in 2002 was generated by Playstations and PS2 consoles. As sales can be expected to level off soon, an ever more elaborate Playstation Portable was recently made public. The head of the successful games division and President of Sony Computer Entertainment Ken Kutanagi was duly promoted executive vice president, a sure indication of greater things to come. It could also be indicative of Sony's future as an electronic toy maker.

Bibliography

Guth, Robert A. and Chang, Leslie, "Is Sony Cool Enough for China?", *FEER*, 2.1.2003.

Morita, Akio, *Made in Japan: Akio Morita and Sony*, New York: EP Dutton, 1986.

Nakamoto, Michiyo, and Burt, Tim, "Consumer Electronics", Parts 1–3, *Financial Times*, 10 — 12.2.2003.

Nathan, John, *Sony: The Private Life*, London: HarperCollins, 2000.

"Sony — Surprise", *The Economist*, 3.5.2003.

"Sony, the Complete Home Entertainer?", *The Economist*, 1.3.2003.

Sir Richard Branson's Virgins

The Road 'Not' Travelled

One of the most recognised names in the United Kingdom, Virgin is a brand that defies the odds and captures the imagination. Never before has a brand been so widely used in sectors that stretch across air travel, financial services, music, beverages, automobiles, telecommunications, retail and fashion. Although one may argue that Hanson, a British-American conglomerate, which makes bricks, cigarettes, industrial chemicals and food, and Proctor and Gamble (P&G), which is engaged in the production of toothpaste, shampoo, peanut butter, paper towels and drugs, are multi-national companies who are also involved in diverse industries, none of them are, however, in the same league as Virgin. Even the likes of Japanese keiretsu companies like Mitsubishi, which are engaged in the automobile industries, steel-making, consumer appliances, electronics and banking, and Yamaha (music and motorbikes) do not come close to the 'magic' of the Virgin brand.

The reasons are obvious. Most consumers are either unaware or does not care about the name of the parent company. They buy Hugo Boss fashion and fragrances, use Pantene shampoo, Pampers diapers, and eat Pringles potato chips, but most do not know that Proctor and Gamble made them. Nor can they find P&G shampoo or P&G potato chips. The Virgin name and logo, by contrast, appears on a huge range of products. Virgin Atlantic Airways, Virgin Cola, Virgin Mobile, Virgin Bride, Virgin Megastores, Virgin Direct and Virgin Books are just a few of the many diverse products that carry the Virgin brand name. When asked, most consumers have no problem identifying the Virgin brand. In their eyes, the brand stands for value for money, quality, fun as well as a sense of competitive challenge. Most importantly, Virgin does not merely sell a product, like most other brands. Instead, it sells an attitude! Its consumers have an emotional association to the brand.

Stretching across five continents, from Japan to Singapore, Australia, South Africa, the United Kingdom and the United States of America, the Virgin group is composed of around 250 companies of different sizes, industries and locations. They are broadly categorised into eight product functions. The Group's total revenues around the world are in excess of £4 billion and it has around 25,000 employees. Led by adventurous entrepreneur, chairman, and owner Sir Richard Branson, the reach of Virgin is extremely extensive. It is involved in three airlines, two rail franchises, holiday tours, wine and beverages, cosmetics, bridal service, balloon flight, health clubs, cinema chains, Internet services, mobile communication, radios, cars, motor bikes, a credit card scheme, a pension fund, a record label, publishing and many others. Given the 'shroud of secrecy' in which the Virgin group operates, it is almost impossible to pinpoint the exact number of companies that carry the Virgin name. It is after all a private company which is run as a network of holding companies and many off-shore trusts, which are designed to cut costs by minimizing the group's tax liability.

The value of the brand and the attitude of its employees appear to be the only thing that holds the Virgin empire together. Virgin strongly believes in giving its customers a richer experience through quality and fun by creating new opportunities and turning innovative ideas into reality. The Virgin vision is the desire to be different by being better, by giving better quality, better service and better value to its customers, with a tradition of doing it with a bit of style and having fun. Its mission is to provide premium quality to the consumers at first class discount price.

Virgin also empowers its employees to deliver a quality service and facilitates and monitors feedback to improve continually the customer's experience of the brand. By adding the fun element into business, Virgin is able to stand out from the serious and mundaneness attached to many companies, especially the established ones.

The Virgin Chronicle

With the aim to avoid retail rental costs, the company started out as a mail-order record business. Toying with various names, which include Slipped Disc, the name Virgin was adopted for its easy application to many different products and the fact that its founders were all business world virgins.

Business was booming until labour strikes by the postal service in 1971 threatened to bankrupt the up-starts, forcing them to open their first record shop, rent-free in exchange for bringing human traffic for the shoe shop landlord, at the cheaper end of Oxford Street. In the same year, Richard Branson bought a manor in Oxfordshire and converted it to a recording studio, adding the 3rd company into the Virgin portfolio. It was also this period when Branson fell foul of the law, resulting in a fine of £53,000 by the HM Customs & Excise for purchase-tax fraud, which nearly crippled the company.

Embracing a customer-first service attitude, Virgin mail order and record shop business grew from strength to strength. However, Virgin's business did not take off until 1973, when Mike Oldfields' Tubular Bells topped the UK charts and earned Virgin enough profit to purchase Necker, a private island in the British Virgin Islands, to set up Virgin's first nightclub, a gay disco and its Event magazine, and most importantly, to finance the expansion of Virgin Records. Throughout the 70s till the early 80s, Virgin Records signed up numerous artists like the Sex Pistols, Human League, Phil Collins, Boy George, Culture Club and later, Janet Jackson and The Rolling Stones, whose chart-topping successes made Virgin Music Group one of the top independent record labels in the country. In the middle of this period, Virgin Records made its foray into the European market through licensing deals in France.

The success of its music group bankrolled Virgin entry into the air travel industry, with the creation of Virgin Atlantic Airways, beginning its first flight between London and New York in 1984 from Gatwick Airport. The airline later started its first Heathrow service in 1991.

By 1989, more companies which carry the Virgin brand were formed. Virgin Vision (forerunner to Virgin Communications) was set up to distribute films and videos, while Virgin Games was founded to publish computer games software. Virgin Holidays and Virgin Cargo and Virgin Airship & Balloon Company were also formed. Mates Condom was launched, with proceeds going to the Healthcare Foundation while Vanson Development was created to develop residential and commercial property. A luxury hotel in Deya, Mallorca was also acquired, spinning off to hotel operations in the UK and the Caribbean. Recognition of Virgin's achievement came when the company won a Business Enterprise Award for company of the year in 1985.

In 1986, the Virgin Group, comprising the music, retail and property, and communications divisions, floated on the London Stock Exchange at 140 pence and later on NASDAQ over-the-counter exchange in U.S. in 1987. However, the decision to list the company was an ill-fated one as the stock market crashed on 16th October 1987, plunging Virgin's stock price from 160 to 90 pence, halting its acquisition of EMI, a rival record label. Together with Branson's dislike of getting permission from institutional investors with regards to Virgin's business decisions, the 'burden' of being a listed company placed heavy demands on Virgin and made it difficult for the company to cope with all the formality that institutional investors insisted they adopt. In the end, the initially promising stock listing plunged the company into heavy debt when the company bought itself out from other shareholders with a loan of £182.5 million from a group of banks.

Between 1989 and 1990, Virgin entered into a period of partnership with Japanese companies. Virgin's 'flings' with the Japanese began when Fujisankei, a media group, bought a 25 per cent stake in Virgin's music business for £115 million. Seibu-Saison, a travel and leisure conglomerate, also entered into a strategic alliance with Virgin through the purchase of 10 per cent stake in Virgin Atlantic for £36 million after the outbreak of the 1990 Gulf War. However, disagreements led to Seibu-Saison pulling out of the partnership, selling back its share to Virgin in 1993. Virgin also entered into alliance with Marui, a department store chain, to establish a 50–50 joint venture company to open megastores in Japan.

This was the same period where Virgin sold off huge stakes of its business to starve off its supposedly perpetual financial problems. 50 per cent of its megastore business was sold to W. H. Smith, while the 'jewel in the crown', Virgin Music Group, was sold to Thorn-EMI for £560 million in 1992. Such was the irony as just a few years ago, Thorn-EMI became a target of hostile takeover by Virgin. However, though selling Virgin Music was a painful decision, the money raised from the deal helped to expand the Virgin empire. One of the biggest beneficiaries was Virgin Atlantic, which grew to become the biggest breadwinner of the company, and was voted airline of the year by Executive Travel magazine for three consecutive years. In 1999, 49 per cent of Virgin Atlantic was sold to Singapore Airlines.

Since the sale of Virgin Music in 1992 until 2000, the company launched Virgin Radio 1215AM (sold for £85 million in 1997), Virgin Cola, Virgin Bride (the biggest bridal retail shop in Europe), entered the internet market with Virgin.net and bid twice for the franchise to run Britain's National Lottery, promising to give all profits to charitable foundations. The company also acquired MGM Cinemas, together with Hotel Properties Ltd and TPG Partners, a major U.S. investment fund. Virgin Direct Personal Financial Service was launched in partnership with the Norwich Union, who was later bought out by Australian Mutual provincial, and in 1997 launched its first banking product, Virgin One Account. The company also won the franchise to run two train services under the name of Virgin Trains. Other Virgin related companies include Virgin Vie, a cosmetics and beauty care company, Virgin Mobile and Virgin Cars.

As we can see, the reach of the Virgin empire is extremely diverse. Many of these companies were formed in partnership with other companies, with Virgin taking a majority interest in the new venture so as not to bear the whole risk of a business by itself. However, to be able to fully see the reason why consumers are so fascinated with the brand and what the company's culture is like, one must look at Sir Richard Branson. Without this peculiar and flamboyant figurehead, Virgin would certainly not be where it is now, entrenched in the heart of many whose paths crossed with one of the most exceptional brands in the world.

Sir Richard Charles Nicholas Branson

A billionaire entrepreneur consistently featured in Forbes magazine's list of the World's Richest People, Richard Branson has an estimated fortune of US\$3.3 billion in 2000. Also a daredevil adventurer, celebrity icon, national hero, prankster rolled into one, Branson is the power behind the Virgin 'revolution'. Flamboyant, fun-loving, caring and a good motivator, his critics would also say that he is scheming, greedy, narcissistic, has a 'grasshopper' mind and a womaniser underneath all that public relation skills. However, there is no doubt that he is the company's best advertisement. Other companies like Pepsi may spent US\$300 million on an advertising campaign, while Walt Disney builds its image around Mickey Mouse, none of them beats Branson who is able to create free publicity for Virgin through his antics and public relation genius.

Born in 1950, Branson still could not read at the age of eight as he was dyslexic and short-sighted. Admitted to Stowe School after receiving numerous cramming sessions to make sure he passed his entry exams, Branson never improved to be an academically smart student. When he left school in 1967, his headmaster predicted that he would either go to jail or become a millionaire. Both which came true.

Branson's first brush with business was his Student magazine, which had very limited success. However, it evolved to become Virgin mail order record business, which was his first 'real' step into the world of business when Student magazine shut down. As we have seen, the 1971 postal strike 'forced' Branson to open his first record store where he fulfilled the first prediction of his former headmaster. For the second part of his prediction, there is no doubt that he achieved it many times over.

Known for his penchant for wearing casual clothing and dislike for business suits, Branson carries an air of informality around him and hates to be caught in an overly formal meeting. However, it can be argued that it is not through his business success story that the world came to know about him, but rather through his many adventures which often endangered him and threatened to deprive Virgin of its inspirational chairman. Branson broke the Atlantic sea speed record in the Virgin Challenger II in 1987, crossed the Pacific Ocean in a hot air balloon and skidded naked down the Swiss Alps.

He is also notorious for his pranks, which are a lot more practical than intelligent. He is known to empty the content of a fire extinguisher onto guests or his employees and up-turning attractive women during parties. One infamous case was when Branson flipped Ivana Trump, then wife of New York property tycoon Donald Trump, upside down at an airline awards dinner. Another incurred the wrath of the late Sir James Goldsmith, a corporate raider and take-over baron, who was pushed into his swimming pool by Branson, even after repeatedly reminding him not to do so before and during the party held at Goldsmith's mansion. Branson is often criticised to be narcissistic. Always wanting to be at the centre of attention, he believes that a party is not a party until he is there to start it. Once, he was stuck in a traffic jam and repeatedly called his hosts every 15 minutes to update them on his whereabouts, saying that he will be there soon to start the party.

As a celebrity icon, Branson is often seen with other more illustrious public figures. He was well acquainted with the late Princess Diana and politicians like Margaret Thatcher and Tony Blair. In 1999, he was knighted in the New Year's Honours List, not too bad a distinction for a person who once broke the law.

Virgin's Organisation Culture

Using traditional management theory, the essence of an organisation can be divided into 7 categories; Innovation and risk taking,
attention to detail, outcome orientation, people orientation, team
orientation, aggressiveness and stability.

The Virgin Group, is a highly risk-taking company. It was
reported that the company bought over MGM Cinema without
due diligence, unaware of its financial and physical condition.
Many of the cinemas were reported to be run-down and in
serious need of maintenance. The Group is also seen, in Wall
Street lingo, as a debt-junkie. The company has no qualms about
going into debts in the name of expansion. Many times, this trait
nearly led to the demise of the company, until a 'white knight'
came along at the crucial moment to buy a part of Virgin's asset
and to refinance the company. This scenario was supposed to
have played out many times, from the various partnerships with
the Japanese to the sale of Virgin Music to Thorn EMI and the
49 per cent stake of Virgin Atlantic to Singapore Airlines. This
high risk-taking nature of the company can be traced to its
chairman. As the main decision-maker of the company, the way
in which Branson does business reflects his tendency of putting
himself in high risk situations, like his ballooning trips and
Atlantic crossing. Therefore, it is not surprising that Virgin has a
highly optimistic outlook with regard to the way it does business
and its speed in picking up business ideas.

Virgin often boasts itself as one who 'seek' justice for
consumers. It prides itself for entering into markets long
dominated by monopolies that overcharge their consumers. An
example is its very first business venture, where buyers of music
records are able to purchase records from Virgin Mail-order
Records at a much cheaper price than from its rivals. The
outcome of this marketing strategy is that Virgin is often seen in a

way in which it wants consumers to see it. However, whether Virgin is really what it markets itself is quite ambiguous, as often the prices which the company charges are not any lower than what its rivals charge. Moreover there is a need to cover the downside, which relates to what Branson would say.

Virgin is supposedly a very people-orientated company. The company strives in an environment of 'business is fun'. Employees are apparently remembered by the first name and everyone is encouraged to walk into Branson's office and give him suggestions on how to improve the company's operation or to come up with a new business idea. Company parties are also held regularly, where alcohol, drugs and sex are supposed to be in abundance. It should be noted that Virgin employees are reportedly not paid well, but are attracted to the company because it is fun to work for Branson.

The company is very aggressive in the way it functions. Often, the management is not shy in making use of the media to create free publicity or in giving writs against competitors, which they allege are trying to drive them out of business. When the company first entered into the Australia market, it threatened to sue anyone who use the Virgin brand, although there were a few native companies who are registered under that name and had a longer history than Branson's Virgin. Being a very growth oriented company, Virgin is often seeking to conquer new markets, sometimes with little regard to risk and reward considerations. Its tendency of engaging itself in almost every industry in the world puts it in quite a fragile position. As the Virgin brand is used on almost all its products, the possibility of brand dilution from products that are out of line with the Virgin image may also affect the rest of its business. Therefore, stability is not a word that can be used smoothly in the same breath as Virgin.

Branson is Virgin, Virgin is Branson

To describe Virgin's organisational culture using traditional management models or organization theories will be 'un-Virgin-al' to begin with. To adequately explain the Virgin culture, we should look at three dimensions. Firstly, the most prominent aspect of Virgin is its irreverent attitude towards establishments. This trait can be attributed to the swinging 60s, in which Branson grew up. Part of this irreverent image is the portrayal of a 'rebellious' Virgin, which can best be illustrated with the 'Sex Pistols' incident.

During the Queen's Silver Jubilee celebration outside Parliament House, Branson rented a boat from a River Thames cruise company and sailed down the river with the Sex Pistols in their perpetual drunken state. At the height of the celebration, Branson's procession stopped directly opposite Parliament House and the Sex Pistols started singing their rendition of 'God save the Queen'! When they touched shore, the police immediately arrested them and the incident was sensationalised by the tabloids the very next day. It could explain why Virgin is more popular among the more rebellious part of the population or with working or young middle class consumers who have more rebellious attitudes but normally suppress it to be in-line with the conformist orderly majority.

Being irreverent towards the establishment was also acted out in the British Airways (BA) 'dirty tricks' incident. By assuming the position of moral authority, Virgin portrayed itself as the upholder of justice, challenging big monopolies who tried to drive small upstarts, like Virgin, out of business, so that they can continue to overcharge the consumers who were not given adequate choices. Virgin Atlantic, the fun-loving and cheeky airline, which had only one leased plane at the time of the 'dirty tricks' incident, was supposedly undercut by British Airways, a former state-owned established airline with 250 planes which, together with United Airlines and American Airlines, had a monopoly of landing slots at Heathrow Airport. Putting itself up against British Airways, which was supposedly managed like a government administrative department and lacked entrepreneur-ship, Virgin charged that BA was trying to remove its competitors by engaging in dirty tricks like reading into Virgin's reservation list and aggressively 'touting' Virgin Atlantic's customers to switch to BA. When Virgin won the suit, it portrayed itself as the people's company, gaining market share as sympathisers started to purchase Virgin's products. Thus, Virgin add a sense of challenge and purpose to its image, not only to its customers, but also to its employees who see that they are fighting for the underdog, enabling Virgin to continue to pay below market rate to its employees.

This image was further enhanced when Branson tried bidding for the National Lottery, wanting to rename it as the People's Lottery and giving all profits to charitable institutions. Branson also injected imagination and responsiveness for the consumers, providing massage and manicure services on board his airline when requested. And by adding a 'cool' alternative image to the Virgin culture, it is no surprise that the brand occupies a special place in the heart of his fans. Surprising, given his many antics and pranks, Branson is on good terms with many celebrities, journalists and politicians.

The second element of Virgin's organisational culture is how it does things the fun and non-conformist way. In Virgin, employees are encouraged to be personal. Dressing down is prevalent, people call one another by their first name and company parties with a lot of drugs, alcohol and sex seem to remain a regular fixture. It is said that money-making is not the motivation that drives the company, but rather customers and employees satisfaction.

The way in which Virgin uses publicity is another major aspect that defines the company's fun and non-conformist culture. The launch of Virgin Coke in the U.S. took place in New York's Times Square with Branson driving a tank down the street, knocking down a wall made up of coke cans. Virgin Mobile, on the other hand, was launched in London with a casually-dressed Branson sitting in a see-through van surrounded by 6 nude models holding mobile phones. The use of sex to sell its product is not new to Virgin. Other than Virgin Mobile, Virgin Coke's bottle are made to shape like Pamela Anderson's famous curves, with slogans like: 'Open your mouth, I'm coming!' and 'You can taste our love every time you swallow!' Semi-naked nurses were also used to launch Virgin Energy. Branson is also known to cross-dress for publicity. He was seen in a bikini, wearing a bridal gown during the launch of Virgin Bride and as an air stewardess on board Virgin Airways serving wine to his passengers.

However, the most outrageous publicity campaign was during the launch of the first Virgin Atlantic service from Heathrow Airport. Branson, covering British Airways' Concorde which was parked at the lobby with Virgin Atlantic' signature red over BA's logo, boarded the plane in a pirate costume, declaring, 'This is our territory'. All the above publicity campaigns, though shocking, were cheap but very effective when compared to the millions spent by other more established companies. Together with the many dangerous adventures that Branson undertook up till today, it emphasises the fun and non-conformist culture of Virgin.

Positioning itself as a large extended family, Virgin culture places its customers and employees first. After the company won the lawsuit against British Airways, the damage handout from the case was famously given to its employees as the 'BA Bonus'. During the airline industry downturn, Branson offered to relocate his airline staff to other parts of his empire instead of optioning for retrenchment. The bid for the National Lottery, the launch of Mates Condom to educate the young about safe sex and chairing the UK2000 environment group were other ways in which Branson claimed to give power to the people.

The Virgin culture also believes in the empowerment of the individual companies and their employees. It is a highly atomised empire, or as some critics will argue, a huge primitive tribal hierarchy. This is done with the belief that 'small is beautiful', and that it encourages entrepreneurship and contributions within the group as decision making is passed on to individual companies and that it minimises tax liability. Except for Virgin Atlantic, which employs 6,200 people, Branson is said to split a company into two once it has more than 50 employees.

Virgin's Future

The corporate culture of the Virgin Group has minimal changes as it achieved global reach. It still functions the same way it did when it was first created by Branson. If there are any changes, it could be that the increasing size of the empire will cause the organisation to turn into more of a 'task' culture. However, the company is still very much a 'power' culture company, with Branson calling the shots. As the company increased its standing in the global business world, its culture remains as atomised as two decades ago. Except for Virgin Atlantic, the rest of the other 200 plus companies are micro-managed by Branson's lieutenants and only once in a while checked upon by him.

When the company was formed, its aim was to provide quality products at lower costs to consumers. 'Power to the People' was a slogan used by Richard Branson during his marketing blitz, which often makes use of free publicity created by the media, notably the British tabloids. An irreverent, rebellious and anti-establishment image took shape as the company grew, and together with the above, are still used to market the company. Fun-loving and informality were never far in association with the brand. Sex, drugs and alcohol are still rumoured to be a big part of the company culture.

As Virgin's fate is heavily tied to that of Richard Branson, it makes one wonder if there will be life for Virgin after the demise of its chairman. As Richard Branson is Virgin and Virgin is Richard Branson, the company may find it impossible to find a replacement for such an inspirational, flamboyant and at time cultist leader. Virgin's survival and growth may rest on how Richard Branson instills his beliefs and image onto the Virgin group. His ability to source out new business ventures with more established partners, taking up majority stake like what he has been doing, will also be crucial. Whether he will be successful in doing so may decide if Virgin will hold on to its irreverent and fun-loving image, or fade into the business world as another of those boring profit-making institutions.

Bibliography

Bower, Tom (2000), *Branson*, London: Fourth Estate.

Branson, Richard (1998), *Sir Richard Branson: The Autobiography*, London: Pearson Education Ltd.

Dearlove, Des (2002), *Business the Richard Branson Way: 10 Secrets of the World's Greatest Brand Builder*, 2nd ed., Oxford: Capstone.

Jackson, Tim (1995), *Virgin King: Inside Richard Branson's Business Empire*, London: HarperCollins.

The Economist, 11 January 1997.

Toyota: The Reluctant Multinational

Toyota Motor Corporation was founded by the Toyoda family in 1937. It is presently the world's third largest carmaker holding 9.5% of the global auto shares after General Motors and Ford in 1997 and by far the leader of all Japanese carmakers (*Business Week*, 7 April 1997). It is famous by being the most innovative automotive manufacturer in process technology and the most efficient in product development. Yet, Toyota lagged behind as compared to its other major Japanese competitors, in international production and regional headquarters (Kumon, 1998). This was due to its prudent strategy of avoiding risky overseas ventures, the importance of its home market and its ultra-conservative financial and management policies which might be a consequence of it being a traditional Japanese family business by origin. Fortunately, there was a change in the attitudes towards overseas investments when Toyota selected Hiroshi Okuda as the first non-family president of the company.[1] Other than investing in the automobile

---

[1] The first non-Toyoda in 45 years to hold this position in 1999, Okuda moved to the chairman's position, *The Wall Street Journal*, 11 January 1999.

industry, Toyota is involved in other business segments which include factory automation, semiconductors, design and manufacture of prefabricated housing, financial services, leisure boats and the IT related businesses and telecommunication.

In order to understand the company, it is helpful to look at their corporate motto. Toyota's motto stipulates to create an affluent society and improve the quality of life through the automobile (Basu, 1999). Therefore, Toyota emphasises on the quality of its products which will be offered to the consumers at a reasonable price. It also aims to be a good corporate citizen by donating money to five main sponsorship activities: Education, international exchange, environment, arts and culture and local communities.

Origins of Toyota Motor Corporation

The founder, Sakichi Toyoda, son of a poor carpenter, set up the Toyoda Automatic Loom Works in 1926. He was also known as the King of Inventors, who had 84 patents for his inventions. He was a humble person, who lived by the maxims of labour, gratitude and service, which would serve as the guidelines for the group's policies and activities (Toyota Motor Corporation, 1988). Kiichiro Toyoda, his son, majored in mechanical engineering and saw how popular cars were in the U.S. and Europe. Therefore, he decided to set up his own automobile company, Toyota Motor Company in 1937 using capital obtained from the sale of the rights of his father's automatic loom to a British company, the Platt Brothers. The first prototype automobile was produced. It was a Model A1 passenger car with a Type A engine.

However, after the Second World War, Toyota was on the brink of bankruptcy due to high inflation. It decided to seek help from the Nagoya Branch of the Bank of Japan. But the rescue came at a very high price as the marketing organisation had to be split off as an independent company, Toyota Motor Sales. Worst of all, a labour dispute culminating in a two-month strike took place in 1950 in response to the substantial personnel cuts initiated by the bank (Basu, 1999). It was only in 1982 that Toyota Motor Corporation and Toyota Motor Sales of Japan merged into one entity again, the Toyota Motor Corporation.

As the company grew in the post-war era, exports became a major part of Toyota's business, thus leading to its venture into the U.S. in 1957 with the establishment of Toyota Motor Sales USA. In the meantime, in order to secure the local market, Chubu Nippon Drivers' School was established in 1957 as part of Toyota's marketing strategy, as it was very difficult to obtain driving licenses in Japan (Toyota Motor Corporation, 1988). When more Japanese obtained their driving licenses, there would be more demand from these new drivers for Toyota cars. It then also sponsored motorcar rallies and shows, to enhance the reputation of its product as a durable and reliable car.

Corporate Culture

Toyota's corporate culture is deeply rooted in oriental philosophical values and beliefs. It stipulates a harmonious existence with the communities, but at the same time is equally aggressive towards its competitors to obtain higher market shares in the Japanese and global markets. Yet, corporate acquisitions and large takeovers are anathema. This culture is consistent with the Confucian values of harmony, order and serving others for the greater good of the society.

Management Style

Toyota is a traditional family-run business that emphasises its obligations towards its workers, customers and suppliers. Japan is a web society where there is great interdependence between all members of a group and an abundance of moral and social obligations, both vertically and horizontally (Lewis, 1999). It has a masculine corporate culture with no female, foreign or outside directors on the nation's biggest company board consisting of 58 members. It also sees very little need to listen to its shareholders as 40% of the total shares in Toyota are held by Japanese banks and financial institutions, in which Toyota also has sizable holdings. Therefore the top management of the company retains the key decision-making authority. The management of the company is strongly segmented on a functional basis with managers having the responsibility for the major vertical operating functions. This causes serious problems as every division works hard but is poorly coordinated, thus causing inefficiencies, unnecessary tensions and frustrations.

Toyota's Production System

"Everyone works desperately, hoping that he is not a burden to others".

— Sachs, 1994, p. 102

Toyota sees the building of vehicles as a community project. There is an emphasis on the quality and the price of its product. Its success is linked to its process technology, the "Just-In-Time" production system, where all resources are minimised and constantly in use. This system has three components: *Kan-Ban*, *heijunka* and *jidoka*, which allows a functionally flexible workforce and products, customised production runs and shorter cycle times and quality control. *Kan-ban* is a process, whereby material and components are supplied to the production assembly line just in time for production. This helps to minimise waste and reduce the storage of unnecessary parts, thus reducing inventory cost. Secondly, the production system involves level production or *heijunka* and continuous flow production. Lastly, *jidoka* is incorporated too to monitor the automated production processes for abnormalities and strives to achieve zero defects (Basu, 1999).

However, there are certainly flaws to the just-in-time system as it is vulnerable to delays and defects. There was an intensification of work especially when the idle time of the workers in Toyota was reduced from 75 seconds to 45 seconds. There is also multi-tasking, including various unskilled tasks. This system works only when there is a cooperative relationship between trade unions and management. After the initial turmoil of the post-war years the industrial trade unions in Japan have subordinated the interests of their workers to suit corporate goals, like those of Toyota (Sach, 1994). There is strong peer pressure among the production workers in Toyota to keep up with the line as all workers are forced to work overtime if the production quotas are not met and the production allowance risks to be cut. It is set according to the amount of labour it takes a given team to reach its production quota. Quality Circles[2] (QC) and suggestion drives implemented by Toyota do not increase the autonomy of the workers, as the management still makes all the decisions and even sets the agenda for QCs. The main advantage to be a production worker of Toyota lies in the security of long-term employment, above average pay, the high bonuses, which can be up to 50% of

[2] Quality circle is a small group conducted by the employees who meet regularly to make suggestions on quality control and production rationalization.

the normal monthly pay, and corporate retirement pensions, which are lost in case the employer is changed.

Overseas Investment

Toyota used to be a very conservative company whose overseas ventures focused mainly on the search for export channels and local distributors for its products. Nonetheless, its approach changed when faced with the impact of globalization, protectionist pressures in the importing regions (U.S., EU, etc.) and the growing strength of its auto rivals. Toyota then reluctantly started to believe in localizing its operations to provide customers with the products they need.

Investment in USA

In 1981, voluntary restrictions on Japanese automobile exports to the United States were initiated (Toyota Motor Corporation, 1988). In response to the protectionist actions from the U.S. government, Toyota decided to enter into a fifty-fifty joint venture with General Motors to reduce the risk of establishing plants in the United States. This cooperation would also allow Toyota to accumulate experience in local production in the United States. This joint venture was marked with the official start of New United Motor Manufacturing, Inc. (NUMMI), capitalised at 200 million dollars at the Fremont plant in California (Toyota Motor Corporation, 1988). In starting the company, NUMMI emphasise teamwork and mutual trust between labour and management, by adopting an "open office" floor plan, the use of a single cafeteria for all employees and common parking facilities for everyone. The company also used a just-in-time production system for the body line. In January 1986, Toyota established Toyota Motor Manufacturing USA, Inc. (TMMU) and Toyota

Motor Manufacturing Canada, Inc. (TMMC) for its operations in the USA and Canada which subsequently set up 4 other plants in North America. In addition Toyota introduced a luxury line in the U.S. — the Lexus in 1989 to shed its cheaper-price and lesser quality image in the American market. Toyota's strategy in launching the Lexus division was to make a luxury car that demonstrates high technology and high quality and support it with the best service to gain high customer satisfaction (Basu, 1999). The consumer response towards the Lexus was overwhelming with annual sales of more than 150,000 units in 1998, surpassing Honda, Nissan and BMW. Camry, another U.S.-produced Toyota automobile, became the number one selling passenger car in the United States in 1997 and 1998 and is still one of the bestsellers of Toyota (*Business Week*, 7 April 1997).

Investment in Europe

The European market holds much potential for Toyota and it demands only the finest products. Toyota is a late-comer in the European market with plants set up in the UK, Portugal, Turkey and the Central and Eastern Europe (CEE) region.

Decision to invest in the Czech Republic

Toyota expanded quickly only after 1999 into CEE to take advantage of the opportunities there. The Czech Republic offers low production costs, stable economic factors and its European Union (EU) membership in 2004 provides access to EU markets. Kolin may not seem to be the best deal as Czech workers already earn more than three times compared to those in Romania, and their wages are still rising (*Business Week*, 15 November 2002). But the productivity of the Czech workforce surely is a compensating factor. The Czech Republic is home to the 100-year-old Skoda, which was acquired by Volkswagen (VW) in 1991. VW introduced western quality controls and work habits to its Czech labour force and further built a network of Czech suppliers, who have since provided half its input by value. When Toyota decided on the location of its new plant, the Czech government granted generous investment packages to the new joint plant of Toyota and PSA. The plant would get public support worth 5–15% of its investment value, that is, €75–225 million (*CTK Business News Wire*, 7 January 2002). Likewise, the package included a token fee of CKr 1 billion for the site and free infrastructure in line with EU competition legislation (*Global News Wire*, 7 January 2002). Job creation and training grants were also given and Toyota was exempted from paying corporate tax for ten years. All these government incentives were a significant pull factor drawing Toyota to invest in the country.

Strategy

Toyota entered into a joint venture with PSA Peugeot Citroen of France, the European champion of diesel cars, for the production of small cars in the $1.35 billion factory in Kolin in 2001. It was the largest single greenfield investment in the Czech industry ever. Starting in 2005, the plant will assemble 300,000 minicars a year, all priced under $7,500 which is 50% less than Toyota's Yaris, its entry-level model for the European market (*Business Week*, 15 April 2002). This joint venture was seen as the best and most cost-effective way to obtain a substantial market share rapidly rather than acquisitions and takeovers of existing plants which remain anathema to Toyota. PSA and Toyota have split the investment costs and hope to generate healthy margins by pooling their expertise in engine and emissions technology. In this joint venture, Toyota will be responsible for the production, while PSA Peugeot will be in charge of marketing. For Toyota this investment is an important brand-building exercise to raise its current 4% share of the European market. Its strategy is to Europeanize design, production and marketing, so that Toyota is seen as a European car, like Opel (which is in fact American being a GM subsidiary) or Volkswagen. The high quality of the diesel engines produced by the French company is able to command a better price for its diesel models as PSA is the European champion of diesel cars, which contributed 49.5% of the carmakers' volume in 2001 (*Financial Times*, 9 July 2001).

Toyota's greenfield investment enables it to build its production system from scratch, thus allowing a full utilization of its modern technology. Toyota's distinctive and highly efficient manufacturing technology of Just-in-Time systems leads to a horizontal spillover to the local workforce by improving their productivity, and to a vertical spillover to the consumers with a rise in the product standards. PSA/Toyota's Kolin car plant also led the entry of other Japanese car components suppliers like TRCZ, Tris and Aoyama Seisakusho into the region, thus providing new employment and training opportunities to the local workforce. The new Kolin-based plant is expected to create 3,000 jobs and an increase in the number of indirect jobs. Toyota's investment venture in the Czech Republic will, in the long run, enhance the benefits for the workers in the automobile sector, also as a result of the entries of the international suppliers.

Toyota's economic involvement in Poland

The Czech project has prompted Toyota to raise investment in its engine and transmission plant in Walbrzych (Waldenburg), Poland, from €100 million to €400 million[3] (*Automotive News*

---

[3] This planned project would add 300,000 engines and 50,000 transmissions to the 250,000 gearboxes already planned.

Europe, 11 March 2002). It also plans to build another 60-million pound gearbox and engine plant in Poland to supply the Czech-based operation. The Walbrzych facility in Silesia would become Toyota's largest auto components factory and should conclude the process of building the pillars of Toyota's production activities in Europe. The decision to supply car components from Poland results from the good infrastructure linking Poland to the Czech Republic, thus allowing for lower transportation cost of components. Furthermore a 110-million pound engine plant is set up in Wroclaw (Breslau), Poland, creating 350 jobs that seeks to serve a forecasted upturn in demand in Eastern Europe and to supply its plants in the UK and Turkey. These greenfield investments offer an opportunity to upgrade the quality of the domestic car components suppliers as cooperation with Toyota will stimulate horizontal spillovers of technology. However, in the Polish case spillover benefits are believed to be patchy due to the limitations of the local banking system. Bank loans are subjected to higher interest rates that hamper the development of local suppliers. Nonetheless, this new project will create new job opportunities in a country, which is troubled by high unemployment. Toyota has now localised the production of its European cars by also setting up components plants in Poland but the positive contribution of such production depends greatly on the policies of the government to upgrade human and technical capabilities of the local suppliers.

Investment in Asia

The first area chosen by Toyota to develop export channels and assembly operations was Southeast Asia, due to its proximity to its headquarters in Japan and cheap labour costs. In the early nineties, many of the Southeast Asian countries had requested Toyota to manufacture automobiles and trucks in their countries.

Toyota spent two years in discussions and negotiations with these countries. Finally, Toyota announced the ASEAN Complementary Program and set up four companies. Toyota decided to build the manufacturing plant for diesel engines in Thailand. The transmission business was given to the Philippines. The steering wheel system production went to Malaysia (Basu, 1999). Its strategy in Asia is to sell sturdy and simply designed cars to withstand the rigours of the local roads. In Singapore, Toyota cooperated with a distributor, Borneo Motors and a new slogan was created, which states "Together, we must be the best". Gateway, one of its plants in Thailand, is rated as Toyota's best factory in the world. The factory employs about 1,800 people who bolt Toyota Camrys and Corollas together, alongside the new Vios. The production lines can produce a complete car every two minutes, while parts shops stamp out enough bumpers and body panels for export as spares to South-east Asia (*The Straits Times*, 18 January 2003).

China is the largely untouched market that probably has the biggest potential after the U.S., Europe and Japan, in the next ten years. The key objective of Toyota's expanding business opportunities into China is growth. Toyota has joint ventures or technological tie-ups with the Chinese enterprises which are mainly state-run, in order to manufacture a lower priced product. This provides the easiest means to enter the difficult Chinese market. Having the state as the partner; market entry and expansion is greatly facilitated (Basu, 1999).

Impact of Globalization on Toyota

There was a major reorganisation and restructuring of the company by Okuda after he was appointed the President of Toyota Motor Corporation. Toyota terrified its rivals by announcing the development of its recently launched Ipsum in a record of 15 months. The designers in Toyota have probably hit the human limit for product development (*Business Week*, 7 April 1997). The company has also created another breakthrough in making affordable hybrid engines that rely on both electric batteries and gasoline. In fact, product cycle speed-up is just one facet of Okuda's strategy to rekindle the killer instinct at Toyota. Other means include extending Toyota's edge in high speed, flexible car-making, shaking up the company's insular, consensus-driven culture and pursuing the most aggressive overseas expansion in automotive industry (*Business Week*, 7 April 1997). First, he reduced the size of its 58 board members, in order to improve management efficiency. Toyota also relocated its production from the home market to larger potential markets with cheaper labour costs such as India, China, South America and Eastern Europe, where there are fewer cars on the roads. This decentralisation is necessary as sales in Japan have saturated

To the Japanese, the company is sacred. Once the employees are accepted, they show complete loyalty to the company and this loyalty in theory and traditional postwar practice is rewarded by life-time employment and regular promotion to important positions, regardless of their effectiveness (Lewis, 1999). However, the impact of globalization and of Japan's structural crisis has forced an overhaul of the wage and promotion system. It is now increasingly linked to the performance of the employees rather than their seniority. Many older executives have been stripped off fancy titles and are given narrower responsibilities in order to create more opportunities for younger executives.

In order for Toyota to improve its profitability, there has to be more efficiency and productivity improvements in the decision-making process of Toyota executives. Evidence indicates that decisions still continue to be made mostly on a regional and divisional basis rather than on a global and company-wide basis. Therefore, a circle "I" team was created to tackle the significant issues beyond the prevailing divisional business units to a company-wide basis (Basu, 1999).

A Business Reform Campaign was launched in 1993 after the plunge of Toyota's profitability, which targeted the productivity of white-collar workers by reducing the entire white-collar workforce in Japan by 20 percent. Toyota had been adding large numbers of top students graduating from prestigious Japanese universities. These people moved up the ranks by way of promotion based on seniority. These past practices have produced a glut of middle managers with little room to move up further (Basu, 1999). Therefore, in order to keep up with its rivals, Toyota reduced the number of new recruits and prepared attractive packages to entice early retirement. It limited the number of working hours and forced the employees to take their vacation entitlements. Operating budgets for most divisions were reduced by 5 percent per year. Thus overtime work among white-collar workers was disallowed, unless critically needed. Annual raises and bonuses were either severely reduced or cancelled.

Nonetheless, the decision to dismiss white-collar workers was not fully pursued as it was in conflict with Toyota's responsibilities and social obligations as the industrial leader in the Japanese society. It would have violated its long practiced corporate values such as family feeling and lifetime employment. Toyota's financial performance acts as a bellwether of the Japanese economy and its performance affects confidence in the Japanese economy. The Business Reform proposal was a unique solution as no one was fired, but redundant staff was deployed to Business Reform (BR) groups. These groups were assigned special tasks within the divisions that included new business areas, new product areas and projects to consolidate tasks of the divisions. Individuals from the BR groups were transferred to new markets such as China, Southeast Asia and Eastern Europe (Basu, 1999). This whole episode shows that Toyota still compromises profitability in view of its social obligations to its employees while other Japanese companies such as Nissan, Mazda and Toshiba had laid off permanent employees in large numbers.

What Lies Ahead of Toyota?

"Toyota cannot control the wind, so it changes the position of its sail to catch the wind".

— Basu, 1999

Toyota will continue to be an influential global carmaker, after the successful restructuring of the company by Hiroshi Okuda. However, the benefits created by the restructuring process might be limited due to its social obligations to its employees and the Japanese society. Toyota has been flexible as an Asian company to adapt the changes that are occurring now due to the impact of globalisation. One significant issue which remains unanswered is whether Toyota will change its focus in the near future from employee care to customer care under the severe pressures of the recession in Japan and the global competition.

Toyota faces the danger of being successful overseas, while losing its top position in Japan. As most of the fat profits come almost entirely from the U.S., Japan which accounts for 41% of vehicle sales is contributing less to the bottom line. Honda, one-third of Toyota's size, has taken a big bite out of Toyota's sales in Japan with the successful launch of its Odyssey minivan and CR-V four-wheel drive sport utility car (*Business Week*, 27 March 2002). That was bad news to Toyota as it has long relied on robust Japanese earnings to finance its global expansion.

Its youth strategy is highly ineffective, as it took Toyota three years to launch a follow-up after it made a splash in Japan with the affordable Vitz subcompact. In the meantime, Honda and

Nissan had grabbed significant market shares with their Fit and March and were then leading the subcompact market (*Business Week*, 27 March 2002). Toyota also launched six sedans in Japan with the intention to steal upwardly mobile customers from BMW and Honda, but it was a flop. Both Verossa and Will are only selling half of what they were targeted. Toyota failed because it has no real brand strategy in Japan, unlike its clearly-defined Lexus and Toyota marques in the U.S.

Toyota has called for tough measures to reconquer its market shares in Japan by selling minicars (made by affiliate Daihatsu Motors) in its showrooms to attract the younger generation and by offering cash rebates: $800 each to buyers of five flagging models, including the Verossa and Will (*Business Week*, 27 March 2002). To survive the competition, Toyota needs to be even more radical by streamlining its lineup and its distribution networks and to come up with a new brand strategy by producing more new hits to cater to all age groups.

Bibliography

Basu, S. (1999), *Corporate Purpose: Why It Matters More than Strategy*, New York and London: Garland Publishing, Inc.

Kumon, H. (1998), "Overseas Production Activities of Toyota Motor", in Mirza, H. (ed.), *Global Competitive Strategies in the New World Economy: Multilaterism, Regionalisation and the Transitional Firm*, UK: Edward Elgar Publishing Ltd.

Lewis, D. R. (1999), *When Cultures Collide: Managing Successfully across Cultures*, London: Naperville, Ill.

Sachs, B. (1994), *Reorganising Work: The Evolution of Work Changes in the Japanese and Swedish Automobile Industries*, New York and London: Garland Publishing, Inc.

Toyota Motor Corporation (1988), *Toyota: A History of the First 50 Years*, Japan: Toyota Motor Corporation.

Newspaper Sources

T
O
Y
O
T
A

Automotive News Europe

Business Week

CTK Business News Wire

Financial Times

Global News Wire

The Straits Times

Fiat: The Festa Is Over

Fix It Again Tony

— popular U.S. pun on FIAT

In its heydays in the mid 1980s, FIAT produced close to 4 million cars, held a 60% share of the Italian car market, and as a group produced 5% of the GDP of Italy. With a 14% share of the EU's car market, it was Europe's largest car producer by volume, even ahead of Volkswagen. Its political influence until the early 1990s permitted import protection from Japanese and Korean competitors in the Italian market, the much delayed obligatory introduction of the catalytic converters, and plenty of public subsidies, including scrapping funds introduced by the government of Romano Prodi in 1997 (then inducing customers to buy new Fiats with catalysts). Not by accident *La Stampa*, the Fiat owned daily, had led the campaign to vote for Prodi's left of centre Ulivo list. When Giovanni Agnelli, Fiat's honorary chairman and capo famigli of the owning clan died in January 2003 at age 81, he was mourned in the streets of Turin by

200,000 people. Obituaries likened him to an "uncrowned King of Italy".

Yet by the time of his death Fiat Auto was hemorrhaging cash. Past policies to cut R&D had left the auto-maker without a competitive new model. The capital accumulated during good years had seen spent on a diffuse diversification binge.

Sitting on €50 billion of loans downgraded to junk bond status, Fiat's friendly Italian bankers were turning less friendly. As General Motors, Fiat's minority shareholder was unwilling to exercise its put option to purchase the car operator, Umberto Agnelli, Giovanni's younger brother, was forced to sell his group's most profitable assets to reduce the debt mountain. The turnaround of the Fiat group's core car operations, however, still remains to be seen.

Fiat started out in style. In 1899, eight bored rich young gentlemen decided in a trendy Turin café to set up a joint company to produce the fashionable new automobiles. One of them was Giovanni Agnelli, the son of a large landlord, who was trained at a military academy. He had left the military at age 23 as a first lieutenant of the cavalry. He first set up a ball bearing plant, RIV, which today is part of SKF.

The new company was called Fabbrica Italiana Automobili Torino (FIAT). It started by copying Mercedes engines. By 1901, 150 workers already manufactured 73 cars with a strength of 2 PS being able to speed up to 35 km/h. As one of Italy's then 30 car producers (including Alfa Romeo and Lancia, both today part of Fiat Auto), Fiat grew happily, allowing it to go public during 1906/7. In a mysterious operation its stock price crashed, allowing Agnelli, who acted also as Chief Executive Officer to buy out cheaply his erstwhile business partners. Later, the share values duly recovered.

When Turin's public prosecutor investigated the incidence, Giovanni Agnelli briefly resigned as CEO, but later resumed his functions as an undisputed majority shareholder when no charges were filed.

Fiat built racing cars, running up to 100 km/h. More importantly, it supplied trucks for the Italian expeditionary forces, which in 1911 moved into Libya against the Ottoman Empire. During World War I it benefited handsomely from military procurement, producing ship engines, trucks and other military vehicles. By 1917, Fiat had grown into Italy's third largest industrial enterprise. During 1914–18, the numbers of its workers, which stood at 4,000 at the start of the war, grew tenfold. Although Italy emerged on the winning side of WWI, there was widespread social discontent, public disillusionment with the conduct of the war and criticism of war profiteering. Fiat was an obvious object. By 1920, Turin had become one of the focal points for postwar labour troubles. As part of the communist uprising in postwar Europe following the October Revolution in Russia armed Red Guards occupied the Fiat and Lancia car plants in Turin. Some 13,000 workers were involved. Violent fights with deaths ensued.

In 1922, Mussolini took power. His blackshirts had provided useful protection for the industrial plants and helped to end civic strife. Although liberal minded as an industrial capitalist, Giovanni Agnelli had to coexist with Fascist rule to assure social stability and continued corporate growth. By 1929, Fiat had become Italy's largest industrial plant, producing 40,000 cars (60% of Italy's output) per year. As leader of a showcase modern industry, Agnelli was appointed senator for life. Aided by Italy's policies of autarchy, Fiat then diversified into steel manufacturing, aviation, shipbuilding and road construction. With Italy's attack on Ethiopia in 1935, armament orders came pouring in again. In 1936, Fiat designed its "Fiat 500", the "Topolino", as the people's car, of which until 1955, 510,000 vehicles would be built. Its new Mirafiori plants by 1939 represented state-of-the-art

Taylorist modernism. Soon 22,000 of Fiat's total of 70,000 workers worked there. Mirafiori and the RIV ball bearing factory were soon hit by Allied bombing raids. As the tide of war turned against the Axis powers, worker unrest began to spread. By March 1943, there were strikes for higher wages, better food supplies and for the delivery of promised government aid for the victims of the bombings. In the confused and sometimes surreal agony of Fascist Italy Giovanni Agnelli and his faithful administrator Valesio Valleta had walked a skillful tightrope act between the ruling Fascists, the German occupation army and the Communist underground, which had re-established its party cells in the Fiat works. After the war, in August 1945, Communist partisans were about to expropriate Fiat, yet U.S. occupation officers objected. In December 1945, Giovanni Agnelli died after having been acquitted from charges to have collaborated with the Fascists. His only son, Eduardo, who had been married with a fairly non-conformist princess, had already been killed in a sea plane accident back in 1935.

Giovanni then had obtained the legal guardianship over his three grandchildren Giovanni ("Gianni") (1921–2003), Susanna, in the mid 1990s serving as a Foreign Minister in Italy, and Umberto (1934–2004). Gianni was favoured by his grandfather as his successor. He was universally described as tough, intelligent and charming. After a gilded youth hobnobbing with Europe's interwar aristocracy and grand bourgeoisie, Gianni served as a lieutenant with Italy's expeditionary corps in Russia and in North Africa, before apparently defecting to the Partisans. After the war, he remained strongly disinclined to engage himself in business, which he left in the able hands of Valetta. He rather indulged himself into a well publicised lifestyle of the new postwar jet-set, consorting with Hollywood stars like Rita Haywood and Anita Ekberg. Corporate duties were limited to his presidency of the family owned Juventus Turin football club (1946–66). In 1953, he married a beautiful Neapolitan princess with expensive tastes. Compulsive partying with beautiful women and fast cars lasted until 1966, when at the relatively mature age of 45, he began to take his corporate and dynastic duties more seriously. Valleta, who had almost despaired about Gianni's lifestyle and business disinterest, had retired in 1964 aged 83 and died in 1967. After WWII, he had to weather a fair amount of labour troubles. In 1948, armed unionists locked him in his office for days. In 1950, a bomb exploded in the Mirafiori plant. In 1952, a senior Fiat manager was murdered. Many of the workers at Fiat and other Turin plants were migrants from Southern Italy. They lived in poor overcrowded areas, were unwelcome by their Northern countrymen, and flocked by the thousands to the communists and their militant trade unions, which had easy answers and promises to their despairing living conditions. Valletta reacted by offering Fiat's 140,000 employees a fair share of prosperity. He provided them with vacation homes, kindergartens, training courses and excursions to remote places like Lourdes, a Catholic faith healing spa in the Pyrenees. Fiat was also known to pay better wages than other industries.

In 1955, the Fiat 600 was introduced and in 1956, the Autostrada del Sole was opened. The new Fiat model (and the smaller Fiat 124) thus became the symbol of the new motorisation of Italy's young and working class families as they moved from scooters to cars.

As Gianni reasserted family control, he introduced U.S. style assembling and controlling operations in the late 1960s. By that time, there was trouble on the labour front again. The 1968 student rebellion in Italy spread also to the working classes, part of which felt alienated from the PCI's then moderated Eurocommunist orientation. For militant students and anarchist workers in the late 1960s, Fiat with its autocratic leadership was easily public enemy Number One. The militant labour fights starting in 1969 were no longer controlled by the PCI and its unions, but by sympathizers of the Red Brigades and other violent communist sects. When Agnelli tried to fire 122 militant workers, he was forced to rehire them in a government brokered peace plan. This was not to last. In 1973, the Mirafiori plants were occupied by armed workers, who held out for one week against the assaults of the carabinieri. Physical attacks on plants and on managers multiplied. There was a need for continuous protection by bodyguards and the police for all Agnelli family members and senior management, affecting their way of life with residences rebuilt into fortresses. In Italy at least, for them *dolce vita* was no longer possible. Nonetheless, terrorists managed to kill 4 Fiat managers and to wound 27 others, mostly by kneecapping.

In Agnelli's view, Fiat had become the victim of Italy's societal crisis, as political scandals eroded public confidence and public services deteriorated. Elected chairman of Confidustia, the association of Italy's employers, in 1974 Agnelli negotiated the (in)famous *scala mobile*, an agreement with inflation indexed automatic wage increases: It starved off workers' unrest and bought time at best. As it also eroded Italy's competitiveness and the lira's value, it took a lot of political courage to rid the country off the *scala mobile* one decade later.

During the 1970s a successful model the Fiat 127 was on the market. Yet when the oil crisis of 1974/75 hit Italy and Fiat sales hard, Agnelli reacted in strange ways: He used Fiat's cash reserves for an ill-advised diversification into the production of buses and trains. In 1975, he also invited Carol De Benedetti (then owner of Olivetti) as a crisis manager in return for 5% of Fiat's shares. After 3 months, it became known that De Benedetti tried to purchase a relative majority of shares via strawmen. Then Agnelli terminated the relationship, whereupon in 1976, another strange bedfellow entered as a major shareholder: none other than Libyan Colonel Gaddhafi purchased 9% of Fiat's shares for $415 million. It took a lot of U.S. pressure and the help of Deutsche Bank to buy out the Libyans for a multiple of their original investment at $3.1 billion one decade later.

In 1979, absenteeism rates at Fiat's workforce had increased to 20%. Labour troubles mounted again as 61 employees were fired due to alleged terrorist contacts. Reduced sales and increased debts forced Fiat in 1980 to dismiss 16,000 workers temporarily. The unions responded with a strike at Mirafiori. In its 55th day, they escalated in calling for a general strike. As Fiat was about to capitulate, a miracle happened. Following the call of a solitary Fiat engineer in October 1980 in what seems to have been a genuinely spontaneous demonstration, 40,000 Fiat workers took to the streets in Turin and called for an immediate resumption of work. The strike collapsed, and for the next two decades, there was to be peace at Fiat's chronically troubled labour front. In 1980, the new Panda was on the market, one of those once-in-a-decade strokes of a genius, which as a smart cheap car saved Fiat from its recurrent financial predicaments. By 1983, Fiat was strongly profitable again. In 1984, the Fiat Uno, as the most produced Fiat models, enabled a Fiat market share of 60% in Italy and of 15% in the EU. Both made the 1980s Fiat's most profitable decade.

In 1969, Lancia had been purchased and in 1986, Alfa Romeo was bought as a defensive move against a threatened takeover by Ford. Alfa had always been a less profitable upmarket competitor sponsored by the state holding IRI, which for political reasons, financed the huge loss-making Alfasud plant near Naples in the South.

By 1980, Gianni Agnelli appointed himself Chairman and delegated everyday management to tough Cesare Romiti as CEO, whose role had been one of "bad cop" during the days of labour strife. Agnelli, however, retained ultimate control. Again, he insisted on a diversification drive creating a conglomerate ranging from publishing to telecoms and pharmaceuticals, which were controlled by a pyramid structure of holdings (called IFI, IFIL, Exor, etc.) at the apex of which sat the Giovanni Agnelli & C family trust. Most of these participations were highly profitable, and gave the Agnellis a strong public voice in the daily printed press beyond its Turin paper *La Stampa* (owned since 1925), but they drained capital from the core car business.

As Europe's car business consolidated, Fiat stood out. Earlier attempts to take over Citroen in the 1960s had been vetoed by General de Gaulle. Now, it was Agnelli who blocked mergers with Daimler, BMW, Volkswagen and Ford for fear of loosing control. Finally only a deal with General Motors (GM) materialised. GM had feared a German takeover of Fiat, which would have threatened its troubled European ("Opel") operations. GM and Fiat in 2000 swapped a 20% participation of GM in Fiat Auto (then worth $2.4 billion) with a 5% Fiat share in GM. GM was given a put (purchase) option to buy the remaining 80% shares in Fiat Auto by 2004. Both sides agreed on joint model development, joint production sites in Europe and Latin America to produce engines and gear boxes. Fiat may also have hoped to conquer the U.S. compact car market with the help of GM from which it had withdrawn earlier.

By 2002, however, GM devalued its Fiat Auto share from $2.4 billion to $220 million (thus valuing the entire company at only $1.1 billion). GM's interest to exercise its put option in 2004 had grown decidedly cold. What would have been the consequences of a GM takeover? Alfa Romeo would have complemented GM's luxury brands (Cadillac and Saab). Fiat's Latin American operations would have been managed from Detroit. And for Fiat itself? Its cars in all likeliness would have become Opels with Fiat's logo stripes.

Independent of GM's capital participation, Fiat continued its boom and bust rollercoaster of an incorrigible one-model company: The "Tipo" of 1988 did well. But by 1993, there were again losses, following the attacks of Ford and the Japanese (allowed full access to the Italian market only after the creation of the EU's integrated internal market in 1992).

In addition, there were embarrassing inquiries by the Italian State prosecutors into donations paid by Fiat to smoothen political connections in Italian high politics. Cesare Rominti was interviewed by Milan public prosecutor Antonio Di Pietro of "*mani pulite*" fame. Apparently up to 3% of Fiat's turnover was paid as contributions to the political system. Relations were particularly close to the DCI's reformist wing led by ex-PM Amitore Fanfani, but also to centrist parties like the Republicans, who under PM Dini in 1995 made Gianni's sister, Susanna, Foreign Minister.

In 1996, the Agnelli's "La Stampa" successfully led the public drive to solicit votes for Romano Prodi's Ulivo center-left alliance. The anti-corruption "mani puliti" campaign resulted in the arrest of a few lower level Fiat managers, but no charges were raised against the top. Fiat is both the victim and the beneficiary of Italy's way of doing politics. It has had more than its usual share of social strife and labour troubles, but it also benefited from generous public procurement, massive motorway construction, import protection and straight subsidisation (estimated by some experts to amount to €5 billion during 1992/2002).

So far back in 1994 Fiat's last hurray was the Punto. In consequence until 1997, Fiat Auto was profitable again. However, in 1996, Romiti was replaced by Paulo Fresco, a long term disciple and deputy to Jack Welch at General Electric. His ambition was to create Fiat as "Europe's equivalent of GE" with the blessing of Gianni Agnelli. All profits and even more borrowed capital were plowed into a massive diversification drive, while the core car business was starved off funds. Fresco's biggest acquisition was the $4.3 billion purchase of Case, a U.S. farm equipment marker, in 1999. Merged with Fiat's New Holland farm and construction machinery producer to form CNH, it made Fiat the world's second largest operator after Canada's John Deere in the sector. Unfortunately, this coincided with a downturn in the global farm economy, and 17 plants of the newly merged company had to be closed with 7,000 jobs lost.

While creating a diversified conglomerate, Fresco also attempted to globalise Fiat's operations with investments in Poland (for Eastern Europe) and in Brazil. However, the Polish market was subsequently conquered by Daewoo (and the rest of East Europe by local products of Volkswagen/Skoda, Audi, Suzuki and Toyota), while the Brazilian market imploded in the crisis of 1998.

Having neglected R&D — expenditure had been cut by Fresco to $4.5 billion (1995/2001), equivalent to one-quarter of Volkswagen's expenditure — the Stilo saloon, which was to redress Fiat's fortune in the time honoured fashion, however duly flopped in 2001. After years of studious neglect for once the magic failed to work. For the Agnellis now (almost) all of their non-car operations were profitable, while only Fiat Auto was draining cash. Brother Umberto reportedly favoured disposing the loss-making car operations altogether, while Gianni insisted on their continuation for reasons of familial piety and pride.

While Gianni became increasingly incapacitated in his battle against prostate cancer, it was the banks, who in early 2002, forced first attempts at restructuring. With debts at €28 billion as a result of Fresco's acquisition spree, and group losses having escalated from €300 million (2000) to €1.8 billion (2001), and €2.1 billion (2002) there was little alternative. As the debt was mostly financed by friendly Italian banks, even their leniency came to an end once Fiat was rated to junk bond status, thus threatening their own standing, given that the exposure of Banca Intesa alone stood at €3 billion.

Milan's Mediobanca had wanted to force Fiat into bankruptcy and to make creditor banks accept debt for equity swaps — all under lucrative Mediobanca control. The Italian government under PM Berlusconi — as an upstart capitalist himself no known friend of the aristocratic Agnellis — made his wish publicly known for an "Italian solution". The government would buy one-third of the shares of Italy's largest industrial conglomerate prior to recapitalising and floating the new "Italauto".

The 160-strong Agnelli clan, with their 80-year-old autocratic capo famiglia and padrone incapacitated, had a definite succession problem. Gianni's only son, Edouardo (1952–2000), had been a troubled soul, more interested in religion, Eastern philosophy, drugs and astrology than in automobile manufacturing. He died by his own hands in 2000. His cousin, Giovanino (1964–1997), Umberto's only son, was more balanced, a keen ambitious sportsman and groomed for succession, but died prematurely from cancer of the stomach. Finally Gianni in 2001, picked his grandson John Elkam, son of his daughter Margherita, in near despair. The 22-year old American was an economics graduate with no practical business experience.

With Gianni's demise in January 2003 Umberto took over, fired Fresco and began a programme of divestment in order to reduce the mountain of debt. Fiat's GM share was sold for €1.2 billion, the airplane engine maker Fiat Avio for €1.6 billion, Toro Assicurazioni for €2.4 billion, and Fraikin, a French long-term truck rental company for €800 million. It also sold one-third of Ferrari, and raised €400 million by divesting its car leasing business. All in all, sales generated €7 billion. Yet, the Agnellis have not become poor. Fiat Auto apart, their holdings still include controlling stakes in CNH, in the truck maker Iveco, in Ferrari, in SNIA–BDP an armament producer, in Magneti Marell, a components maker, in Comau, a robotics producer, Juventus Turin, La Stampa newspaper, the Rizolli publishing group, the

Chateau Margeaux winery near Bordeaux, as well as the sizable shares in Danone, a French dairy producer, Galbani, an Italian food producer, Accor Hotels, Club Med, etc., most of which remain highly profitable, thus putting the family's net worth at $5 billion (*Forbes*, 2000).

The objective of Umberto Agnelli as president and of his new CEO, Guiseppe Morchio, formerly with Pirelli tyres, is to break even with a positive cash flow for the Fiat group by 2005 and for Fiat Auto in 2006. For the consolidated group's turnover of €50 billion, €22 billion should accrue from cars, €10 billion from CNH, €9 billion from Iveco trucks, €1 billion from Ferrari, the rest from construction and parts.

Cost cutting for Fiat Auto — 12,000 jobs are to be axed — will have limited utility. The one-model company is in urgent need of rescue by a new model in order to revive its slagging sales. With the onslaught of Japanese and Korean competitors in the Italian home market, Fiat's image of a cute cheap car is no longer exclusive and good enough. Market shares have halved to 30% in Italy and to 7% in the EU. Capacities aim at an annual output of 4 million units, but now produce less than 2 million. Previous cuts in R&D and in investments have truly taken a heavy toll.

Bibliography

Avantario, Vito, *Die Agnellis*, Frankfurt/Main: Campus Verlag, 2002.

"Fiat's running out of gas", *Bloomberg*, 31.7.2003.

"In Search of Fiat's Soul", *The Economist*, 3.6.2000.

"Fiat. Under Siege", *The Economist*, 19.10.2002.

Edmondson, Carl, "More smoke is pouring from Fiat's engine", *Business Week*, 23.12.2002.

"Fiat after Gianni Agnelli, "The party's over", *The Economist*, 1.2.2003.

Schlamp, Hans-Jürgen, "Clan auf Crash-Kurs", *Der Spiegel*, 29.7.2002.

Piller, Tobias, "Die Automisere von Fiat", Frankfurter Allgemeine. 1.6.2002

Piller, Tobias, "Der schwierige Neuanfang von Fiat", *Frankfurter Allgemeine*, 23.6.2003.

Piller, Tobias, "Fiat will bis 2005 wieder die Gewinnschwelle erreichen", *Frankfurter Allgemeine*, 27.6.2003.

Betts, Paul, "Italy's firm family ties", *Financial Times*, 24.3.2003.

Kapner, Fred, "Fiat drama produces cast with a past", *Financial Times*, 14.1.2003.

Kapner, Fred, "Fiat's day of reckoning", *Financial Times*, 24.1.2003.

Betts, Paul and Simonean, Haig, "Obituary Giovanni Agnelli", *Financial Times*, 25.1.2003.

Corporate Mergers, Merged Brands in Trouble: DaimlerChrysler and BMW–Rover

These are two of the largest takeovers of the late 1990s. There are many parallels between the two cases: Both were originally applauded as brilliantly executed merger operations, and both went badly wrong after two years of German *laissez faire* management.

Both were the consequences of discarded management fads and the product of a new one. In the 1980s diversification was the craze of most management gurus. It would liberate companies from the cyclical downswings of product cycles, allow new synergies and limitless prospects of growth. When these visions turned sour, strained management resources and persistent losses began to threaten core business operations. In 1995, British Aerospace put Rover up for sale, which was promptly snapped up by BMW. Daimler's new chief, Jürgen Schrempp had begun to sell off or close down his predecessor's dream of a diversified high tech conglomerate. The aerospace and defense interests, purchased and operated together with troublesome minority shareholders, such as DASA (consisting of MTU, Dornier, MBB and Fokker), the electrical engineering (AEG), software and service (Debis) branches were either scaled down or closed down altogether. The new fad of the mid-90s was to refocus on one's core business. In order to survive as an independent company producing cars, one was supposed to become a multi-brand, full-range vehicle producer with global reach and enjoy lower per unit costs with an annual output of between 2 to 4 million units at least. BMW and Mercedes as leading up-market high margin producers had neither of them, but they had a well-filled war chest (Daimler as a result of restructuring since 1996 had become profitable again) and the ambition to join the global top four players.

For Daimler the new deal meant to utilize Chrysler's dominance in the U.S. growing mini van and sports utility segment — as well as a regional complementarity in utilizing Chrysler's marketing network in the U.S. For BMW it meant acquiring Rover's four-wheel drive technology and a range of small- to medium-sized mass-produced cars.

The logic and the execution of both takeovers was praised as brilliant and faultless by analysts and the business press at the time, creating high expectations, although the seeds for the future managerial and financial disasters were sown at that time already. Both Daimler and BMW undertook great efforts to accommodate perceived political sensitivities, also in order to protect the precious reputation of their cash generating main premium brands.

Given the "latent hostility to things German at senior levels of the British establishment" (Brady/Lorenz, p. 179), BMW chief Piechetsrieder announced a policy of no redundancies for Rover's over-manned and outdated operations and left an under-performing British management team in place, which in the view of the authors was "tantamount to negligence" (Brady/Lorenz, p. 69).

In the case of Chrysler, which as the U.S. third largest car manufacturer was historically particularly prone to the up-and-down swings of car demand in the U.S. market, and which had been bailed out at U.S. taxpayers' expense at its last crisis in 1981, both sides insisted in public on a friendly myth as a merger of equals of what in reality was a friendly takeover. Daimler in fact paid a premium over Chrysler's then current share price (Waller, p. 191). The results were over-sized management boards, sweet, expensive compromises, resistance to change in Chrysler with encouraged score-keeping, and a two-year "power vacuum" at the top of Chrysler (Waller, p. 266), as its U.S. managers began their mental divorces from the company and ultimately left in large numbers. Suddenly enriched with generous options packages they were left with little incentives to work.

Both Daimler and BMW allowed *laissez faire* with mounting losses to rule for two years. Then, under public pressure due to continuing losses and depressed share prices, they suddenly shifted into reverse gear. Daimler managers replaced Chrysler's top staff, ending the expensive illusion of a merger. After Piechetsrieder's dismissal, hundreds of BMW engineers were flown in to Rover to rescue the British operations with micro-management. This was as insensitive with its "sledgehammer approach" (Brady/Lorenz, p. 197) to amount to a "human relations disaster" (Brady/Lorenz, p. 142).

Brady and Lorenz conclude that a more rational hard-headed honest approach like the one Volkswagen adopted with Skoda (Brady/Lorenz, p. 53) would have been preferable than to shifting between two undesirable extremes. In retrospect it appears that only the British workers, their union, the TGWU, and their industrial negotiator, Tony Woodley, recognised early enough that BMW was Rover's only hope for survival and that this required thorough tough restructuring from the start, not the *laissez faire* injection of funds into a company suffering from 20 years of under-investment by British Leyland, with endemic quality problems and a seriously damaged brand.

The inter-cultural differences between the merged companies could not be removed by extensive and expensive get-to-know sessions and funny seminars organised by intercultural communicators.

To the Germans British management appeared as intransigent, arrogant, grasping and egoistic with an aversion to risk (Brady/ Lorenz, p. 62). In the U.S. they were shocked at the Americans' insistence on hierarchy and multiple earnings of top management, their humourless political correctness in racial, sexual, and no drinking/no smoking codes, and their refusal to socialise after work (Waller, pp. 251/4).

In return, the Anglo-Saxons were annoyed by the Germanic habit of decision-making at formal meetings in a memo-based corporate bureaucracy.

In the end, after billions of losses Chrysler ended up as the U.S. sports utility and four-wheel drive subsidiary of Daimler, and after having swallowed an investment of £2.5 billion, Rover in early 2000 was sold for £10 million to the capital-starved Alchemy syndicate, whose ambition was to allow Britain's last independent car production to survive on the basis of a positive cash flow only.

In all fairness, there were other contributing factors, which conspired to these spectacular merger failures in the global car industry in the late 1990s. They are in Rover's case: the appreciation of the pound Sterling to levels of DM3.10 — far above the levels of the price competitiveness of the British export industry, the hesitant and delayed delivery of UK government aid for Rover, aggressive pricing by Rover's competitors and waning demand for its products. Chrysler was mainly hit by the contraction of the U.S. car market in the late 1990s which once again affected Chrysler most dramatically.

All in all, these are two sorry tales of well intentioned cross-national mergers gone wrong. They went wrong due to cultural reasons, for which most cross-national mergers and takeovers — from Swissair to Vivendi — usually fail: the unhappy mixture of managerial hubris, faddish wishful thinking, and persistent incompatible national business cultures. Perhaps a growing realization of the importance of the latter could not only save capital and human resources, but also be helpful for much needed, more differentiated corporate approaches to globalisation.

Six years later, Daimler is still struggling with its Chrysler subsidiary. It still has cost problems with U.S. made steel, labour and pension obligations. Worse, in spite of strong cuts in purchasing costs, GM and Ford had started an aggressive price discount war to fight back the recurring Japanese competition. After losing sales, Chrysler responded with financial incentives, cash back schemes and a free 7-year engine warranty. With a squeeze on margins and declining sales, even further cost cutting could not prevent further losses. As a result, Daimler Chrysler shares by April 2003 traded at €29, down 70% from their €96 levels a few years earlier. The value destroyed represented more than the US$36 billion which Daimler had paid for Chrysler. It is now valued as nil by the stock market.

In the meantime, German managers had taken over key functions at Chrysler. When David Eaton retired as CEO in 1980, Dieter Zetsche succeeded him. Yet it took 3 years to use joint components between Daimler and Chrysler models — things which are usually cited as the key advantage of corporate mergers and their fabulous synergies.

BMW – ROVER

By 2003, Chrysler put two new major models on the market:

◊ a two seater rear wheel drive sports car called "Crossfire" (which finally had 39% of its components produced by Daimler), and

◊ a blend of a mini-van and a sports utility car named "Pacifica".

Both are positioned as newly invented "premium brands", below the luxury level and above the mass market. So far nobody in the U.S. had been aware of this market segment (which is very much in existence in Europe with its sizable upper middle class).

It remains to be seen whether Chrysler with its fading mass market appeal will manage its 'upgrade' with crossbreeds. If successful, it would be the most surprising stroke of a genius in the world's best researched car market. If the strategy flopped, a sizable divestment would probably be in order before long.

In contrast, BMW seems to live happily ever after its costly divorce from Rover. Rather it was Ford who eventually acquired the loss maker and continued to struggle with Rover's problems, which BMW left behind.

According to Helmut Panke, BMW's new CEO (2002–), BMW has learnt its lesson not to venture into the mass market again. With its 11 different series, it rather aims at the top segment of each vehicle type. This not only applies to sports cars and off roaders, but also to Minis, the only successful brand retained from the Rover adventure.

Although their margins have become smaller than in BMW's traditional luxury segment, demand growth has been particularly strong in Asia and in the U.S., especially for the more expensive elaborate versions. Production at its Spartanburg plant (South Carolina) had to be increased to 150,000 units p.a. (accounting for 15% of BMW's total production). BMW also went top market with its Rolls Royce production at its new plant in Goodwood at the English South coast.

Originally, BMW had lost a bidding war for Rolls Royce and Bentley manufacturing against a £470-million bid from Volkswagen back in 1998. Once it acquired the overpriced works from Vickers, VW then discovered that the Rolls Royce name was owned by Rolls Royce Aerospace, which sold it to BMW for £40 million, probably the largest amount ever paid for a trade name, but still a bargain compared to Volkswagen's purchasing price for the decrepit Crewe (North England) plants, which needed another £600 million from VW for an upgrade.

BMW and VW then agreed to split operations, with VW producing 7,000 Bentleys p.a. in modernised Crewe facilities, with BMW assembling its new RR01 in the south of England. There its German-produced body, its 460PS strong engine and gear boxes are put together, painted and the extensive trimming done by craftsmen, who earlier built luxury boats along the coast. BMW's new Rolls Royce starts with an asking price of £208,000. An annual production of 1,000 units is envisaged.

The lesson of the two costly mergers is pretty straightforward: Mergers don't create synergies for brands. They rather pose mortal threats by diffused images and inconsistent qualities and pricing. BMW rescued itself with a clear refocus to its traditional brand strength with a careful expanded up-market scope.

DaimlerChrysler, however, still struggles. Its national and segmental brand identities are more diffuse than ever. As success remains persistently elusive, even Daimler's highly profitable core brand could ultimately be threatened.

Bibliography

Brady, Chris and Lorenz, Andrew, *End of the Road. BMW and Rover — A Brand Too Far*, Harlow: Pearson Education, 2002.

Waller, David, *Wheels on Fire. The Amazing Inside Story of the Daimler-Chrysler Merger*, London: Hodder and Stoughton, 2001.

"DaimlerChrysler learns to share, 5 years later", *International Herald Tribune*, 25.3.2003.

Grant, Jeremy, "Chrysler chief faces twists and turns on road to rebranding", *Financial Times*, 16.6.2003.

Grant, Jeremy, "The heat is on for DaimlerChrysler costs", *Financial Times*, 3.9.2003.

Harnischfeger, Uta, "Daimler profit target looks a long way away", *Financial Times*, 10.4.2003.

Fockenbrock, Dieter, "Daimler und Chrysler. Ein Stern auf der Erde", *Tagesspiegel*, 7.5.2003.

Griffiths, John, "Bavaria tries to make a British marque", *Financial Times*, 4.1.2003.

Harnischfeger, Uta, "BMW in drive to maintain goals", *Financial Times*, 9.5.2003.

Burt, Tim, "Profile Helmut Panke, BMW", *Financial Times*, 13.5.2002.

"BMW erwaegt mehr Produktion und höhere Preise in Amerika", *Frankfurter Allgemeine*, 26.5.2003.

The Lego Universe of Building Bricks

All of Denmark is basically a small Legoland.

— Frits Brendal

Today Lego is active in 33 countries with 10,000 employees achieving a turnover of €600 million per year with production sites in Denmark, Switzerland, the U.S., Brazil and Korea. Lego aims to become the world market leader for construction toys, preschool and school materials, family parks, and for lifestyle and media products in its target group of families with children of up to 16 years of age. In some of these segments, this third generation owned and managed company is quite close to its declared objective.

It all started when in the poor farming village of Billund, located in Central Jylland, a pious carpenter and cabinet-maker named Ole Kirk Christiansen ran out of orders during the world economic crisis of 1929, which hit Denmark and its farm sector hard as it depended on livestock exports.

Rather than firing his redundant craftsmen and apprentices, Christiansen reacted by diversifying his artisanal production in offering a wider product range to his rural clientele, like ladders and wooden farm implements. When orders did not pick up, they produced toys from scrap wood like walking ducks, fire engine cars and furniture for puppet homes. His son Godtfred, a trained carpenter with only elementary school education as well, proved to be a gifted salesman.

Through commission sales in village Kobmands stores all over Denmark, he assured the survival of his father's workshop. They also used the short-lived yoyo craze in the mid-1930s well. During this time the fledgling company shortened its slogan "Leg godt" (play well) memorably to 'Lego' as its future trademark.

In 1942, fire destroyed the wood workshop in Billund. It was soon replaced by a then modern toy factory where 40 workers began to produce foremost wooden animals, coloured toy cars and railway carriages.

During World War II, plastics saw a quick and dramatic development. Hence Ole fatefully in 1947 decided to purchase a plastics injection molding machine — for experimental purposes for the time being. In 1949, the original Lego stone was invented and patented as an 'automatic building brick'. Although packaged in bright colourful packages, the toy trade was slow to accept the new product. After Denmark, in the 1950s the West German market was targeted. The rest of Western Europe followed.

In a toy factory in Rudolfstadt/Thuringia in the prewar years already a similar toy brick had been invented. As Rudolfstadt became part of Soviet-occupied East Germany, Communist state management held the poor plastic brick in neglect and poor quality and thus left the field to Lego (this author had both types in his toy collection and definitely preferred the Danish variant, which unlike the East German product, never lost its shape and hold). In 1958, Ole's son, Godtfred Kirk Christiansen took over.

He had been the inventor of the improved combination technique of the adhesive bricks and defined the timeless principles of the 'Lego System':

Unlimited possibilities to play, be attractive to both boys and girls, all juvenile age groups, invite healthy and quiet play, develop fantasy and creativity, with new elements easy to add on, and those add ons to enhance the play. Finally: to insist on perfect quality.

In 1960, a fire once again helpfully destroyed the wood-processing facilities. Godtfred decided to discontinue the wooden toy lines. His older brothers, who disagreed, were bought out and set up their own companies.

Given the Lego system, there was a permanent need for new product ideas to complement the staple brick. Initially ideas originated from Godtfred's hobby cellar. But in 1959 a development department ("Lego Futura") with 5 employees was set-up. 40 years later this unit employs 300 creative people in 3 continents and in sites like Boston, Tokyo, Milan and London, apart from Billund. The plastics used were improved to be ever safer, more indestructible and to keep brighter colours (1963). Duplo bricks were developed for the little hands of two to six years old (1969). Plastic tools for kids were invented.

The first Legoland Park was opened in Billund (1968). At its origin was the nuisance value of an ever increasing stream of visitors, who began to obstruct smooth work operations. Special permanent exhibits were set up for them, which with continued attractivity were expanded into a well designed mini-world of Lego-build world sites, castles, harbours, fairy tale landscapes, jungle paths, Western towns, pirate hideouts, Indian camps, goldmines, Lego ships, cruises, rafts and Lego cars. Originally designed for parents with children aged 3 to 12, soon it was found that one-third of the 1.4 million annual visitors in Billund were unaccompanied adults, attracted by the notion of the big wide world turned into small format, a Gulliver's perspective, which lends an illusion of power and oversight.

Following Billund's success, in 1996 in Windsor, UK, a derelict safari park was turned into another Legoland with plenty of British themes, like replicas of the Tower, Scottish castles and Welsh mines, thus providing edifying features for compulsory school excursions. Soon afterwards, in the course of a sustained market penetration effort in the U.S., in Carlsbad, California on an abandoned tomato plantation Legoland No. 3 was opened. Two more openings followed: in Makuhari on reclaimed land near Tokyo for Japan's captive parents, and in Günzburg, Swabia on an abandoned U.S. army base located in between Munich and Stuttgart in May 2002.

Half a century of growth left their traces on corporate culture. But its unique pietist origins are still visible in pronounced intentions of good corporate citizenship and worthy educational aspirations.

Founder Ole was a devout Protestant, whose poor childhood years were followed by an apprenticeship in Norway and Germany. His son, Godtfred engineered the 1960s boom, but still insisted on egalitarian structures. He dispensed paternalist goodwill, and accepted subordinates mistakes while insisting on tight frugal cost management. Up to the 1960s, each working day would still start with a voluntary common prayer session for all staff in Billund.

The village was gradually transformed into a corporate small town. In the 1940s, Lego financed the sidewalks, piped water and sewage systems and a crafts school. In 1964, Lego initiated the set-up of a regional airport in Billund. Located in central Jylland, today it is Denmark's second largest after Copenhagen. Contemporary Billund has 8,500 inhabitants, out of whom 1,200 work full-time for Lego, and some 700 as seasonal helpers (March/October) in Legoland.

Observers like Margaret Uhle have noted the strong nexus between the Lego designs and the country of Denmark itself: Both are clean, well ordered and functioning smoothly with small homes, small towns and neat roads with lots of traffic lights, trees and respectable people on bicycles and in small cars — about as exciting like a real-sized Legoland. At the same time, Danes are reputed to be gifted craftsmen and creative tinkers who love their children. This amounts to a corporate identity well matched with national culture.

As a well intentioned pragmatic Danish company, Lego so far also provided for smooth generational transition. Successors were well-groomed in due time. The old generation faded away in due course. 100% family control remains assured. For once in Scandinavia transparency is thought dispensable. Balance sheets remain confidential.

In 1979, grandson Kjeld Kirk Christensen took over. He inherited the need to improve management and to streamline production. Lego had adhered to the laudable principle of "few chiefs and many Indians", with strong roles of senior Indians like foremen and industrial craftsmen, with weekly planning session of senior management as a relatively feeble link to arrive at and to communicate management direction to the ground troops.

With a staff of 2,300 in 1980, Kjeld felt the time had come to introduce proper middle management to take care of the increasing complexity of decisions. It was also clear that there were too many Lego products on the market. Even for Lego staff, it had become difficult to keep track.

Output was then streamlined into 3 product lines:

◊ Lego Duplo for small children;
◊ Lego construction toys for the basic boxes and for thematic programmes like City, Castle, Space, Railways, Technic;
◊ XYZ: other quality toys.

2,000 elements were sorted along basic, decorative, functional and figurative lines.

Lego research found that its products were rather boys' favourites. They like to build massive structures, preferably towers, who could dramatically crash, or set up street crossings, where masses of cars could wonderfully crash as well. Girls also did play with Lego, but usually lost interest after ages 5–6. They preferred to work with wide-open structures: to furnish homes, populate streets, coffeehouses and beach sites. In order to service the quiet social games which girls prefer (different from the boys' explorative action games), Lego provided rounder, softer figurines with a bit of glamour for the girls' preferred role-plays. Dream houses and assorted decoration, including flowers, were designed for this purpose.

Faced with shrinking markets for educational toys in Europe and in the U.S. in the 1990s, under license from Disney figures like Winnie the Pooh were produced as Duplo figurines, with others to follow. This was a significant departure from Lego's doctrine away from educational toys.

Already earlier since 1983, in cooperation with McDonald's small Lego sets were included into Junior packs ordered at their fast-food outlets. This spread basic Lego bricks all over the U.S. and generated the demand for follow-up purchases. This strategy worked well in most other countries except Germany, where McDonald's is met with poor parental acceptance. In fact, it is seen not as a family restaurant, but rather as a sub-standard junk food provider and hangout for delinquent, mostly immigrant, kids. This led Lego to the correct conclusion that an association with McDonald's would hurt its very positive brand image in Germany.

Starting out with its Lego figurines (1974), its Legoland features (1978) which allowed whole townships to be built and settled, Lego went on to produce successfully Duplo zoo animals and thematic figures as casts for Robin Hood scenes, castles and pirates.

Faced with computer toys in the mid-1990s in core European markets, Lego sales began to shrink. Lego responded by producing Lego Robots and Technic computers, which could be used as educational toys for school use. Efforts were undertaken to design digital bricks, which would be programmed by children — and hence thought to be more exciting than the pre-programmed Tamagochi blurps. Yet the "programmable brick", which in 1998 was put on the market, remained too expensive for mass marketing so far. Also with many of the complicated Lego Technic toys, it was frankly getting difficult to recognise the basic guiding Lego principle: Never to produce a 'ready' finished product for a child, to make it easy for assembly, disassembly and for recombination to develop his own new toy.

These slow and painful departures from corporate philosophy were triggered by mounting heavy losses, which started in 1998. In 1999, 1,000 employees had to be laid off. In 2002, 200 more were fired. Growth in the 1980s had been brought about by achieving global reach. 300 million children by the time had played with Lego bricks. Yet the lives of middle-class children was about to change. Their days became programmed with extra-curricular activities. Toys had to compete with electronic games and instant media access. The sad truth was: There was simply no time left to play the slow paced games which Lego offered. With licensed toys — from Star Wars Legos to Winnie the Pooh and Harry Potter — there is a definite departure by Lego from the ideal of open-ended self-guided play. As Charles Fishman rightly observed, this may be trendy, but it is not a sign of leadership, which Lego 30 years earlier had exercised.

Lego remains very adept at the right PR: to stimulate the highest Lego tower construction (currently at 25 meters) and other very visual Guinness Records; to have UNHCR in a celebrated poster and free advert campaign pose 40 Duplo figures of all colours, occupations and ages, and ask "Who is the refugee?"; to organise civic-minded sponsoring for the reconstruction of Frauenkirche, Dresden's largest landmark baroque church, which was destroyed during Allied bombing in February 1945; by popular model competitions; and last but not least by having the Danish mail issue a Lego postage stamp.

A fair amount of merchandising has started, with Lego toothbrushes and kids wear: true to Lego style it is colourful, solid and highly priced.

Marketing is done increasingly through 'Lego shops in shops' in department stores or at special counters in toy shops or duty free shops, where pricing and display are under control. Yet at the same time, there is also a fair amount of Lego discount sales by larger retailers. Perhaps the company is resigned to this, as there is a major market entirely out of its corporate reach: Lego, indestructible as they are, form a staple of flea markets across the globe as children sell the bricks which they have outgrown. It should come as a comfort to the good people in Billund that even second-hand Legos regularly fetch good prices. And in clinching the deal, the Lego box does one last pedagogical service to the budding 14-year old salesman: His entrepreneurial spirits have been encouraged. No small feat for a bunch of coloured plastic bricks.

Bibliography

Fishman, Charles, "Why Can't Lego Click?", *Fast Company* 50, September 2001, p. 144.

Uhle, Margaret, *Die Lego Story. Der Stein der Weisen*, Reinbek/Hamburg: Rowohlt, 2000.

Wiencek, Henry, *The World of Lego Toys*, New York: Harry N. Abrams, 1987.

www.lego.com/info

L
E
G
O

The Magic of Disney

There is little doubt that the magic behind Disney lies with the man himself. Indisputably, the driving force and the direction of the company stem from Walt Disney's creative X-factor and his abiding influence. The 'Disney Image' is one emanating the realisation of dreams, the perpetual state of childhood and the enchanting lure of escape into a fantastic and happy world of childhood innocence. Behind this surreal world of magical dreams lies the history of a company that is not unlike other successful companies of today. The struggling start experienced by its creator(s) in the early years, the internal disputes that weighed the company down time and time again and the takeovers and the financial battles that took place — these were all present throughout the formation of what is today greatly loved and widely known as The Walt Disney Company.

The Beginnings of Magic

Before Walt Disney became the man who opened the creative door to popular accessible children's entertainment and made it, as such, globally appealing, it is said that he first received such creative inspiration as an ambulance driver during WWI, often coming across great castles in Europe (Grover, 1997, p. 1). In the years to come, the fruit of such inspiration would present itself as the magnificent imitation castles that one finds in Disneyland these days. Before the internationally renowned icon Mickey Mouse (who curiously enough nearly became Mortimer Mouse[1]) came to dominate the hearts of many, it must be mentioned that Walt started off dealing with a rabbit instead — Oswald the Lucky Rabbit to be exact. Drawing crude cartoon strips for local theatres and sketching advertisements for a barbershop, together with the Oswald and Alice Comedies projects he involved himself with in the early 1920s, comprised Walt's first business ventures which ultimately failed, though, on hindsight, served as important stepping stones in the whole scheme of things.

Walt and his older brother Roy Disney later became partners and started the Disney Brothers Cartoon Studio in 1923. Here, the starkly different characters came out strongly in the often un-smooth working relationship. Walt was decidedly the more creative, let's-give-it-all-we've-got person while Roy seemed to provide the business expertise his brother lacked. Roy was in charge of persuading the bankers and investors to lend Walt money but at the same time, often dissuading Walt from spending money the company managed to receive. Having prudence and extravagance working alongside each other, it was little wonder friction arose between the two brothers. However, it seemed that Walt was the one who called the shots as the studio later changed

---

[1] Walt Disney had initially wanted to name this 1928 creation "Mortimer". It was his wife who suggested the (more appealing and appropriate) name "Mickey" instead (Grover, 1997, p. 2).

its name to Walt Disney Studios in 1926, and later Walt Disney Productions in 1929. Given that, clearly much good came out of this partnership, and the linking between the two brothers would set the pace for many other alliances that would develop in the future. "Partnerships were obviously an integral part of Walt Disney's business strategy ... and agreements between Disney and the likes of Exxon, AT&T and General Motors ... still contribute thousands annually to the Disney coffers". The examples in later sections will demonstrate the prowess of partnerships and how they can truly rake in the cash.

The Disney Service Culture

Orlando Disney is an example which the Manchester Business School, University of Manchester, has chosen as a model for emulation. In the school's opinion, "Walt Disney World has achieved an enviable reputation for outstanding service that has made it the premier entertainment centre in the World." Working closely with the Disney Institute, tailored programmes are made available for companies who wish to come and pick up essential business skills. Delegates are promised an in-depth experience on how Disney's service strategy actually functions. The Institute provides extensive training in the following areas: Quality Service, Leadership Excellence, People Management, Loyalty, Organizational Creativity and Value Chain Management.

According to the school,

$$Leadership\ Excellence + Cast\ Excellence +$$
$$Service\ Excellence = Future\ Success$$

Disney defines its excellence in the ability to accurately empathise with customers as "guestology". This means "to identify their customers through a compass model that focuses on needs, wants, stereotypes and emotions." Both in theory and in practice, the importance of a "service philosophy" is greatly stressed upon. As such, the legacy of Walt and his detailed attention to customer experience lives on even after his death in 1966. Each customer is treated exactly the way Walt would have treated them himself. This is the key to Disney's lasting, enduring appeal. People feel like they are important, apart from the fact that they are simply out there having a good fun, worry-free time.

There is indeed little wonder as to why "the Walt Disney Company is repeatedly hailed as a superior service provider, perhaps the best in the world." (Capodagli and Jackson, 1998, p. 59). Essentially, Walt Disney recognised and had great understanding of his customer base. An example given in Tom Connellan's *Inside the Magic Kingdom: Seven Keys to Disney's Success* demonstrates how successful the Company is in reading and subsequently meeting the needs of potential guests. It is widely known that Disney sees people more as guests and less as customers per se. On the day Disneyland opened, Walt Disney announced the theme park's motto: At Disneyland, the visitors are our guests. Connellan tells in his book of how a couple at Epcot could not afford to go to France or Italy for their vacation at that time and so, as an almost equally appealing alternative, replaced such an experience with a more inexpensive trip to the Epcot's (The Experimental Prototype Community of Tomorrow) French Pavilion. Of course, they knew it was not the real thing, but as Connellan explained, the experience and illusion of it all provided a sense of real magic that was quite wonderful altogether.

An illustration of how Disney's attention to detail is in fact two-fold — i.e. for the park visitor and the employee — is seen in the imprinting of names on the second-story windows on Main Street of people who contributed to the design, implementation and running of Disneyland. One of the most recently added name is Charles Boyers, who is noted for his famous Disneyland artwork. Not only are Disney's employees appreciated and honoured, the customer also receives a sense of family-warmth and aesthetic value from it all. Another example of Walt Disney's attention to customer satisfaction is demonstrated in the fact that he was adamant that the designers take the perspective of young children into account when designing the park. Walt would frequently stoop down while looking at a partially constructed building to consider how smaller people would see things.

The employees at Disney are also trained in team commitment. Besides the not-to-be-taken-for-granted mission statement comprising the company's mission and goals that guide employee vision, it is known that Disney often groups the same people when working on various projects. For example on a certain movie project, the teammates are all staff who have worked together before. Thus, a solid sense of rapport and effective group dynamics are fostered amongst the teams.

The Company also recognises the pointlessness of having a mismanaged, ineffective and rigid hierarchical organization. As such, "top Disney executives go out of their way to solicit advice from staff members ... frontline people who hear guests' comments and see their reactions." Efforts are thus made to go beyond the strict hierarchical chains of information and, instead, to get direct, and ultimately advantageous, information for those who really need to receive feedback and for those who, in effect, have the powers to make the necessary changes. One sees that the lower rung staff works together with those higher up in the corporate ladder.

Also, Disney works by a process called "co-locating" where the emphasis is on bringing teams together to work in a central location. At Disney, these "planning centres" have proven to be highly successful, especially when it facilitates brainstorming sessions amongst the staff.

We have seen how Disney's success is strongly factored by the Company's painstaking efforts at providing excellent customer, or rather guest, service. Quite simply, the success of Disney has to do with two chief factors: Firstly, a tapping into and a sound understanding into the psyches of people — that ultimately, all people want to have a good time. Secondly, utilising the above knowledge to its fullest potential, to extend it in an all-encompassing reach to all the possible markets, as we will see in later sections. In effect, it attempts to meet the demands and wishes of the people, both physically (thrill rides), emotionally (happy feelings, a sense of return to normal irretrievable childhood innocence and memories), and socially (family unit and strengthened ties, friendships).

More Than Just Child's Play

The Disney Company is certainly more than just a happy place for people to visit. Behind the wondrous experiences the Company offers via its various resort lands, the Disney Company is primarily a place of business. The people behind the company are foremost there to see that profits are made and business is booming. The company, unlike what most of its customers are inclined to assume, represents more than Saturday morning cartoons and the Disneyland theme parks. To say the least, takeovers and acquisitions are not the kind of things that make up a happy state of affairs (at any rate, surely not for those who are at the losing end of the deal). Michael Eisner, who took over the leadership of the Company in 1984, continued in a different manner from Walt Disney by maintaining that an effective partnership requires "… nurturing, hand-holding, head-cracking, and once-in-a-while arm-twisting."

Besides the already established four destination resorts in the United States, Japan and France, a fifth addition to the group of successful resorts is Hong Kong Disneyland, which, "subject to the Government's completion of reclamation and infrastructure by specified target dates," will open in late 2005. However, the company's business is reaching ever further and it has diversified into many other profitable organizations since.

Anaheim Sports, Inc., operates the Walt Disney Company's two professional sports franchises, Major League Baseball's Anaheim Angels and the National Hockey League's Mighty Ducks of Anaheim. The Walt Disney Internet Group (WDIG) provides a platform where Disney operates some of the more highly trafficked Internet properties, including ABCNEWS.com, Disney.com and ESPN.com. "Through Disney Auctions, the Internet Group, in partnership with eBay, offers consumers the opportunity to purchase authentic Disney memorabilia sourced directly from business units of the Company." Disney is also working hand-in-hand with MSN to provide comparable Internet services at affordable prices to the entire family, with unlimited dial-up service, Disney Games, smart junk mail filters and powerful parental controls. All of this is, of course, in line with Disney's wholesome family-oriented image.

The Disney Mobile and Phone Center, working jointly with Motorola, has come up with a range of themed phones and thus entered competitively into the profitable handphone market with its own unique brand of Disney Character Graphics, Ringtones, Logos, Animations and Games. There is now, too, a Disney Visa Card from Bank One where members are provided full Visa platinum benefits and no annual fee. A scheme also set in place that works such that one can earn one Disney Dream Reward Dollar^{SM} for every one hundred dollars in net purchases, up to a maximum of 750 Disney Dream Reward Dollars^{SM} on $75,000 in net purchases in a calendar year. Linking this with their own Disney Cruise Line® and Disney Vacations, one also pays zero interest for 6 months on cruise packages or ticket-inclusive Disney vacation packages when booking through the Walt Disney Travel Company and charging the package to the Visa card prior to arrival.

Disney's Studio Entertainment arm comprises the following: Walt Disney Feature Animation, Walt Disney Television Animation, Walt Disney Pictures, Touchstone Pictures, Miramax, Giant Screen, Buena Vista Theatrical Group, Buena Vista International, Buena Vista Home Entertainment — Domestic/ International and the Buena Vista Music Group. It would surely be striking to many "lay persons" not in the media loop to realize that the company has dealings with movies like The Rookie, The Sixth Sense, In the Bedroom and Gangs of New York, apart from the obvious Disney productions like Lilo & Stitch and Treasure Planet, via all the above groups involved.

Disney's longstanding relationship with the media conglomerate American Broadcasting Corporation (ABC) is, however, well-known. In the early years, ABC invested $500,000 outright and guaranteed a $4.5 million loan in order to purchase 34.5% of Disneyland (opened 17 July 1955) and a commitment from Walt to produce a regular TV show. The power relations reversed later when in the mid 1990s Disney acquired Capital Cities/ABC for $19 billion. With ABC News, ABC Sports, ABC Daytime, ABC Kids and ABC Radio underpinning the media network as such, Disney's overall stand in the media industry strengthened further. Notably "Disney is the #2 media conglomerate in the world", only behind AOL Time Warner. Competition is tough though with the likes of AOL Time Warner, Viacom and NBC being the top competitors in the field.

The hugely popular EPSN — together with ESPN2 (sporting events and news), ESPN Classic (historical sports footage), and ESPNEWS (24-hour news and information) — that reach more than 87 million U.S. homes, also reaches another 119 million homes worldwide with its ESPN International unit — is clear evidence of what some might call the Disney Phenomenon, that Disney has truly diversified from funny cartoons with its mounting stakes over various entertainment groups. In addition, ESPN creates content for TV and radio and operates one of the most popular sports sites on the Internet. ESPN has also lent its name to a magazine and a chain of eight sports-themed restaurants. Disney's 80% stake in ESPN is indeed strengthening its financial standing.

Equally important to note is that Disney manages an extensive range of consumer products as well. Disney Licensing consists of Disney Toys, Disney Softlines (apparel and accessories) and Disney Hardlines (packaged goods, stationery, home furnishings and consumer electronics). The popular products comprise Disney juices developed with the Minute Maid division of The Coca-Cola Company, cereals, two-way radios and 2.4 GHz cordless telephones manufactured and distributed by Motorola, Inc, all of which have varying levels of success upon their entries into the North America, Latin America, Mexico, United Kingdom and Japanese markets. "Under the direct-to-retail model, Disney Consumer Products licenses its characters and brands to select retailers globally, rather than to third-party manufacturers and distributors. Retailers will source and manufacture products directly, for sale exclusively through all channels of their retail outlets." This, in turn, leads us to Disney's entrance into the European market. Characteristically, German and U.K. operations were driven by merchandise licensing while French and Italian operations by book and magazine licensing (Bartlett and Ghoshal, 2000). In Europe, Disney's direct-to-retail agreement with Carrefour, the largest retailer in Europe, resulted in the launch of an exclusive line of children's clothing and accessories at Carrefour stores in 30 countries. Agreements with major retailers H&M, C&A and Tesco also resulted in placement of exclusive Disney product lines in key European markets. Disney

Publishing, the world's largest children's publisher with books and magazines, sells 345 million copies annually. Publishing is also responsible for the highly successful publications like Eoin Colfer's hit *Artemis Fowl: The Arctic Incident* — the sequel to the best-selling children's thriller *Artemis Fowl and W.i.t.c.h.*, a monthly comic magazine developed in Milan, Italy, which claims be the no. 1 children's magazine title in Germany, France, Italy, Benelux and the Nordic markets.

The above shows the impressive range of services provided by Disney. On the other hand, unlike in any one of Disney's own fairytales, not everything is perfect. There is increasing discontent and less agreement amongst shareholders within the Disney Group. Of late, ABC has suffered from weak ratings and its theme parks have been receiving fewer international visitors. Michael Eisner, the man who took over at the helms of the Company in 1984 and who pretty much sees himself as a populist communicator to be regarded as the rightful heir to Uncle Walt, ascribes the flounder, as do operators, to mainly external factors beyond the group's control — September 11 attacks that hit tourist traffic, ABC suffering from global advertising downturn and the emergence of a host of rival studios in the animation business. DreamWorks, Warner Bros and Nickelodeon serve as tough competition to Disney, portioning off terrain once previously exclusive to Disney. The Disney theme parks also face the rivals of Legoland, Magic Mountain and Knotts Berry Farm. As one media insider succinctly and accurately put it, "They [Disney] no longer own the kids demographic." Juxtaposing all the above factors against the lack of confidence by U.S. consumers and security concerns of travelers effectively puts Disney in an unfavorable position as such.

Against professional opinion, Eisner, according to one board member, maintains that the purchase of ABC and the integration of ESPN sports businesses have always been the right strategic move, despite disappointing downturns. There is confidence in the management that in spite of economic downturns, with people having less disposable income during times of recession, that ultimately, "America and Americans always bounce back" and that "people hardly ever actually cancel their Disney vacations ... they only defer them until the time is right." There is great belief amongst the Disney management in the lasting attractivity and enduring power of the Disney brand. Recent laws passed also strengthen the safeguards with which the Company's holds to protect her aging brand name and products by upholding "lengthier copyrights protecting the profits of songs, books and cartoon characters." Michael Eisner wrote: "Frankly, with the Disney brand and the great assets of our company, it isn't easy to fail. It's much easier to succeed. And we will." Shareholders' main concern, however, is not so much the potential earnings capacity of Disney's assets, but whether it has been, as promised, managed effectively to deliver growth and shareholder value. Facing increased intense competition in the areas of media networks and theme parks, the Disney Company indeed has much to live up to. Maintaining its unrivaled position as a service provider, therefore, is one of the key areas that, if continued excellence is pursued, will ensure The Disney Company as a magic kingdom.

Bibliography

Books

Bartlett, Christopher A. & Ghoshal, Sumantra, *Transnational Management: Text, Cases, and Readings in Cross-border Management* 3rd ed., Boston: Irwin/McGraw-Hill, 2000.

Connellan, Tom, *Inside the Magic Kingdom: Seven Keys to Disney's Success*, Austin, Texas: Bard Press, 1997.

Capodagli, Bill & Jackson, Lynn, *The Disney Way: Harnessing the Magic of Disney in your Organization*, New York: McGraw-Hill, 1998.

Grover, Ron, *The Disney Touch: Disney, ABC & the Quest for the World's Greatest Media Empire*, revised ed., New York: McGraw-Hill, 1997.

Newspaper Article

Christopher Parkes, Christopher Grimes and Tim Burt, "The Fairytale may end in tears as Eisner's Magic Kingdom shows signs of crumbling", *Financial Times*, September 24, 2002.

Online Sources

Welcome to the Disney Institute
http://www.csm-europe.com/study_tour/disney3.asp?community=csm

Disney Institute
http://disney.go.com/vacations/websites/disneyinstitute/

Creating the Customer Experience
http://www.csm-europe.com/study_tour/disney4.asp?community=csm

Just Disney.com Home
http://www.justdisney.com/disneyland/waltdisney_touch/

The Walt Disney Company: Parks and Resorts
http://business.virgin.net/daniel.jesudasen/film/parks.htm

The Walt Disney Company: Walt Disney Internet Company
http://business.virgin.net/daniel.jesudasen/film/int_group.htm

Disney on MSN
http://register.go.com/disneymsn/ss/indexhome

Disney Mobile and Phone Centre
http://disney.go.com/mainstreet/mobile/

Disney's Visa Card
http://disney.go.com/visa/index.html?CELL=6RHH19

Studio Entertainment
http://disney.go.com/corporate/investors/financials/annual/2001/
keyBusinesses/studioEntertainment/theWaltDisneyStudios.html

The Media Monopoly
http://www.chicagomediawatch.org/01_3_chiseven.pdf

Hoovers Online: ESPN, Inc
http://www.hoovers.com/co/capsule/3/0,2163,103583,00.html

An annotated bibliography of literature relevant to the Disney
Phenomenon
http://www.uvm.edu/~tstreete/biblio_of_disney-lit.html

Disney Consumer Products: Hardlines
http://disney.go.com/corporate/investors/financials/annual/2001/
keyBusinesses/disneyConsumerProducts/hardlines.html

Motorola Disney Two-way Radio Classic
http://www.motorola.com/radios/disney

Disney, JCPenney to Develop Apparel Lines under Retail Licensing
Agreement
http://www.laughingplace.com/News-ID10005390.asp

Walt Disney International
http://disney.go.com/corporate/investors/financials/annual/2001/
keyBusinesses/waltDisneyInternational/waltDisneyInternational.html

Walt Disney Co. Presents Address to European Analysts
http://www.laughingplace.com/News-PID10004750-10004754.asp

Letter to Shareholders: To Fellow Disney Owners and Cast Members
http://disney.go.com/corporate/investors/financials/annual/2001/
introduction/letterToShareholders/introduction.html

The Miami Herald: Supreme Court gives victory to Walt Disney
http://www.miami.com/mld/miamiherald/business/
4952857.htm?template=contentModules/printstory.jsp